Presented To

St. Mary's
College of Maryland
Library

By *Eleanor Reeves*
Cooney '25

Date *May 1966*

In Memory Of

Mary Garner Reeves,
her mother

THE SOCIOLOGY

OF

COLONIAL VIRGINIA

THE
SOCIOLOGY
OF
COLONIAL
VIRGINIA

By
MORRIS TALPALAR, LL.B.

Philosophical Library
New York

Printed in the United States of America

16236

TABLE OF CONTENTS

CHAPTER ONE
THE BACKGROUND OF VIRGINIA'S LAUNCHING

CHAPTER TWO
THE RISE OF COLONIAL VIRGINIA'S ARISTOCRACY

CHAPTER THREE
THE MIND OF COLONIAL VIRGINIA'S ARISTOCRACY

CHAPTER FOUR
COLONIAL VIRGINIA'S LABOR BASE

FOREWORD

Virginia is a landmark in the history of the Anglo-Saxon people.

The Anglo-Saxon people developed towards their position of world domination during the last several hundred years, when they showed an unusual initiative in exploration, discovery, conquest and colonization. As England's first colony Virginia is the genesis of the British Empire, [1] and as the first Anglo-American colony she is the genesis of the United States of America.

During the War for Independence there rose from Anglo-America, especially from Virginia, the greatest political leaders in the history of the American people. The British Prime Minister Gladstone is quoted as having said:

"Virginia produced more contemporary great men than any other piece of real estate on earth, Greece and Rome not excepted." [2]

Colonial Virginia — a world that no longer exists — was much more than a geographical demarcation; she was a culture. She contributed Thomas Jefferson, James Madison, John Marshall, George Mason and George Wythe. The brilliance of her apex is not dimmed by the sordidness of her base.

These men nursed and matured in a time when Americanism was yet to be; they knew themselves primarily as Virginians. Their genius is embodied in American institutionalism, and a true appreciation of their life and work is hardly possible without a thorough understanding of their social milieu — its polity, economy and values.

There is a wealth of writing on colonial Virginia, but there is no objective, logically coordinated presentation of her sociology.

The present work is an attempt to make good this need.

INTRODUCTION

Technology has introduced a new era in the history of man. This may cause the present historical dichotomy (BC-AD) which is restricted to a part of the world, to be replaced by a universal historical dichotomy in terms of Before Technology and During Technology.

Mankind has never had a universal-eternal standard of values in terms of which a local-temporary way of life can be appraised. It is competently held that a code of ethics is authoritarian, and without rational foundation. The absence of a common denominator in values, and their authoritarian derivation; the fact that a world view is basically emotional rather than logical, and is subjectively accepted as superior — all this results in the isolated (in space or time) ideological world-in-itself.* Where contact between such mutually exclusive mental entities is unavoidable a meeting of minds on fundamentals is precluded, and one side must impose its will on the other. Thus under such conditions objectivity can only describe — it has no way to evaluate.

With the development of inter-continental communications America became the meeting place of people from various parts of the world — people of differing values, who had had hardly any previous contacts with one another: American colonial history therefore confronts the student more often with the ideological *cul-de-sac* than any subsequent period; and it is impossible to say where the justice

* Eighteenth-century Virginia and Massachusetts are examples of two wholly different worlds in space, while eighteenth-century and twentieth-century Virginia are two wholly different worlds in time.

THE SOCIOLOGY OF COLONIAL VIRGINIA

lies in the struggles among the multitude of ideologies that was brought to the new world, from which in time — through the process of the fusion of mind and blood, and of elimination — emerged the present American way of life.

Seventeenth-century England seethed with ideologies: although the ideological strands were quite involved, they were sufficiently definitive to turn the realm into a battle-field. As the fortunes of war fluctuated representative groups left home for a remote unknown wilderness which was big enough for each to find a place where they could settle and freely organize and live their lives their own way. They came to America with a given state of mind, about which they were persistent — their purpose was to translate their mind into reality. Virginia was in the control solely of Cavaliers, Massachusetts Bay of Puritans, and Pennsylvania predominantly of Nonconformists (Quakers). Each of these colonies— which is a good index to the social system of its neighboring settlements — was organized strictly in terms of its own way: its isolation— both physical and mental— was complete; and Virginia and Massachusetts are each a clear-cut example of basic mental uniformity. Thus the English colonies in America offer an unusual opportunity for a study in sociology.

The social evolution of America does not follow in a straight line: there are abrupt breaks or qualitative departures, which introduced and in time crystallized new principles in institutions and values. The event that is isolated from its context has no more than statistical value: an understanding of the colonial period is predicated upon an insight into its mind; and this can be achieved by sensing what is implicit, since the explicit alone is not a literal index. There was plenty of the past in the Puritans, little of the future in the Cavaliers. Pre-technological Americans just simply did not think, believe, act, as do their atomic-age descendants: the historical epoch is created by mind— not by time; and the sociology of colonial Virginia is more like that of ancient Rome than of twentieth-century America.

Each colony had an aristocracy. Aristocracy is never qualified—exalted, debased, comical; it is simply an institution in social phenomena, which must be described. The existence of aristocracy in all times and climes is historically justified, since it was the creator, the patron, and the custodian of culture; it preserved and handed down to posterity everything that is associated with the good, the beautiful and the true. The colonial aristocracy was true to form— culture was its supreme value. The fact of culture and the differences in values, which alter the use and understanding of many words, create an opacity between the present and past American eras that is not easy to penetrate.

Beginnings are often regarded as simple per se. The colonies were offshoots, and they appear picayune in terms of time, space, power. The pre-technological history of America covers little more than two hundred years: the "weight of the past" is hardly felt; and the tendency to think quantitatively brings a diminishing respect for the old era that discourages its study purely for its own sake, and that may even lead towards its erasure. Yet the colony has its qualitative implications: it looms in sociology, for it was the parent of the state; everything fundamental — in institutions and values — was determined by the colony, and was inherited from it by the state.

Contemporary values tend to dim past achievement: the attempt to adjust the past to present thinking is the falsification of history — the past cannot be explained in terms of the present. No age will ever have the right to make its progenitors in its own image, and it neither truly describes nor exalts the Fathers so to treat them. The colonial era is historically fixed — its interpretation may vary, but only as within its own context. When we deal with colonial America we are in a different world.

CHAPTER ONE

THE BACKGROUND OF VIRGINIA'S LAUNCHING

Part One: SOCIAL CHANGES IN ENGLAND

At the beginning of the seventeenth century the Stuart family became the royal house of England, represented by James First as king. On their accession the Stuarts found themselves at the crucial stage in the "long contest which ultimately transferred purse and sword from Crown to Commons".[1] The struggle was between feudal landowners and traders for control of the realm: their differences were fundamental, being based on sociology and values.

The traditional aristocracy in England was based on land or realty, which is limited: this created a stationary society; the class differences were qualitative; the landholder was a gentleman — which the commoner could never be. In the previous century the traders had gained considerable power, especially during the reigns of Henry Eighth and Elizabeth First — and James First was selling titles of nobility at £10,000 sterling each, for which he found ready purchasers. This was fabulous money in the seventeenth century: and it could happen only, it seems, in England — which was indeed the land of "merchant princes". The merchants who had bought their titles acquired the external habiliments of station — the life of the country gentleman in terms of manor, title, culture, mannerism; and to the aristocracy of land and blood was added the aristocracy of capital. The economic potential of capital or personalty is illimitable: the newly titled had industrial enterprises in the towns,

1

foreign investments, ships at sea; and their manors could be given some adjustment with a view to the raising of produce for profit. This created a fluid or dynamic society: the class differences became quantitative; the trader was based on "the People" — his values included everyone. The differences in way of life — hopes, ambitions, pursuits, interests — as between land and capital based aristocrats were real and profound. The former regarded the newcomers as interlopers, or pseudo-aristocrats.

James First sided with the traditional landholders, and he attempted to curtail the gains that the traders had made. The king's position was challenged, and the struggle between the two ideologies began to take on political division as the traditionalists were identified as the "Court" party and the capital people as the "Country" party. During the four decades of bickering that ensued the royalist position came to be identified as "Royal Prerogative", while that of the traders was known as "Rights of the People". The king claimed that the People had privileges, not rights, of which the Crown's grace was the source; the traders held, on the contrary, that the People is the source of the Crown's power, and they declared that "the voice of the People is the voice of God".

By 1642 the two factions had taken on definite shape, and civil war broke out between them. England was organized politically in terms of shires: each shire had a town; each town had a gate — which it lowered, when news arrived that war had begun. The alignment was predominantly one of town and country: the war at first took the form of a series of sieges — each town was invested by the men of the surrounding countryside; and dissident elements in both places were easily overcome. Both sides accepted help from their sympathizers on the European continent.

The supporters of the feudal society, called Cavaliers, were dedicated to three basic principles: no country without a king, no church without a bishop, no land without a lord — which established a union of state, church and property (realty). They comprised the royal house; the traditional land based aristocrats — who included the large landholding nobility and the smaller landholders or gentry; and the Anglican Church conservatives or Churchmen. Loyalism is essentially monolithic — it is dedicated to the continuation of the past, and it has precedents to go by. The Cavaliers were for an absolute monarchy as modified by the federal political doctrine — the autonomy of the shires was not to be infringed. The Establishment — the Church of England, was to be preserved, on the basis of the Anglican theological system. The union of property with state and church was to be continued by the feudal laws of primogeniture and entail. Under primogeniture the family's entire real property was automatically inherited by the eldest son, and entail precluded its alienation and encumbrance. The operation of these laws created and perpetuated the aristocracy by freezing a landed estate with one family indefinitely, for without them estates could be broken up by descending divided and be subject to continual change of hands.

Those who fought for a new social order were predominantly town folk, and they were called Parliamentarians. Their doctrines revolved around the problems of state, church and property — whose status they wanted to change. They were agreed on the principle of nationalism: they wanted the abolition of federalism, or the subordination of the shires to a strong central government; and this brought the corollary doctrine of the limited, or controlled, monarchy. The rebels were thinking more or less in terms of the future — they were stepping into the unknown: and as their theories on the complex social institutions tapered towards detail they revealed profound disagreements concerning the kind and degree of change that should be made, which caused them to separate into three groups — Presbyterians*, Puritans and Nonconformists. The Presbyter-

* "Presbyterian" had then also a political signification.

ians were capital-based noblemen who had recently bought their titles, and the Puritans comprised members of the gentry and commonalty who had acquired substantial merchant interests: both were not averse to a continuation of a good part of the past; they wanted to continue the monarchy, but with limited powers; and they were both members of the Church of England, as they accepted the principle of the Establishment or the union of state and church—each in terms of its own theological system. The Nonconformists were commoners who were beginning to develop as merchants: they wanted to supplant the monarchy with a republican form of government; and they were outside the Church of England—they were for disestablishment, or the separation of state and church. The Presbyterians, on acquiring the status of aristocrats, preferred to retain the basic implications of the feudal land laws. The Puritans, together with the Nonconformists, were independents of property: they chafed under the fetters of the feudal realty laws, as they wanted to be masters of their own land; and they demanded the freeing of property, and the market turnover, which would result from the introduction of the fee simple independent title to realty. Thus the Puritans were independents of the land — they wanted the separation of property from state and church. The Nonconformists were for a complete break with the past — they demanded the separation of all three.

By 1646 the Cavaliers were beaten. The victorious Parliamentary forces then underwent a split: a conflict arose between the conservative Presbyterians, and the radical Puritans and Nonconformists, for control of the British state. As it became evident that the radicals would triumph a union took place between the capital and land based aristocrats: the Presbyterians were joined by the Cavalier remnants, and together they began "the second civil war"[2] to resist the radical supremacy. By 1648, however, Oliver Cromwell, who had emerged as the radical leader, over-

4

came the conservative coalition.

Oliver Cromwell now proposed the abolition of the monarchy — through the execution of the reigning king, Charles First — and of the House of Lords, which would leave the House of Commons as the sole legislative body. This brought another split among the rebels: the Puritans were monarchists and opposed to Cromwell's program, while the Nonconformists were republicans or Oliverians. Cromwell carried his point by purging the House of Commons of royalists, and the king was condemned to the block by the "Rump Parliament". Charles First's condemnation by "the People" set the precedent for the right of subjects to sit in judgment on royalty.

Cromwell's political order, which began as the "Commonwealth" and developed into the "Protectorate", continued until 1660. The Protector initiated the rise of England as a commercial power when he made trade the paramount object of foreign policy, sought a favorable trade balance, and enacted the Navigation Act which introduced the protective tariff. During the Commonwealth the Puritans laid the foundations for what eventually developed into the capitalistic society.

Meanwhile the Presbyterians or titled merchants had entered into conversations with the exiled heir to the throne, from which resulted an agreement known as the Declaration of Breda. The merchant aristocracy agreed to restore the monarchy with the Stuart family as the reigning house, as well as the House of Lords, provided, in effect, that it be accepted as the power behind the throne. In 1658 Oliver Cromwell died; his son, Richard, who succeeded to his position, resigned a year later; and the Restoration of the Crown took place in May 1660, with the Stuart heir becoming king as Charles Second. Thus the restoration of the monarchy in 1660 did not constitute a reversion to the status quo ante.

England's sociology was developing towards capitalism

but the Stuart family plotted against it. In 1689 the
merchant interests made a revolution, and they enunciated
the "Bill of Rights" whose contents assured them undis-
puted control. They kept the crown, but changed the reigning family by expelling the Stuarts and importing the Dutch
House of Orange in the persons of William and Mary —
no British subject could achieve royalty. Since the new
royal family was invited to reign by Britain's lords and
commons its powers were derived — not inherent, which
predicated monarchy upon the will of the People, repudiated
the tradition of the reigning family as hereditary, and in-
sured the Protestant royal succession. Thus the feudal institutional forms—crown, as well as aristocracy and church
— were retained, but their content was adjusted to the
interests of the new society. Parliament — comprising
crown, lords and commons — was definitely established as
the British state: its summoning and dismissal became its
own power, and a member could not be arrested during its
sessions; the royal succession was predicated upon its act,
and the royal negative was rendered innocuous; and it took
control of taxation, of the armed forces, and of foreign affairs. The oath of allegiance and supremacy, which confined the final authority on all political and theological
questions to within England, continued to be the *sine qua
non* of office holding. The Toleration Act was introduced,
which legalized Dissent and gave it some rights. Nationalism began to displace the federal concept of government, the
policies of mercantilism and colonization were strengthened,
and the Bank of England was established in 1695 and the
Board of Trade in 1696.

The substantial victory of the rebel elements made England the pioneer of social revolution in the modern world.

Part Two: THE PROJECTION OF ANGLO-AMERICA

Europe's discovery of the western hemisphere brought a
struggle between some of her national groups for the

domination of the new world: Spanish, French and British imperialism were competing to bring home the riches of remote continents — but this presupposed mastery of the Atlantic Ocean; and ocean traffic began to become more important than riparian. There was no accepted international law to regulate navigation on the high seas, and everyone felt free to act on his own. The Spanish were the first to rule the Atlantic, and together with the French they had been active in America from the sixteenth century. The former were mainly conquerors and explorers; their explorer Balboa had discovered the Pacific Ocean in 1513, and their town of Santa Fe was more than a half century old when Virginia was founded.[3] But they were not colonizers, and their role in America is comparable with that of the British in India. In Mexico and Peru they had discovered the most populated and prosperous parts of the new world already organized on a master-serf basis, so they simply threw out the aboriginal masters and installed themselves. Soon cargoes of precious metals were being sent home. Says Fiske:

"By the year 1609 ... Spain ... had taken from America more gold and silver than would today be represented by five thousand million dollars." [4]

The French were active in Canada but they too were not colonizers. They were mainly explorers and fur traders spread thinly over a vast area who never achieved self-support, and whose gregariousness discouraged the life of the frontiersman. They took easily to the free life of the wilderness, learned the continent well, understood the natives' ways and dialects, didn't bother their occupancy of the land, and accepted them as racially assimilable; and the two were always allied against settler whites. The Spanish and French governments promoted and protected their enterprises in America, and there was little private investment and initiative. By the end of the sixteenth century the Spaniards were gradually working their way up from

Mexico, and the French were moving southward from Canada. The intervening area was unsettled.

During the reign of Elizabeth First England's commercial interests achieved great power in the government; they were convinced that their country's future greatness depended on her gaining a foothold in the western hemisphere, and they began to make plans for overseas ventures. The British Crown therefore pre-empted North America by virtue of the Cabot discoveries, and enterprises were organized for its colonization. The merchants were interested chiefly in locating sources for precious metals and for the raw materials they had to import. But England's inexperience as an empire builder and her lack of sufficient sea power frustrated her colonizing efforts. Meanwhile, the English merchants challenged Spain's Atlantic supremacy by subsidizing expeditions under Sir Francis Drake and other sea captains to prey on her shipping. Spain sent her Armada in 1588 to attack her enemy but it was defeated, and England began to emerge as ruler of the seas. The ability of England's commercial economy to produce much more surplus wealth or capital than the feudal economies of her rivals made her people successful empire builders. The buccaneers had paved the way for the traders and colonizers, and by the end of the sixteenth century the English were thoroughly familiar with the North American Atlantic coast.

The Stuart accession brought peace with Spain, which made the seas more secure for Englishmen. Around the beginning of the seventeenth century the British Crown made land grants in North America to its colonizing enterprises. But the continent was a thinly-populated wilderness; colonization had to begin from the ground up, and with such expense too much even for the royal treasury private share-selling monopolies, especially the "joint-stock-company" which was introduced under Elizabeth, undertook responsibility to finance it. Edward Rider, a member of the Virginia

Company with investments in the colony, declared:
> "there was a material difference betwen the Spanish
> and English plantations. For the Spanish colonies
> were founded by the kings of Spain ... out of their
> own treasury and revenues, and they maintain the
> garrisons there, together with a large Navy, for
> their use and defence; whereas the English plant-
> ations had been at first settled and since supported
> at the charge (expense) of private adventurers and
> planters ..." [5]

England's colonization in North America was her greatest
achievement during the seventeenth century.

Part Three: THE BRITISH-COLONIAL CONNECTIVE PRINCIPLE

Seventeenth-century Anglo-America — which comprised
several colonies on North America's Atlantic coast and in
the West Indies — is incidental to, and can be understood
only in terms of, the social upheavals which were revolu-
tionizing life in England. These enterprises were projected
under Stuart hegemony, although the merchants had a determining say depending on the degree of their influence.
The colonies were founded separately at various times by
different interests, who received from the Crown* vaguely
demarcated grants to land under conditions which made
them either "royal", "proprietary" or "chartered". The
royal colony was the property of the king, who appointed
the governor to whom he *delegated* the pre-emptive right
within the colony area with power to make individual land
grants. The proprietary grant was the property of one or of
a group of royal grantees and their heirs forever, and the
chartered grant was the property of a joint-stock company,
to whom the Crown *transferred* its pre-emptive right to a
section of the continent. Thus the grant was a private

* The king was an individual, while the Crown was a social institution.

estate, owned in fee simple.#

The Monopoly, i. e., the owner, whether king, proprietary or company, had to swear allegiance to the British Crown. Thus the colonies were members of a federal union headed by the Crown to which their inhabitants, as subjects, owed allegiance and from which they expected protection; the federal form of political organization respected, and remoteness from authority necessitated, local autonomy. The Monopoly had the right to transport British subjects to its grant; and it could alienate, bequeath or encumber the colony in whole or in part and sell or lease special interests in it, such as fur-trade or fishing rights — although only to British subjects. Whether it remained in England or emigrated to its colony the Monopoly had complete immediate power over its grant. It could organize a government in its executive, legislative and judicial branches; regulate the Church, which had charge of morals and education; organize and command armed forces, suppress insurrection and declare war on and make peace and trade treaties with Indians; draw up a civil code and inflict capital punishment, arrange its own economy, issue legal tender, levy taxes, charter municipalities, decide on franchise requirements, admit or exclude immigrants, etc. It appointed the settlement's governor and other officials, usually from its membership. For anyone within the grant to impugn the Monopoly's pre-emptive right to its land was a capital offense; all title to land was predicated upon its bona fide grant and reverted to it, and unauthorized purchase of land from Indians was forbidden. Under the federal political organization the colony was not involved per se in Britain's wars, and its trading with the enemy was not clearly treason.

The Monopoly's title compared with the Crown's was the same in degree but different in kind. The former's right

In 1612 the Virginia Company of London sold for £2000 sterling the Somers Islands (Bermudas), which were included in its grant, to a group of merchants.

was derived, not inherent; it could grant land only to British subjects, its legislation could not contravene the fundamental law or interest of England, and a share of the precious metals found on the grant belonged to the royal treasury. Thus the Crown had ultimate power: land in America by whomever granted originated from its grace; it could transcend colonial law to protect British creditors, and reverse colonial judicial decisions; its banking laws were enforceable in the colonies whose money values were determined on the London exchange; it had the power of intercolonial arbitration, and extradition; it could take command of the Monopoly's armed forces, and order it to refrain from or participate in war.

The royal and proprietary colonies were economically largely feudal with primogeniture and entail governing the realty laws, and politically Cavalier. There was a basic similarity in the social organization of all chartered colonies; they tended towards commerce with fee simple title to realty introduced, and were politically Puritan. Their charters were obtained while the merchants were an influence, but a colony's status could be changed and the Stuart policy was to make them royal. The royal and chartered colonies instituted the union of state and church, being respectively Anglican and Puritan. Some of the proprietary colonies had no state church.

References

FOREWORD

[1] J. R. Seeley, Expansion Of England, p. 10.

[2] Robert B. Bean, The Peopling Of Virginia, p. 48.

CHAPTER ONE

THE BACKGROUND OF VIRGINIA'S LAUNCHING

[1] Moncure D. Conway, Barons Of The Potomack & Rappahannock, p. 3.

[2] Oxford History Of England, 9; 144.

[3] Temple Bodley, History Of Kentucky To 1803, p. 9.

[4] John Fiske; Old Virginia and Her Neighbors, ed. 1897, 1; 9.

[5] Alexander Brown, English Politics In Early Va. History, p. 145.

[6] Alexander Brown, Genesis Of The United States, 2; 594.

CHAPTER TWO

THE RISE OF COLONIAL VIRGINIA'S ARISTOCRACY

First Period: 1607—1660; PRE-RESTORATION VIRGINIA — THE PURITAN DOMINATION

King James First granted a charter in 1606 to a joint-stock company identified as,
>"The Treasurer and Company of Adventurers and
>Planters of the City of London for the first Colony
>in Virginia",

in which he transferred to it the Crown's pre-emptive right to a section of North America for the establishment of a permanent settlement. Preparations to found the colony had been going on for some years, and its launching was a great national enterprise to the extent that it influenced the literature of the period.

The Virginia Company was the Monopoly: it held in "fee simple by socage tenure"; it was complete master of, and sole source of title to, land within the grant — with all due respect for the Crown.* It remained at home, and in 1607 sent settlers to the grant which it named "Virginia".# The members of the Company who stayed home were known as "adventurers of the purse", while those who went to supervise the founding of the colony were called "planters" or "adventurers of the person".

The colony was projected to expand the home country

---

* Known in a republic as "eminent domain".

The first Anglo-Saxon name permanently applied to a place outside the British Isles. "Virginia" was at first also sometimes understood to designate North America.

by locating sources of precious metals and of the raw materials she had to import, finding a passage to the East, trading with the natives, and establishing a base for operations against Spanish galleons.[1] Another purpose was,

"to check the dangerous power of Spain and Rome by attacking the Spaniards in America; by subverting their government there and laying in its place an English Protestant settlement".[2]

Everyone in England at the time was politically conscious and had a sense of belonging in some group, although only a few were articulate. The members of the Company were all of the Parliamentary-Puritan party, and they avowed the principles of monarchy and of the union of state and church. Their colonizing venture was not a flight from overt persecution.

Thus within twenty years of the Spanish Armada England's men of capital founded her first colony, and launched the British Empire.

Several previous costly attempts at colonization on North America's Atlantic coast had miscarried, and the Virginia Company had to work on a background of failure. The continents being separated by an ocean the basis of communications was the ship. America was a state of nature. A state of nature is not land, and it has no economic value per se. Land — in the sense of ground ready to the hand of man for agricultural settlement — is a social phenomenon created by man through capital investment; it is not found in nature. The foundation for the establishment of a colony — an arable land area — had first to be laid since people, like grains, cannot be planted in a wilderness. Wilderness is natural resources: it can be turned into arable by reclamation, which was then based on the axe.

Colonization is a commercial undertaking, which is based on collective planning: it presupposes sufficient capital accumulation for the achievement of transportation, and of establishment — which means long-term investment with no immediate returns; and it is dominated by the ledger mind — assets and liabilities. Wrote the English philosopher-statesman Sir Francis Bacon:

"Planting of Counties is like planting of Woods, for you must make account to loose almost Twenty yeares Profitt and expect your recompense in the end: for the Principall thing that hath bin the destruction of most Plantations hath bin the hastee drawing of profitt in the first Yeares." [3]

"Private property" is a social, not a natural, phenomenon: a state of nature having no economic value per se the substance of private property is non-existent — America to the Englishman was an opportunity to invest for potential profit. It was the pre-technological world of the economy and the values of scarcity: nobody — whether man, king or God — gave away anything for nothing; men had to start from scratch, they had to be economically calculating, and each venture had to be made to pay for itself. The Company accumulated its capital by selling shares of stock at twelve pounds and ten shillings per share. The ship sailing to the settlement, which had to be bought or rented, was a unit of capital owned by the Company — people, animals and implements for laboring and fighting; and food — without which there could be no settlement.

The wealth of nations in pre-technology rested on land, and settlement of and within a colony was based on the land grant. What did the settlers understand by the phrase "land grant"? "Land" meant wilderness — there was nothing else. Was "grant" understood in the sense of "bestowal", or simply as "allocation"? Royal grace was the ultimate source of everything: wilderness territory, whether for jurisdiction or for individual, is an opportunity to invest for its potential economic value; there was selectivity in that the grantee, royal or colonial, had to be a British subject and take the oath of supremacy; and the royal grant

15

was a pledge to protect the colonizing investment against rival imperialisms — all of which gives the impression of bestowal. Yet there could be no conveyance of economic value per se in any kind of grant to territory in America. The settlement and expansion of a colony were predicated upon investment capital — cash, chattels, labor; there was abundant land potential, but the acreage of land actual was determined solely by the amount of capital available. The accumulation of a unit of capital for investment risk, by group or individual — especially in view of the dearth of capital, was much more of a problem than the procurement of a grant. Virginia was a naked wilderness; there was no land (arable), and there could be no benefit of station; all the grantee could get was a forest tract upon which to create land; the acquisition of land was entirely the grantee's investment risk, there could be no "corruption" — favoritism or discrimination — in its distribution, and nobody in Virginia ever got land for nothing. Thus the practical understanding conveyed by "grant" must have been simply allocation.

Man is a social animal, and there are different forms of social organization: man's sociality is natural, but the particular form it takes is determined by man himself. The colony is per se a planned society—the colonist arrives at his place of settlement with a pattern of social organization in his mind. The Company was the only organized group constituting "Virginia", and it took full direct charge in the founding of the colony. The settlers' primary purpose was to project civilization—the way of life, the values and the culture, of Europe—into America. They intended to continue being English: they brought with them to the new world the ways and the values of the English community, to which the wilderness about them was to be adjusted; and they planned to build their community in terms of the principle of private property, which was to take the form of the trading kind of economy. The joint-stock company form of organization planted itself in the settlement: it contained within itself the social principles which were to be introduced in the colony; and it constituted the bud from which sprouted the social order of pre-Restoration Virginia.

"Land" may be understood in terms of the colony territory, which was thought of in units of square miles: and of the individual estate within the colony, and of the plantation or arable area within the estate, both of which were measured in units of acres. The first two were wilderness areas having no economic value per se, while the last—arable land—had economic value. Accuracy is unimportant in an isolated pioneering community: time, weights and measures are usually estimated, as professional skills and instruments—surveyors, compass, scales, calendars — are lacking; and wilderness "land grants" are demarcated by natural landmarks rather than by surveying. The unit of measurement is indifferently understood, and acreage numerals as in relation to a state of nature do not have literal meaning.

About one hundred men—listed as "gentlemen, carpenters, laborers"—were transported by the Company to found the colony. Further shipments of proportionately more laborers soon followed—and in 1609 a batch of women was sent over, which transformed the venture from a base into a settlement. A civil community cannot be established in a wilderness, as it presupposes an arable area—the settlement had first to be prepared for private enterprise. Starting from scratch—the necessity to create the foundation upon which to build—means reclamation, which could be undertaken only collectively. Everyone worked for the Company and consumed from the storehouse it had set up, and the ship was at first used for shelter. The work consisted overwhelmingly of reclamation—the alteration of nature to suit the needs of man. The woods and the waters provided some food, but the consumer goods—most food, and all clothing and implements—were imported since local labor could not produce them. Reclamation was based on the axe: arable land was wrested from the forests at cruel cost in capital, and in human blood and life; and the acre of virgin arable was gold — it was the settlers' most precious possession. There had to be a plan of reclamation: this was determined by the intended layout of the colony — which was based on the parcel of land, or the individual farm unit. A Virginia historian says:

> "it was ordered that the tradesman who preferred to follow his trade should be allowed a dwelling house and four acres of land to be held in fee simple". [4]

Thus the reclaimed area was not one vast mass of arable: rather was reclamation carried out in terms of scattered small patches; forest tracts of roughly one hundred acres each were set off contiguously — on each of which four acres were reclaimed and fenced in, and a log cabin was thrown up; and each of these was considered an individual farm unit. This was known as "seating" — preparing the tract for private establishment, or potential occupancy and producing. The Company transported and seated — it did not establish. The transportation of the emigrant, and the creation of the farm unit on which he was to be established, were enabled by the share of stock — which was the unit of capital, and sold at twelve pounds and ten shillings. By 1619 the Company had a solid decade of constant labor behind it — all investment and no returns: a sufficient arable area — several thousand farm units, as yet unoccupied — which was the basic substance of private property, had been created; there was now a consciousness of difference between wilderness and arable— which gave the founders a sense of accomplishment, and of value as inherent in the settlement; and a foundation had been laid upon which to build what the Company had intended from its inception — a civil community. The settlement took on perforce a social pattern: a government was set up; there was fundamental harmony concerning the economic organization of the colony; and private property in realty and personalty — in terms of "fee simple by socage tenure" or complete mastery — was introduced.

The transportation of an emigrant and the seating of a tract were covered by the share price: the Company, by operating collectively, could save money, and it made a profit; if the profit was twenty percent then the Company could create one hundred-twenty farm units for the income from one hundred shares. The reclaimed area was the only unimported socially valuable article in the colony, since capital had been invested in it. This could not be granted away for nothing as the Company would have been bankrupted. The vast majority of the shares of stock had been sold to purchasers, while some were conveyed to Company members as payment for their personal supervision in the founding of the colony. Thus the Company alienated its land through sale and pay. The introduction of private property in 1619 meant the distribution of the farm units to private owners — in fee simple independent title, unencumbered; distribution was based on the number of shares each member owned. Thus the absentee shareowners (adventurers of the purse) were proportionately provided — while the rest was distributed among the local members (adventurers of the person) by virtue of the shares they had acquired through purchase and compensation. A few of the members were big shareowners: it is said that the family of Captain Christopher Newport, who was a leading figure in the founding of the colony, was made a grant of land equivalent to seventy-one shares — which came to as many seated one hundred-acre forest strips, or a total of two hundred eighty-four acres arable.

With the introduction of private property in 1619 the shareowners inherited from the Company the skeletal framework of an economic organization, on which they were to put the flesh. The private owner, like Captain Newport, proceeded to organize his hundred-acre prepared units in terms of an estate which was known as "Hundreds"* — and this constituted the nucleus of the colony's economy. The Hundreds was organized on what may be called the "corporate farm" system, which took the following form: a few of the farm units were merged to make up the owner's own "domain"; and radiating from the domain were the remaining units, each of which could in time be conveyed on the family farm system to an occupant. It had been the Company's responsibility to transport, and to seat — as within the hundred-acre wooded strip four acres were reclaimed and fenced in, and a log cabin was thrown up: it now became the responsibility of the private owner to "establish", or to activate each strip; he conveyed to the occupant — in fee simple independent title, in most cases encumbered (mortgaged) — the seated tract, and stocked it with a cow and some agricultural implements; and this constituted an activated farm unit. Thus the family farm existed as within the corporate farm estate. The owner's domain — within which was a "plantation" that was cultivated by his laborers — was the center around which the life of the estate revolved, for on it were concentrated the indispensable craftsmen — blacksmith, carpenter, tanner, brickmaker, glass-blower. The family farm could not be autarchic: many goods and services necessary for the proper maintenance and operation of a farm—grinding grain into flour, churning milk into butter and cheese, breeding livestock, sharpening and repairing implements, buying manufactured articles, disposing of surplus produce, shipping facilities — were available only on the domain. The corporate farm estate was rendered autarchic by the domain, which was the nub of the estate's commer-

* There was a jurisdictional division at home called "Hundreds".

cial activities and the nucleus for the development of a town.

In the founders' world back home the manorial estate was in a transition stage: it was departing from traditional ways of doing things, its occupants were acquiring rights in the land they worked, and the farming system in agriculture was slowly emerging from within the manorial system. The Virginia Company contained within itself the principles involved in this movement for social change, which it transplanted to the colony; it constituted the framework— in state, church, economy, class—from within which the colony's sociology was a logical emergence. Thus pre-Restoration Virginia's corporate farm estate followed the organizational pattern, and was ultimately an evolvement from within, England's feudal manor — but the social relations as between owner and occupants were radically different.

The corporate farm estate was organized and maintained primarily with a view to economic gain, and it presupposed substantial capital investment. The creation of the domain required a minimum number of farm units to make it economically possible, and it had to service and supply several hundred inhabitants as well as some animals. Shelters for human and animal labor, warehouses for the storage of surplus produce, a store to be stocked with imported manufactured articles, facilities for shipping, and for churning milk and grinding corn — had to be built; it was indispensable to import craftsmen — who had to be supplied with work sheds and the necessary tools; and farm animals of good stock — cows for the conveyed tracts and several bulls, work horses and some stallions, as well as sheep, hogs and poultry — had to be brought over. The corporate farm estate also had to be limited to a maximum number of farm units: with communications primitive, each estate could not be unwieldy as its occupants had to be within practical reach of the center; and Captain Newport's seventy-one farm units probably had to be divided

21

into two separate domains.

The Company had been originally organized, and empowered as the sole authority, for the initial achievement of two concomitant objectives: colonization — to transform a wilderness area into a civil community; and sociology — to give this civil community a certain social form. The share of stock, its cost to the shareholders, and the benefits derived therefrom, constituted the nucleus for the social organization of the colony. With the introduction of government and private economy in 1619 the initial objectives were considered achieved. The Company had labored for permanence, and succeeded well: although it continued to exist it withdrew as the visible active head of the venture, and the government took over the management of the colony. This introduced a new principle: with all the land apportioned and beginning to produce the settlement was started towards self-sufficiency — Virginia was a fact. The Company had given the colony its social pattern, along which lines it continued to develop after the former's withdrawal and subsequent disappearance. Authority ceased to be monolithic, and there took place a separation of powers: property became independent of state and church; the government had nothing to do with the creation, stocking and conveyance of farm units, as this became the responsibility solely of private capital. Now came the problem of expansion: a land office was set up; areas ungranted were public property reserved for the people, and men turned their gaze westward to the forests; and private capital could now undertake to do on an individual basis what had previously required collective effort — furnish the unit of capital, and assume the responsibility to transport and seat and, in addition, to establish.

The colony's expansion was derived: it had to be based on immigrant capital, and it maintained an office in London for information and help to intended settlers. The fundamental problem for the prospective colonist was to get a start, which involved his transportation and establishment. This presupposed a cash outlay: the sum of twelve pounds and ten shillings — whether through the Company share, by the emigrant on his own, or by a colonial's advanced subsidy — constituted the unit of capital necessary for the emigrant's settlement in the colony.

The people who went to found and settle the colony were all English. They were mainly small town folk who planned their settlement in terms of the only world they knew — their world back home. They were of different social status: gentlemen, commoner country folk and town craftsmen, and unskilled laborers; and they introduced in Virginia the hierarchical or class system of society. Economically they were of two kinds: those who could finance their own transportation, and those whose transportation had to be financed for them. This forced colonial society into a retrograde move, unknown at home—the division of its inhabitants into the primary categories of "freeman" and "bondsman". The freemen, who had to be British subjects and were identified under the Puritans as "the People", had social status and rights to property in land; while the bondsmen, who did not need nationality and were known as "indentured servants", had no social status and no rights to property in land. Those who were self-sufficient came into the colony as freemen, while the great majority of the impoverished came in as bondsmen. Each category had subdivisions. The freemen were classed as "gentry" and "commonalty", and this had its corresponding economic differentiation known as "rich" man and "poor" man. A few emigrants had sufficient capital with which to acquire estates, and they constituted the gentry who exercised leadership in founding and governing the colony. The country folk and town craftsmen were classed as commonalty. Many of them had enough money to emigrate on their own and get themselves a good start. But there were also many skilled workers without funds, and the colony needed them badly. Arrangements could therefore be made through the London office for well-placed colonials to finance the start of such emigrants, on the understanding that it would be repaid by their skill over a period of time. Skill was respected: the master's investment was well protected but the agreement was a contract, not an indenture; and the assisted craftsman came in as a freeman. So long as the accumulation of a labor class had to be subsidized bondage was inescapable: the ordinary laborers had neither money nor skill; they could come in only as bondsmen — owned by the Company and afterwards by the landowner — and their status came to be subdivided as temporary and permanent. The foundation for colonization was the creation of arable, which rested on the back of the man who wielded the axe: clearing tangled forests with an axe is excruciating labor; most of the bondsmen, who were gathered from the distressed elements of England's population, had never been workers or of the wage-earning class; and martial law had to be imposed on the settlement, under which severe measures were sometimes used to coerce the men into laboring.

The Company and afterwards the government had the monopoly, the pre-emptive right, to all the territory within the Virginia grant, which was a state of nature: it alone could grant title to land; but this right was identified primarily with the principle of sovereignty — it had no economic meaning since the wilderness was vast and bare, had no sales value, and was not taxed. The government derived part of its revenue from a tax on realty, but this presupposed productivity or private capital investment. The government's jurisdiction over its territory is remote from everyday life: it cannot grant anyone an estate; all it can do is grant whoever has capital the right to create an estate. Natural land (wilderness) is transformed into social land (arable) by reclamation. This was by far the most arduous and expensive problem: there was no farm machinery in pre-technology; the creation of arable was based upon the sinews of living labor — men and animals, and also on implements, and they had to be imported and maintained, which meant capital investment; the man of capital had to get consent (title) from the established authority before he would invest; and the government grant of title simply authorized and secured the investment. Thus the acquisition of land was a double process: it had to be received from the government through title grant, and reclaimed from nature through capital investment. The legitimacy of title, and of the source of title, was paramount for it involved investment — and the colonial authority had to be empowered by the London government, whether royal or rebel, to grant title to land.

Pioneering in colonization — man's challenge to nature— makes man conscious of the limits of his physical strength, endurance and courage. It is a practical impossibility for any one man working by himself to reclaim an acre of land with an axe, or to throw up a log cabin of any degree of comfort even with tools. A colonial writing of 1682 says:

"six men will in six weeks time, Fall, Clear, Fence in,
and fit for Planting, six Acres of Land." [5]

Thus it took one man fully provided for and supervised almost a half year to reclaim and fence-in four acres of land — the throwing up of the log cabin took additional time. The individual could not by his own efforts acquire a base to start from: this could be achieved only by forces outside himself — by an organized group, created and directed either by a Company or by a person with sufficient capital. But given a shelter and several acres arable the individual can by his own work produce enough to feed his family. Virgin soil remains fertile for about ten years — and once started off the settler has a base to work from, and he can clear more of his tract at his leisure. Thus a one hundred-acre wooded tract is far more than enough to enable a farmer to support his family for a natural life span. The Company, and afterwards the landowner, took the responsibility to throw up a log cabin and to reclaim sufficient of the area within which it stood: this meant capital investment — the putting of economic value into a state of nature, which rendered title automatic. The invested area was regarded as "realty" — and there was a practical exactness, sense of private property, and trespass sensitivity, concerning it. On its activation — actual occupancy and producing — the government put on a tax, which was restricted to the producing area.

The conveyance of the family farm unit by the domain owner to the occupant was made under a "leasehold" arrangement, which introduced the principle of the "mortgage": the man who was destitute of capital could enter into an agreement with the man who had capital whereby the latter advanced the former the amount of capital necessary to give him a start, on the understanding that the advanced subsidy—in terms of principle and interest—would be repaid over a period of time, after which the mortgagee owned the property in clear title.

Capital investment in reclamation transforms the anonymity of wilderness into the identity of arable. The man of capital achieved a corporate farm estate or status as head of Hundreds by a method known as the "head right", which was introduced by the government. This meant that a fifty-acre tract of wilderness would be granted to whoever paid for the transportation of an individual, whether freeman or bondsman, who came into the colony. The head right claimant was issued a paper by the land office certifying his claim, and this was entered into the office realty records. It was the grantee's responsibility to seat, and there was an immediate relation between granting and seating: on the grant's seating a contiguous fifty-acre tract accrued—and the land office paper automatically acquired integrity as title. But not all land grants materialized: failure to seat within a given time—which was determined by land tax receipts—brought lapse, as there can be no hiatus within a settled community; the lapse of the head right was nugatory, since there is no gain or loss in the absence of economic value per se. Thus the man who imported a hundred persons was entitled to a hundred head rights—to a hundred individual fifty-acre tracts, not to five thousand acres: the grant was officially neither specifically located nor surveyed; the vastness of the spaces enabled the grantee to select his own area of investment—no particular location advantages had as yet developed, and safety dictated proximity to areas already invested; and on the seating of each tract, as this was accomplished, title and accrual were automatic. The head right was an opportunity to invest, and was valuable only to the man with abundant capital: it presupposed a base to work from—the laborers had to be imported and paid for, and they had to be provided with food and shelter, and also with implements. The principle of increasing returns through large-scale undertaking seems to apply here: the man who imported a hundred laborers, twenty work animals and plenty of implements—if he knew how to use what he had with a view to utmost exploitation—could probably seat more than a hundred head rights before his labor force withered; but it was hardly practical for five percent of this labor force to seat five head rights. Thus the head right was not the conveyance of economic value per se—rather was it a form of government consent and regulation in the taking up of lands. There could be no creation of estates without population: it was inherent in the colonizing endeavor during pre-technology for land and labor to blend; they implied each other, for the creation of arable was predicated upon the importation of labor; the head right system was a way of relating the two, and it became the basic method of acquiring land in pre-Restoration Virginia.

The settlers intended to establish cities, and the domain of the most important estate in the colony was chosen as the capital—which was named "Jamestown"*, where the land office was located and the government met once a year. The settled area was divided for political purposes into counties, which were "a reflection of the old Shire system of England". Defense is of paramount importance to a pioneer community: the settlers were in fear of Indians and Spaniards, of political malcontents and of the bondsmen; and the county served especially as the defense unit. Thus the colony's organization was essentially military, and each county had a "county commander" who bore a military title and was its supreme head. Forts also were built for the colony's defense.

The titles in landholding known as "fee tail" and "fee simple independence" are not simply matters in legislation: their differences are profound, as each is the foundation of a distinct sociology or way of life.

The change of landholding title in Anglo-Saxon law from fee tail to fee simple was incidental to the sociological evolution from feudalism to capitalism, and property ultimately achieved independence from state and church when movable property (personalty) acquired greater value than immovable property (realty). This social process—although punctuated by periods of violence—was gradual and stretched over several centuries. During the transition fee simple gradually emerged from fee tail, and there was a complication of the two forms of title in landholding. When James First ascended the British throne the realm was at a critical stage in its process of social change.

The Virginia Company, as founder of the first colony, had to operate under unprecedented conditions. The charters were obtained by the Company at a time when the atmosphere of the Elizabethan era still prevailed in Parliament, and capital was the ruling power. Thus, although

* The naming of an area after one's sovereign was regarded as a claim to possession by that country, and as a mark of the settlers' loyalty.

28

everything was done in the name of the king, there were no requirements in the charters concerning subinfeudation. The original charter granted to the Virginia Company says:

"we . . . grant and agree to . . . nominate and assign, all the lands, tenements, and hereditaments . . . in free and common soccage".[6]

The title of "free and common soccage" empowered the grantee to eschew the manorial form of agricultural organization, and to establish the settlement in terms of full mastery in land ownership. Thus the king conveyed to the Company, the Company to the head of Hundreds, and the latter to the family farmer—all in fee simple independent title.

The laws of "primogeniture" and "entail"—which create and perpetuate the feudal form of landholding known as the "proprietary"—are the cornerstones of feudal aristocracy: they held good in a society consisting of vast landed estates, such as the manorial system in England; and they applied to "lands, tenements and hereditaments", or to corporeal and incorporeal property that is "immovable" in nature, and "fixed" in artifice or in law. Lands are corporeal property immovable in nature. Tenements are corporeal property fixed in artifice. And hereditaments may be a complication of corporeal property benefits such as income from rents and annuities, and proximity to communications or to a beautiful landscape or remoteness from unhealthful spots; of incorporeal property benefits such as rights of way or security from danger; and of corporeal property benefits that are fixed in law, such as the slaves in eighteenth-century Virginia who were legally classified as "real-estate-entailed" and were annexed to the land. If the feudal realty laws are to apply de facto the lands must be developed to the extent that they have intrinsic value; the tenements must be enduring; and the hereditaments—which are peculiar natural advantages and artificial adjustments facilitating exploitation and enhancing the value of the property—must be established. This type of economic organization presupposes: a knowledge of the area — topography, climate, flora and

29

fauna, nature of the soil, most suitable crops—which can come only from the accumulated experience of gradual development; the existence of a traditionally established community in which realty is the most valuable source of wealth; and a land-limited country in which all the arable land is taken up, and a large part of whose population has to find other sources of livelihood. Primogeniture and entail are the result of the urge to protect the holding of that which is basic in its value.

The feudal system is a hierarchy: under it the land-occupant "held"—he did not "own"—by grace of a superior or overlord; the king was at the apex of the system, and he held by "the grace of God". The occupant of the soil had to pay his immediate overlord a "quit-rent"; this was an acknowledgment that he held the land by inferior title, or by grace of his overlord. Thus the quit-rent was simply the due of an inferior to a superior.

"The quit-rents were not regarded as a fiscal measure, or a tax; they were a recognition of the king's ultimate sovereignty, in whom the title of all lands was vested." [7]

The "fee simple independent" title—under which land is owned by right or in complete mastery—arose from a cheapening of realty values which was due to the availability of land, the insufficient development of the occupied lands, or the rise of other sources of wealth which make personal property more valuable than real property.

In England at the time the fee simple independent title to realty was clearly understood in principle, but its application was hedged in by the traditions and practices of feudal land-holding. The establishment of the colony was the first opportunity to introduce the complete separation of property from state and church, which enabled the fee simple independent title to flourish in full freedom: the settlers had a general knowledge of its practice, but the detailed understanding of its operation within a new social complex—rights and obligations of parties in relation to alienation (sale, gift, exchange); encumbrance (trusts, mortgages, principle, interest) which leads to banking; inheritance—had to wait on experience.

To the seventeenth-century Englishman land was very valuable. His country is a land-limited island: the city—of which there were many—endows land with its greatest value, and litigation over land disputes abounded; moreover, as a navigator his land experience was chiefly with small islands, of which there are many along the American Atlantic coast—the Elizabethan Englishman did not think in terms of the vast land mass. The settlers envisaged the rise of cities, and they thought that their experiences at home would be repeated in the colony. The land grant was delimited in terms of acres—which gave it identity, and also gave the courts something to go by in case of litigation. With the passing of time, however, the comprehended area was increasing at a much faster rate than the population; their experiences at home in relation to land were not repeated; and as the English mind began to be displaced by the colonial mind a consistent diminution in the value of land took place.

The corporate farm estate was comparatively small, as its domain had to be within easy reach of the outlying farmers. The primitive condition remote from home is not conducive to a sense of security concerning life and property, grants are contiguous to reduce dispersal, and concentration is welcomed since men find safety in one another. As late as 1646 the Indians were still permitted to hunt north of the York river, and pre-Restoration Virginia's basic activities centered in the area between the James and York rivers. The pioneering Englishman, who thought in terms of a land-limited country, soon found himself with a far greater land potential than he could ever hope to populate. Land in early Virginia—a scattering of scraggly clearings in a mass of forests—was virtually without intrinsic value: the value of a tract was computed by the labor and implement costs necessary to reclaim it from the forests; the tenements were logs, and no advantages had as yet accrued that could be prized as hereditaments. There was insufficient capital—

cash and labor—necessary for the establishment of baronial estates: the land taxes could have no more than token value in order to encourage investment; up to 1641 men were taxed per head of the cattle—rather than on the realty— they owned[8], and in 1662 the Assembly declared that "land is yet at a low value"; and the indentured servant, who was always classed as personalty, was the most important item of taxation. Moreover, the Puritans planned to develop manufactures and commerce—which introduce the principle of intensive economic expansion. Attempts to give natural land some intrinsic respect could be made through pre- emption—the established authority alone could grant title to such land. The settlers' economic plans and the conditions under which they had to operate were inimical to feudal realty laws, and the land grants were in "fee simple by soccage tenure" or for all practical purposes in fee simple independent title.

> "The corporations held their lands of the king by a socage tenure, and . . . no rent was demanded by their charters because the latter were in origin the instru- ments of trading companies and not of feudal lords".[9]

Thus in pre-Restoration Virginia no one paid quit-rents.

With the introduction of private property an attempt was made to encourage investors by giving them a say in the colony's management. In addition the growth of the colony in population and settled area gave rise to complications which necessitated the establishment of local government, and in 1619 the Virginia Company created the "Virginia Assembly" which was called "the popular government". It comprised the Governor, appointed by the Company; the Council, having about eight members—which acted as a "Council of State" or advisory body to the Governor—ap- pointed by the Company; and the House of Burgesses*, which consisted of several representatives elected periodi- cally at first from each plantation# and afterwards from

* The word "burgess" denoted a citizen or city-dweller.

There were a few corporate farm estates or Hundreds near the Virginia settlement but independent of the Company's jurisdiction, and the Assembly refused to admit their representatives.

each county. A Secretary and a Treasurer of the colony were also appointed by the Company. Jamestown was the capital. "The 'popular government' . . . was really that of a joint-stock company";[10] with the Governor comparable to the President, the Council to the Board of Directors, and the House of Burgesses to a meeting of the stockholders.

"There was a marked similarity between the government of the colony and that of the Company after 1619, which suggests that the latter's organization may have been a model." [11]

The Puritans were for a strong central government, and the counties had no local autonomy. The Assembly could convene only once a year and during emergencies; it met and voted as one body—the "Grand" Assembly—and performed executive, legislative and judicial functions; its members were above arrest during sessions; and its legislation was subject to the governor's veto, and remained nugatory until ratified by the Company. The Assembly, in turn, was promised the right to ratify the Company's orders. Martial law was supplanted by the English common law; the rights to private property, protection against search and seizure without warrant, trade and correspondence with the outside world, petition for redress of grievances, habeas corpus, trial by jury, and suffrage—for freemen—were introduced; and a Code of Laws was drawn up for the colony's guidance. All freemen, regardless of property, were enfranchised.[12] Church (Puritan) and State were united; and the parish was the ecclesiastical unit administered by the "vestry", whose members were elected periodically by the parishioners.

Thus the rise of the Virginia Assembly—whose enunciated rights embody many of the demands of Parliament from the Crown—coincided with the introduction of private property. Virginia's legislation could not be "repugnant to the laws of England" but the Company realized that lack of colonizing experience would render its instructions inadequate, and that local peculiarities would preclude entire reliance on Lex Britannica, and it recognized the colonists' right to local autonomy and initiative. The colony was transformed from "the Company as a corporate body, (to) the community as a body politic": it had attained the dignity of political organization or self-government and of recognition, the inhabitants were becoming mentally settled to it as "home", local interests were arising, and Virginia began to lead a life of her own.

Agriculture, which includes both planting and farming, was the base of the colony's economy. This was due to the as yet inchoate condition of the manufacturing economy in England, the inevitable recessiveness of a colony, the need for colonists to be essentially self-sustaining, and to the comparative simplicity and cheapness of land cultivation. But the differences between planting and farming can be fundamental. The planter raises the type of crop which grows thickly and provides constant employment. The high yield per acre sufficiently concentrates labor to enable efficient supervision. This made slave labor, which must be constantly supervised, very profitable. The plantation must have a large area because soil exhaustion is rapid, and it is devoted to a specialized crop which is raised primarily for sale. There is some division of labor, and class distinctions between owner and laborers are sharp. Planting agriculture can operate very successfully on a system of feudal land tenure. The farmer raises the kind of crops that grow scattered and provide only intermittent work, his labor must have a promise of reward since it cannot efficiently be driven, and class distinctions between owner and workers are slight. Thus farming never used slave labor profitably. The tract may be small because soil exhaustion is relatively slow, different kinds of crops are raised which eliminates specialization, and they are used primarily for home consumption. The basis of farming agriculture is fee simple land ownership: the fee simple independent farmer is the capitalistic expression in agriculture, for under feudalism with its land laws there can be no farmer class.

Personalty was more valuable than realty in pre-Restoration Virginia and allodial landholding, rather than feudal tenure, prevailed. In 1633 the Assembly enacted that,

"it shall be lawfull and free to buy and barter for tobacco at such rates as the parties can agree, any lands, leases, houses".[13]

The Assembly of 1639 legislated on deeds and mortgages; the one of 1643 required that to "convey over the estate by way of mortgage" would be recognized if the conveyance is registered in a court of law, which protected creditors; and the property of minors was safeguarded so "that no land belonging to any orphant . . . be alienated". Thus the colony's landholding classes—which consisted of the owners of corporate farm estates, and of the occupants of these estates who constituted the majority of the commoner freemen—rich and poor, all owned their land in fee simple which made them independent farmers. The colonists had become rooted in the land, and this created consciousness of permanence as a community.

There was no London governmental agency to rule and regulate the colonies in America before 1660, and the Virginia Company was freely committed to the establishment of manufactures and commerce—as an integral part of the colony's economy; and it spared neither trouble nor expense in its efforts to advance towns and trade. The Company's instructions to Governor Wyatt in 1621 order him to "review the commissions (of) 1618 . . . for dividing the colony into cities, boroughs, etc." [14] That honest efforts were made in this direction is attested by some of the early place-names, such as James City, Charles City and Elizabeth City. The site of the capital, although unhealthful, was picked for settlement as a precaution against Indians and Spaniards, but especially because its proximity to rivers would facilitate commerce.

The Company advertised for men to go to the colony who are "of good Trades, of skill in husbandry, or industrious labourers";[15] and its "Orders and Constitutions" of 1619, drawn up for the governance of the colony, says:

"In all Patents or Indentures of Grants of Lands, the Grantees shall covenant to employ their people in great part in Staple Commodities, as Corne, Wine, Silke, Silke grasse, Hemp, Flax, Pitch and Tar, Potashes and Sope-ashes, Iron, Clap-boord and other Materialls: and not wholly or chiefly about Tobacco, and Sassaphras." [16]

Governor Wyatt was instructed in 1621,

"to put prentices to trades, and not to let them forsake their trades for planting tobacco, or any such useless commodity." [17]

The colonists were directed also to prepare works for the production of brick and glass, for the building of ships, and for the cultivation of grapes and silk worms from which to manufacture wines and silk. British as well as foreign experts in these occupations were promised homes and land grants and were sent over to organize the industries and instruct the workers. Beads were manufactured to be traded with the Indians for skins and furs. The existence of ore deposits near the colony was soon discovered, and the virgin forests necessary to make charcoal for iron manufacture were there.

"Within three years of the . . . settlement . . . they set up machinery in spite of dire hardship, and as early as 1609 a ship sailed proudly away to England with seventeen tons of crude iron, which the East India Company promptly purchased at four pounds sterling a ton and declared to be the best they had ever secured from another country." [18]

The search for a passage to the East was intensively pursued. The American continent was then thought to be a narrow strip of land; and the colony was visualized as a stopover between the far East and Britain, from which its wealth was to flow. Said a contemporary:

"Virginia shall gain the rich trade of the East Indies, and so cause it to be drawn through the continent of Virginia." [19]

There was also some activity towards locating sources of precious metals.

But the nature of colonial society creates a craze for immediate returns with indifference to the future. In their agricultural activities the Virginia colonists discovered that the raising of tobacco brought high profits immediately, and a clash arose between the plans of the Company and the local interests. It seemed that the "useless commodity" alone could lift them quickly from the severe conditions of frontier life into the comforts some had had at home. Despite the Company's strenuous efforts to push manufactures the colonists continued to engage chiefly in tobacco planting, and King Charles First wrote in 1627— "this plantation is wholly built upon smoke".

Nonetheless the Company succeeded in establishing manufactures and commerce as an integral part of the colony's economy—although evidently not to the extent desired, as urban ambitions declined from the city to the town; Jamestown was at first called "James Cittie". The author of "A New Description of Virginia", published in 1649, shows that trade had grown up with the West Indies, the parent country and the other colonies; small vessels had been built for the coasting trade and for fishing, large amounts of pitch, potashes, furs and lumber were exported, and "the colony was becoming a granary for New England" [20]; the first brick house was built in 1639, and within a decade bricks were being manufactured in abundance; the imported cattle, pigs and chickens thrived and multiplied into herds and flocks, which are sure signs of permanency and well-being; "as early as 1646 . . . considerable wealth had been accumulated in the Colony" [21]; and by 1660 the population had risen to 15,000 whites and 300 Negroes. John Hammond in his "Leah And Rachel",[22] published around 1655, says of Virginia:

"The profit of the country is either by their labour, their stockes, or their trades."

"By their labours is produced corne and Tobacco, and all other growing provisions, and (from) this Tobacco ... a good maintenance may be had."

"Of the increase of cattle and hoggs, much advantage is made, by selling biefe, porke, and bacon, and butter, &c. either to shipping, or to send to the Barbadoes and other Islands."

During Virginia's first century there was great difficulty protecting sheep from predatory beasts and there was no sheep herding, no textile manufacture, little pasturage, and a scarcity of mutton.

"By trading with Indians for Skins, Beaver, Furres, and other commodities oftentimes good profits are raised."

The "Indian trade" was evidently very important for beaver skins were used as circulating medium. Laws were passed in 1645 "for the encouragement of trade"—

"it is to be desired that all manufactors should be sett on work and encouraged in this collony",[23]

and ten years later the Assembly "further ordained,"

"that all freedom of trade shall be maintained, and all merchants and traders shall be cherished, and receive all lawfull assistance and incouragement." [24]

Premiums were voted to stimulate the production of silk, flax, hops and other staple commodities "except tobacco." The king's debts took precedence; but an act protected debtors who came to the colony against process from England, which tended to the increase of population by securing each man the fruits of his labor. One or two places were set apart in each county to which the trade of the county should be confined, which laid the nuclei for towns; a section of Jamestown was set aside for a market place to be held twice weekly; and plans were made to mint coins for circulation among the colonists. Everyone was employed: there was no pauper class; and anti-social activity—crime, vice, beggary —was non-existent. Skilled workers were carefully protected:

> "all gunsmiths and naylers, brickmakers, carpenters, joyners, sawyers, and turners, be compelled to worke at their trades and not to . . . worke in the ground . . . and the commissioners . . . to see that they have good payment made unto them for their worke." [25]

Arable land and indentured labor were the most valuable property, and the great majority of the commoner freemen were independent farmers. The material conditions were tending towards the creation of the "entrepreneur": and the ambition of all men—including those of the "vast submerged"—eventually to accumulate a personal estate, was beginning to emerge as a value. The colony was progressing towards an economy of graduated wealth and income; a class of "freemen that are hired servants" or wage workers was developing, and there was a tendency towards the rise of social classes with conflicting economic interests.

Seventeenth-century Englishmen were sharply divided on political issues, and an organization for whatever purpose had to consist of politically like-minded people. The Virginia Company membership soon revealed itself as made up chiefly of Puritans, and of some Presbyterians. Although there was enough common ground between them factionalism soon set in, and the life of the Company was rent by a continual embittered strife between the controlling Puritans and the minority Presbyterians. This had its reflection in the colony.

> "What may be termed the Puritanical cast of mind, moulded so largely upon the Levitical law of the Old Testament, was dominant among the English people and was strongly reflected in the Virginia Company and in the Colony." [26]

The supervision of Virginia's founding was at first entrusted to a "council" of eight men, of whom one was its president. Both factions were proportionately represented in the council. There was perfect harmony concerning the economic organization of the colony, but on problems of political control the cleavage was serious. A series of acrimonious struggles followed within the council, in which some members were charged with attempts to incite mutiny. This resulted in the execution of one member, and in the expulsion and imprisonment of several. In 1609 and 1612 new charters were granted, and as the Puritans gained definitive control the Company abolished the method of multiple leadership as it vested absolute authority in an individual whom it sent over as "governor."

Meanwhile the political struggles in England were developing clear-cut party lines.

Colonizing projects are per se political, as well as economic, undertakings; problems of the colony's government, and of its external relations, are involved. The Virginia Company was a business corporation organized with a view to making profits, but it was also part of a political movement which attempted to gain control of the realm. This movement was opposed by the powerful landed interests, and the business corporation of seventeenth-century England was more often primarily political than economic in its purposes.

The Virginia Company was described by King James as "a seminary for a seditious Parliament," [27] and it became identified as a political group supporting the Parliament-Puritan cause. By 1624 the Presbyterians had become sufficiently embittered against the majority to adopt the policy of rule or ruin: they went over to the king;* this resulted in the dissolution of the Company and the liquidation of its charter, which meant expropriation of its grant. The Crown

---

* For purposes of the Company; they did not become Cavaliers.

acquired the Monopoly, which put the colony into the hands of the court party; and Virginia was unified as all settlements, including the independent Hundreds, came under one jurisdiction. Thus Virginia became the first royal—as it had been the first chartered—colony, and since the distinction was then dependent for elucidation chiefly on experience there was uncertainty.

The transfer of ownership changed the political alignment in the colony: the Presbyterian was replaced by the Cavalier in the opposition to the Puritan. There were remote areas of agreement between Cavalier and Puritan: they both avowed the principles of monarchy and of the union of state and church, and they were both members of the Church of England. But the differences between them were profound and irreconcilable: tradition wanted the union of state, church and property; while the cornerstone of the Puritan sociology was the freedom, or the separation, of property from state and church; and theirs was a struggle for mastery, not as between persons or political parties, but as between sociologies or ways of life—each with its own institutions and values.

The Puritans in Virginia had had things entirely their own way: the Company had organized the colony in terms of the commercial sociology, which had taken root. The most powerful heads of Hundreds were members of the Council, as they were of the Company: they preferred the charter—which gave the Company the power of pre-emption and made it the direct source of title to land—because in the colony they were the Company; and they had a community of interest with the Company-appointed governor, who was sometimes chosen from among themselves.

Now the Crown was to appoint the governor to whom was delegated the preemptive right, and it became the direct source of title to land. The Puritans disliked the reigning king, and they regarded his governor as an alien, hostile interest.

In 1630 Sir John Harvey arrived as royal governor—the first Cavalier ever to set foot in Virginia—and he immediately proceeded to do what was necessary in order to take away the colony from the Puritans. Distance necessitated local autonomy and the king permitted the framework of representative government—essentially as the Company had organized it—to continue, but the governor was to appoint the Councillors and other political functionaries subject to royal approval. In 1632 the governor revised the Virginia Code to the extent that all previous legislation was nullified, and the colony was to begin again with a clean slate. A good deal of the former legislation was re-enacted, but all law now derived its validity directly from the Crown. Sir John is said to have declared that "the power lay in himself to dispose of all matters as his Majesty's substitute," while the Councillors were merely "assistants to advise with him." He ordered that the clergy observe the Churchmen's creed as differentiated from the Puritan, and that use of the term "Sabbath" be changed to "Sunday."

Governor Harvey had come to the colony with instructions from Charles First to introduce the proprietary system with its implications concerning entail and sub-infeudation, or the reunion of property with state and church. This meant the bringing about of a social transformation in Virginia, by replacing the commercial economy with feudalism through the imposition of the Cavalier principle of no land without a lord. The institutional framework for this transformation was there: the Puritan corporate farm system was an evolvement from England's manorial system, and it could easily revert; a simple change in the land laws could bring this about, and there was no need for confiscation or dispossession. This meant the super-imposition throughout the jurisdiction of a class of proprietary overlords—most of whom were members of the English nobility resident at home, there being no Cavaliers in Virginia; and the liquidation of the class of independent family farmers by changing their status to that of sub-infeudated tenants. And the principle of absentee landlordism would be introduced. Wrote Robert Beverly in 1705:

> "by the Contrivances of the Governour Sir John Harvey ... not only the Land itself, Quit-Rents and all: But the Authorities and Jurisdictions that belonged to that Colony, were given away; nay, sometimes in those unjust Grants he included the very Settlements that had been before made." [28]

Thus the revocation of a colony's charter had much more than incidental implications: it was a problem in sociology, as it meant the liquidation of a way of life; the Puritans' power rested on their kind of social organization; the change from chartered to royal was the first step towards feudalism. In 1721 Jeremiah Dummer of the Massachusetts Bay colony wrote of another such instance:

> "Their Title to their Lands was absolutely deny'd by the Governour and his Creatures upon two pretences: One, that their Conveyances were not according to the Law of England; the Other, that if they might be thought to have had something like a Title formerly, yet it now ceas'd by the Revocation of their Charters." [29]

Governor Harvey declared all patents to land as held of the Company per se invalid, and he required the taking out of new patents in terms of the new social order. Rent was to be paid to the proprietors and quit-rent to the Crown, which changed the title in land occupancy from "ownership" to "possession."

The governor's program immediately brought into question the subjects of state and church, and also the problems of the source of title and of the kind of title to land. Pre-Restoration Virginia's connective principle with London was based on the federal political doctrine, which the king had no intention to change: but the Puritans regarded the royal governor's attitude on local political power as a threat to the principle of popular government; and they also objected to the proposed changes in church ritual. Moreover, land was the foundation of everything: the validity of title was basic, and the idea of the king as the direct source of title caused consternation especially among those who had distinguished themselves by opposition to royal prerogative. Yet the Puritans had an aptitude for wrangling; and, in view of man's inherent disinclination to rebel, they could have compromised on the subjects of government and church, and even on the question of the source of title to land—but never on the problem of the kind of title to land. The *kind of title to land* penetrated to the very roots of human relations—it was a problem in sociology: the Puritan's categorial imperative was the separation of property from state and church; what he wanted above all else was to be master of his own land, which expressed itself in the fee simple independent title; the sub-infeudated status appeared to him as expropriation, and when this seemed to be his alternative he was ready to fight.

Thus the attempt to introduce in Virginia the Cavalier principles on state, church and land meant the liquidation of the Puritan power. This engendered a morbid partisan rancor, and the king's men had to take careful measures against malcontents. In 1632 Harvey's Assembly passed the following law:

"Noe person within this colony uppon rumour of supposed change or alteration shall presume to be disobedient to the present government, nor servants their private officers, maysters and overseers, at their uttermost perills."

The colony produced no arms, and they had to be imported. Legislation was therefore enacted forcing ship captains to submit a statement of all goods brought to Virginia, before its unloading, as well as to submit to search of their ships for verification, and penalizing them severely for unloading any goods anywhere in the colony outside of Jamestown without official consent. This was evidently due to fear of clandestine importation and distribution of arms.

As the bickering in the colony's government worsened London tried to bring about a compromise; the colonists were assured that the change would not deprive them of their estates; and in 1634 London decreed "that the Governor and Council, as was the custom before 1625, might grant lands to freemen." But this was not sufficient to placate the infuriated Puritans: the introduction of the principle of "no land without a lord"—total feudalism—would have subordinated them either qualitatively by reducing them to the status of sub-infeudated freeholders, or—if some of them were promised admittance into the class of lords proprietor—quantitatively, since their estates were much smaller than those intended for the absentee landlords. The problem was resolved when the Puritans, no doubt confident of their party's power in England, rebelled against royal authority by expelling Harvey from the colony. The governor's land program was liquidated, and Virginia continued under the domination of the Puritan Councillors.

As it began to become evident at home that the status quo would continue in Virginia, the king decided to create a base of his own supporters in the new world. He therefore made the Maryland grant in 1632 to the Cavalier George Calvert, with the understanding that it would be organized on the feudal proprietary system. Located in Chesapeake Bay and considered as within the confines of the Maryland grant is Kent Island, on which the Puritan William Claiborne—who was an important official in the Virginia colony—had built for himself a corporate farm estate. By virtue of the feudal way Calvert became lord proprietor over everything within his grant—and Claiborne's property was thus sub-infeudated, although there was no intention to dispossess. To the Puritan this was expropriation, and with the failure of attempts at negotiation there followed the

Calvert-Claiborne affair, in which several fights occurred between their partisans. Thus was set in the new world the preliminary stage for what was to come at home.

In 1642 England burst into civil war; and the Empire found itself with two governments as each contending faction declared itself the legitimate state. In the same year there arrived in Virginia King Charles First's newly appointed governor, Sir William Berkeley.

The atmosphere in Virginia was wholly temperate: she had been founded three and a half decades before war began at home, when English blood was as yet far from the boiling point; there was no accumulated bitterness due to flight from persecution; the founders had transmitted their attitude to their sons, who breathed the uncontaminated air of virgin America; their experience with Governor Harvey had accentuated their self-confidence, and the new governor was an unknown factor. Virginia's Puritans had not stopped at militancy, yet they did not feel the need for the rabid partisanship that their beset comrades showed at home—and they tended to a comparative political apathy. Jamestown hearkened unto the rebel government in London from the beginning of the war, and she began to revise her Code in terms of the Parliamentary decrees. Her House of Burgesses was elected by the people, and in 1643 the Burgesses enunciated the principle of popular sovereignty when they declared their own enactments higher than gubernatorial proclamations and judicial decisions, and when they monopolized the power to tax. Two years later Parliament granted Virginia freedom of religious worship, and it was considering a proposal to hand the colony back to the Company.

In 1648 Oliver Cromwell overcame all opposition at home and made himself supreme master of the realm, which put the ultra radical rebel wing, the republican Nonconformists, into power. Virginia disapproved of many Oliverian acts. The Puritans adhered to the principle of limited monarchy: and their consistent control of the colony, and easy

THE SOCIOLOGY OF COLONIAL VIRGINIA

victory over Harvey, made them amenable to the royal status; and advocacy of the Company's restoration was made treason. Nor were they enthusiastic about religious freedom: steps were taken to suppress the Nonconformists;[30] and although the governor had to be provided with a bodyguard—the Assembly "being sensible of the many disaffections to the government from a schismaticall party" —the malcontent were well under control. More than a half century had passed since the Spanish Armada, and as the power of Spain noticeably waned Virginia's fear of and hostility towards her subsided. The Puritans were shocked by Cromwell's act of regicide, and they immediately recognized the executed king's son monarch of the realm as Charles Second so as to continue the royal status—which gave Virginia the title of "Old Dominion." Thus Virginia's government was anti-Oliverian.

The new governor Sir William Berkeley was a Stuart zealot and his mission to Virginia was the same as Harvey's, but the political situation disabled him from attempting to impose on it the feudal way. At home Puritanism was an embattled principle, which made men objectively conscious of it: in Virginia Puritanism was life; the capital sociology was entrenched and dynamic, and expanding in wealth and power; its denizens—especially the new generation—had a subjective attitude towards its ways, values and institutions; and it was no easy matter to uproot it. Sir William knew what had happened to his predecessor: moreover, the war at home was going badly for his cause; England's sea power was in commercial hands, and Parliamentary war vessels were haunting North America's Atlantic coasts—and in Maryland, where the social set-up was feudal, they had put a rebel government into power. Yet the Puritans' profound resentment of regicide gave them and their governor a kind of community of interest; Virginia's government was as clearly pro-royalist as it was anti-Cavalier; Sir William Berkeley evidently felt that time was on his side, and he was a perfect gentleman as he remained tactfully restrained throughout the full decade of his administration.

In 1652 several of Cromwell's warships anchored off the coasts of Virginia—they were not resisted. The principle of the Commonwealth was extended to Virginia: the Puritans accepted the new order without enthusiasm, but there were no social complications since the colony's previous development tended towards facilitation of the change; and Sir William was retired from the governorship.

Virginia's adjustment to the Commonwealth, 1652-1660, gave the local Puritans complete autonomy. Just as in Cromwell's England the House of Commons became the basic principle in government, so the House of Burgesses played the same role in Virginia—and the Puritan principle of "government by the people," or in the name of the "commonalty," was introduced. The House of Burgesses—most of whose members had important commercial interests—elected from the colony's citizenry the governor, the Councillors and other officials, so that their power was derived from the people: legislative sessions included all members of the government in one "Grand" Assembly; it exercised the power to tax; its enactments took precedence over gubernatorial proclamations and, as the court of last resort, over judicial decisions; and it had the final say in the distribution of lands.

> "The house of burgesses being in possession of all power, granted it out as they thought proper, and resumed it at pleasure." [31]

There was little interference from London, and "the colony was virtually independent during the Commonwealth period." [32] Her Code was again revised: London preferred religious freedom and, says Hening;

> "act 1. of March, 1657-8 ... instead of enjoying obedience to the doctrines and discipline of the Church of England, left the people to the exercise of their own judgments." [33]

The Assembly acknowledged obedience to Richard Cromwell on his rise to leadership in 1659. But no Oliverian ever had power in Virginia: her leading Puritans had been well satisfied with Sir William's administration; there was no bitterness between them and their erstwhile governor, and he and his friends were in retirement and unmolested; and there was widespread doubt of the permanence of England's "regicide republic."

England's civil war created an emigre problem; the defeated Cavaliers were persecuted, and many of them fled the "little Isle" for continental Europe or for North America. The emigre Colonel Henry Norwood described his wanderings during 1649-50 in "A Voyage To Virginia," in which he says:

"a very considerable number of nobility, clergy, and gentry ... did fly from their native country, as from a place infected with the plague." [34]

Virginia's dislike of Cromwell and the fact that she was the last to accept his rule were well known in England, and many Cavaliers emigrated to the colony. Says an historian:

"At any moment the tramp of a Roundhead detachment, coming to arrest them, might intrude ... In Virginia there were no enemies to lurk, and eavesdrop, and betray them." [35]

Meanwhile negotiations were going on in Europe between powerful English political interests and the exiled royal heir, which resulted in the agreement known as the Declaration of Breda. The Declaration legalized the principle of limited monarchy, which left capital in practical control. England's Commonwealth government was overthrown, and in May 1660 the monarchy was restored with the Stuarts as the reigning family represented by Charles Second as king.

Political trends at home had been apparent in Virginia for some time: the Puritans took it for granted that the principles embodied in the Declaration of Breda would apply also to their colony, especially since its status quo ante had been all along commercial; and they looked forward to the Restoration. The Grand Assembly had to choose a governor because of the Commonwealth incumbent's demise, and— after declaring that "the supreme power of the government of this country shall be resident in the Assembly" [36]—it elected Sir William Berkeley to the governorship two months before Charles Second's accession.

Pre-Restoration Virginia was under the practical control of the Puritans. An organization of seventeenth-century Englishmen had to have a political complexion: it was the Puritan whose interests ranged across the seas in search of trade and raw materials; and the charter was his kind of license for colonization. The rights enunciated by the Virginia Assembly as organized by the Company in 1619 embody many of the Parliamentary demands from the Crown: it had rebelled against the Stuart king by expelling his governor, Sir John Harvey, from the colony; and the Assembly sympathized with, and hearkened unto, the rebel government in London from the beginning of the war. But much more important than this—man is a social animal: a settlement of people perforce takes on a social pattern; the Puritans were pioneers in colonization, and also in sociology —they had their own plan of social organization; they wanted to establish a colony, but they wanted to establish it according to their way. King Charles First's two Virginia governors both had orders to infeudate the colony—the absence of infeudation means the presence of Puritans. Yet Virginia's Puritanism was never monolithic: Presbyterianism under the charter, feudalism from the royal status to regicide, Nonconformity during the republic—each strove to have its way in the colony. The challenge of Puritanism's anti-Stuart allies was wholly political, as they were basically agreed on economy: while that of feudalism was profound, since it involved sociology. The results of the colony's change from chartered to royal were superficially political.

While ultimately all power was exercised by—and everyone's rights emanated from—the Crown, the chaos at home precluded royal self-assertiveness overseas, and there was no success in the attempt to introduce a radical social transformation in Virginia.

During her first half century the colony had more clergymen in proportion to population than at any subsequent period. Old Testament names—Adam, Abraham, Isaac, Samuel; Puritan trait names—Thoroughgood, Temperance, Obedience; and trade names—Smith, Sheppard, Brewer, Butler—were common. The Church statutes "inclined to the strictness of the Mosaic system";[37] "popish recusants" were denied the status of freemen; it was thought "that there be great witches amongst them (Indians) and they very familiar with the divill";[38] adultery was a capital offense; and blasphemy, drunkenness, gambling, ostentation, flirting and play-acting were legally and morally condemned. The Church had charge of education, and a will of 1635 granted it lands for the building of a "free school." There was a tendency to evangelism, and to toleration of Separatists: the Nonconformist Pilgrims* were given permission by the Company to settle in the colony, and in 1658 the Assembly granted freedom of religion.# Church attendance on the Sabbath day was compulsory on pain of severe punishment, and in times of danger the parishioners were to "bringe their pieces to the church uppon payne for every offense." After the Indian massacre of 1644 the Assembly ordered that "a day of fast and humiliation ... dedicated to prayers and preaching" in church be observed each month, and the worshippers were to congregate well armed. The "day of fasting and prayer"—a thoroughly Puritan institution—was really a call to arms or mobilization, and the church was a military rendezvous; the ministers had charge of the armed congregations, and the government had to be

* They founded the Plymouth colony in 1620.
# Except to Quakers.

51

sure of their loyalty; and no writ or warrant could be executed by the sheriff on the Sabbath day or at muster.

The Puritans' way of life was based on "the People": its values comprehended the entire population—everyone could be a Puritan. They understood "the rights of the People" as both political and economic: they placed great emphasis on the commonalty—commonweal, common law, House of Commons, Commonwealth; their power rested on capital, and they were convinced that capital is more competent than land in managing the affairs of a country. The Puritans were a social revolutionary force—they were fated to bear the chief responsibility in the struggle against feudalism. Pioneering in sociology—the move from the past into the unknown—is without tradition: precedents must first be established, and the colonists had to grope; and pre-Restoration Virginia is the world's first, if rudimentary, example of the kind of society which is known as the "people's capitalism." The Puritan lived by "the Book"—scripture for ethics, and the ledger for economy; there was never a complete separation of the two. His was a dynamic world of changing status: man's leadership qualities expressed themselves predominantly in the field of economic endeavor; he regarded the profit motif as a positive good; he identified individual improvement—to "rise" or "work one's way up" —with the change from a wage income to a profit income; his supreme ambition was to build up a private property estate; he normally began with humble stakes, and he could hope to achieve his purpose only through gradual economic accretion, which necessitated the concentration of his life on the pursuit of gain. He was economically calculating: thriftiness was a value, and everything had to be budgeted and accounted for—which tended to produce miserliness, and he was often penny-minded and close-fisted. This caused him to develop the ledger, or quantitative, type of mind, which is a dichotomy—one side marked "assets" and the other "liabilities," with the one in excess spelling the difference between success and failure in life. He had little time and mind for cultural pursuits, and even for play. Nobody was per se above labor in the Puritan's world: he regarded labor as a blessing, had contempt for the man who didn't want to work, and he respected the bona fide workingman— who as such was characterized by a measure of intelligence, reliability, ambition. Capital was eager to take utmost advantage of, and continually to improve, the power of production; and the existence and the presence of an "owner" were indispensable to the operation of the economic enterprise, which precludes the conclusion that the worker was robbed of the product of his labor. Yet a straight line could not exactly be drawn between capital and labor—the property owner was often himself of proletarian antecedents, and it was not uncommon for him and his men together to bend over the same tasks. He had no particular interest in land for its own sake—vast non-producing wilderness estates: he regarded land as a business investment subject to market turnover, and his *summum bonum* was to be master of his own land—which meant the separation of property from state and church, and took the form of the fee simple independent title.

Had the settlers "found a continent of land" in America then the material conditions would have existed for the possible realization of the following supposition by Bruce:

"Virginia, without laborers from England and without slaves, would have become a community of peasant proprietors, each clearing and working his ground with his own hands and with the aid of his immediate family.";[39]

and the failure to achieve such an equalitarian social arrangement could plausibly be traced to favoritism and discrimination. But the alleged "continent of land" is a myth —all the settlers found was a continent of gloomy wilderness. Land has to be created: this predicated colonization upon labor; and the existence of a class of propertyless people who had to trade their labor power for a living was unavoidable. Starting from scratch—the necessity to create the foundation upon which to build—renders the pioneer community inherently recessive, and the Company had to establish in Virginia the social categories of "freeman" and "bondsman." Moreover, the individual family farm cannot be autarchic, or an independent economic entity in its own right—which necessitated the domain, and brought about the corporate farm system of organization. This divided the freemen into classes: the "gentry," who had enough capital with which to create the corporate farm estate—the domain and the individual family farms that clustered around it—and who were few and constituted the governing group; and the "commonalty," who comprised the mass of the free settlers, and were the independent family farmers. Thus the creation of a labor base, both bonded and skilled—and of a class of commonalty farmers, was enabled solely by the advanced subsidy, which presupposed substantial capital. In the economy of scarcity of pre-technology only a few could have capital, and the many had to be without capital: this resulted in economic classes—from bondage through commonalty to station—and rendered inevitable the conical social arrangement. The economic differences between the head of Hundreds and his family farmers were enormous: the latter were mortgaged to him, and were dependent upon his domain; and this was the foundation for the division of the freemen into gentry and commonalty— each of which had its own inner gradations. The Puritans instituted the class system of society in Anglo-America.

The commoner freemen consisted predominantly of fee simple independent farmers, of some entrepreneurs, and of a few hired wage workers. It is declared that:

"The original intention of the Virginia Company ... was to promote the growth of an independent yeomanry." [40]

But rather was it inherent in the Puritan way of life for a

strong class of small property owners—the backbone of the people's capitalism—to develop. The workingman of that day, even unskilled, was producing much more wealth than was necessary for his own preservation, and he was beginning to demand more than a bare subsistence return. Puritanism regarded this demand as legitimate: the attempt to translate it into reality meant the bringing about of radical social changes; and it was chiefly through the introduction of the "mortgage" system that the worker was enabled to realize his aims. The unit of economic organization: the share of stock, the twelve pounds and ten shillings, the individual family farm—constituted the original base plan of settlement; the Company had planned and built for the commonalty. The *modus operandi* in colonization that the Company had introduced became the foundation of the colony's social organization and of its peopling, as it continued to be followed by the private landowners. The farm is the capitalistic expression in agriculture: it was the Puritans who created the "farming" system, from which developed the "farmer." This was enabled by the application in the colony of the mortgage system—under which the laborer in the ground escapes the "tenant" status, so that he is not obligated in perpetuity. The Puritans were the pioneers in extending to the common man the benefits of the mortgage relation: for the first time in history a form of social organization had developed that enabled the man at the bottom to work for himself, and gave him the hope of becoming a property owner—it was the opportunity of the ages. The head of Hundreds had to get occupants for the farm units he had prepared with his investment—and he conveyed each of them in one of several ways: by outright sale at a profit, where the occupant took unencumbered; through contract with a craftsman, or payment in skill over a period of time; but predominantly through an arrangement with the discharged servant known as the "leasehold."

There were a few farmers of whom each owned unen-

cumbered several farm tracts, but not enough with which
to create a domain as a profitable economic entity. The person so situated had to attach his property to another's
domain: he took over one of the farms for his own use;
and the rest he conveyed by mortgage to individual family
farmers, who paid him fifty percent the increase of stakes.
This gave him an income from the labor of others—which
distinguished him from the rest of the commonalty, and
could enable him in time to achieve a domain and admittance
into the gentry.

The overwhelming majority of the commoner farmers
each owned one farm on which he lived and worked—and
they were really a laboring class of people, whose living
depended entirely on their own labor. A very small percentage of these had each, through cash or skill, acquired ownership of his farm in clear title: he kept the full product of
his labor, which could enable him to buy a horse or a servant,
and maybe eventually another farm. But the mass of the
farming commonalty was mortgaged to the domain owner.

Some of the fee simple independent farmers had their
origin from the class of craftsmen, who were imported
chiefly from the old country. A few workers of special skills
—vintners, silk experts—were recruited by the Company
from foreign lands, but since they were not British subjects
they had to be offered inducements to emigrate. The same
had to be done for native skills. Skill is a mark of the
civilized community: it is intrinsic, and cannot be coerced;
it gets respect as such regardless of circumstances; and it
was always an indispensable part of the colonial economy.
The craftsman's ability to do certain necessary things that
others could not do gave him a degree of independence as
compared with ordinary labor: his skill was regarded with
awe—it was "mistery"; he was none too numerous, and not
easy to get; and he agreed to emigrate only on an assurance
of the eventual improvement of his condition. He was a man
who was willing to work: he could never be other than a

"voluntary" servant; he had to be content, or he couldn't give the best in him; his papers of agreement were freely entered into at the place of origin—he accepted his obligations; and his benefits—during, and after the expiration of, his term—were clearly enumerated. The colonial who imported skills had to pay an agency for this service, but the craftsman was never literally "bought." He was "bound out"—"under papers," which was a privileged labor status —to a master, usually for from three to five years, but the "papers" seem more like a contract and less like an indenture. He entered the country as a freeman, but not as a citizen—he could not hold office, vote, sit as a juror, while under papers. The craftsman had a say over his own life: he had a choice of masters; of the type of work he would do (he could not be put to laboring in the fields) ; and to some extent also of the conditions under which he worked. The master was to supply the work shed, the tools of the craft, and several helpers; and he was to furnish the immigrant and his family with the basic necessaries of life—living quarters, food, some clothes. Everyone in Virginia was liable in the law: the contract in the Anglo-Saxon law of the time did carry a criminal liability; the master's investment for the recruiting, transporting and providing of the immigrant and his family had to be protected; he had a property right in the craftsman's skill, not in his person—which he could "sell," or transfer, to another; the craftsman was faithfully to perform his obligations, on pain of punishment—he could forfeit his benefits by misbehavior. Yet the fact that the contract carried property rights and criminal liability could not of itself reduce to bondage any of its participants. The man of skill felt at home in the Puritan atmosphere—he was indispensable to the proper functioning of the corporate farm estate. The individual farmers had to use the domain for the procurement of skilled services, for which they paid with their produce. Thus the head of Hundreds also had an income from his craftsmen—the pay for their outside work was his property. Each craftsman had several boys apprenticed to him, towards whom he was in a relation of "master" —which implied authority, and a measure of status. Thus the craftsmen rendered the domain owner necessary services, gave him an income from their outside work, and trained apprentices. At the expiration of the contract the craftsman, native or foreign, was to be conveyed unencumbered and in "fee simple by soccage tenure," the equivalent of a share of stock—a farm unit. It was through the former master's capital investment that the discharged craftsman was provided within the estate with the economic unit required for his establishment—several acres of arable within a granted forest tract, a log cabin, the necessary implements, and a cow—which enabled him to achieve the full status of freeman, citizen and property owner. Thus skill was potential capital: the voluntary servant became a property owner through craftsmanship, and there was never a fixed division in Virginia between white labor and the freeman status.

The farming commonalty was almost entirely a development from within the bondsman class. The head of Hundreds had to find occupants for his many seated tracts, and he could make much more money from a man by using him on a farm than by working him in the forests. The likely servant was early manumitted, and given his start—conveyed a farm unit—by virtue of the master's advanced subsidy, under a "leasehold" arrangement which was in principle a mortgage. Half the increase of this stake was to be paid to the head of Hundreds, which went towards liquidating the mortgage; while the rest of the increase became the farmer's property—all of which made him a freeman, citizen and property owner; and there were more such people in Puritan Virginia in proportion to population than at any subsequent period. There was no "freedman" class: a law passed in 1670 refers to,

"the usuall way of chuseing burgesses by the votes
of all persons who haveing served their tyme are

freemen of this country." [41]

The social conditions enabled the owner-occupant relation to be mutually beneficial: the laborer paid for his transportation with servitude, under which he kept nothing of the product of his labor—and for his establishment with leasehold, where he was entitled to at least half the product of his labor; and the man who arrived on his own fare but without money for establishment could also get the same deal. The leasehold arrangement created the commonalty freeman class. Capital is concentrated labor of brain and brawn: the principle of the mortgage enabled the impoverished person to achieve capital, and all of the social rights flowing therefrom, through labor—it was the only way the freed servant could come by land. The leaseholder was a man who was buying his own farm: he was both a laborer and a property owner; he worked, but for himself; and the best part of the produce he paid to the domain owner went towards the accumulation of equity in property, which is capital. The bondsman as such, in having this opportunity, was a beneficiary of the labor of his class; and as leaseholder he had the potential in principle—even though remote in fact—of himself acquiring a servant. The master had the legal right to free his servants at any time, and manumission—as a sound business practice, not as philanthropy—went on apace. Thus everyone in pre-Restoration Virginia had a legitimate place, actual or potential, within the social framework—no one was on a permanent nonfreeman status. This was enabled by the fact that the labor system was based on economic condition, which is subject to change—not on race or blood, which is immutable: by the limit on indenture, through legal termination and the right to manumit; and by the existence of the commonalty freeman class, within which those released were automatically absorbed, and of which they made up the bulk. The bondsmen, craftsmen, and commonalty farmers made up the colony's laboring classes—they were established by the advanced subsidy, which rendered them subordinate to capital. Capital was the social revolutionary force—labor itself was not such a force: the absence of an "owner" would have meant the disintegration of the economic enterprise, as labor had not yet developed the ability and the self-confidence to assume responsibility in the management of economy—and labor control was not necessary to the continued improvement of the power of production; severe measures often had to be taken against labor, but not because it was revolutionary. The new way of life opened up opportunities and held forth a promise of reward to all; and indentured labor did have a community of interest with—a sense of belonging in, the Puritan society. Thus the bondsman could hope to rise from servility as within the social order: he was not hopelessly condemned, and he did not have to identify his salvation with flight from the jurisdiction; and Puritan Virginia produced neither the "mean white" nor the frontiersman on a social scale.

Under the Puritans the entrepreneur values—the act of engaging in the pursuit of gain, the right to own property and the social opportunity to do so, the ambition above all else eventually to accumulate a private property estate— were first beginning to penetrate also to the submerged masses; they were coming within the reach of the common man, and they were acquiring a popularity they had never hitherto anywhere had. The domain was the nucleus for the development of a town, which gives rise to the entrepreneur. The steady growth of the economy brought complications in relation to the numerous activities on the domain to the extent that it did not pay the owner himself to handle it all. He usually kept his realty interests and became the local banker: but his store, warehouse, shipping and dairy business, he had to sell; while the blacksmith and other craftsmen eventually set up for themselves, rented the sheds they worked in, and acquired ownership of the tools of their trade. Some discharged craftsmen continued their relation with the master as hired wage workers. Thus the people's capitalism introduced the principle of intensive, in addition to extensive, economic activity and expansion: this brought a rapid increase in the production of personal property to the extent that it was becoming more important than real property; and "reality" was subordinated to, and included within, the laws governing personalty—capital ruled over land. Personalty is movable, which renders wealth fluid: this tended towards its diffusion among the populace, and more people were acquiring property than ever before. The absence of fixity in wealth ownership, both real and personal, and the consistent increase in the production of personalty, introduced a social dynamism which brought a vertical fluidity—chiefly upward—as within each class, and to some extent even as between the classes. The move from working for a living to engagement in the pursuit of gain presupposes capital, or the ability to accumulate an economic surplus: the social conditions did give the commoner freeman an opportunity to rise from the "poor man" status —to become the entrepreneur; some of the members of the upper class had risen from the ranks, and they were an inspiration to the lowly freemen.

The foundation of the colony, of the estate within the colony, and of the farm within the estate, was arable—which is a social phenomenon that is produced by capital investment. The jurisdiction, head of Hundreds, commoner farmer —each had to have an initial capital base from which to operate, and the creation and acquisition of realty was enabled solely by capital—which could take the form of cash, chattels or skill. Capital investment was title. The estate constituted a man's total landholdings: the domain was the head and center of the estate, which rendered the estate autarchic or a self-sufficient economic entity; and the corporate farm system was the peculiar social organization of the estate. The man with enough capital organized himself a corporate farm estate, which made him a head of Hundreds or owner of a domain; and the man with abundant capital could own several separate such estates. The Head of Hundreds was a rich man, who engaged in the pursuit of gain: he owned many laborers who cultivated his plantation; he received a given time of the craftsmen's skill, up to half of his leaseholders' yield, and payment in produce for use of his domain; and the surplus he accumulated from all this he could sell at a profit. On the owner's domain was the plantation, which was given over entirely to tobacco: the independent farmer concentrated on the edible crops, and the domain depended upon the farmers' payments for its food and produce. The owner who had less than the minimum number of farm tracts necessary for the organization and maintenance of a corporate farm estate as a profitable economic unit could attach his tracts to another's domain. The man with small capital could buy, and the craftsman through skill could in time achieve, clear and unencumbered, a one hundred-acre farm; while the impoverished freed servant could get a farm on the advanced subsidy, or in terms of the mortgage. These men were the occupants of the corporate farm estate—the independent family farmers: they owned their farms—even if encumbered—in complete mastery, which made their tracts technically free of the estate; but they were subject to the rights of the mortgagor, and they had to use his domain. They were classed as the commonalty, and they were economically poor men whose life was confined to earning a livelihood.

Farming was Puritan Virginia's most important source of wealth—it is inherent in the colonial venture for agriculture to precede industry. The majority of the "adventurers of the purse" either sold their interests to colonials or came over to settle, and absentee landlordism was never a problem. A powerful class of small fee simple independent farmers had taken root in the colony, and they constituted the bulwark of the economic status quo: they abhorred Governor Harvey's principle of "no land without a lord" or total feudalism; and the ungranted areas in the jurisdiction were public property reserved for the people, they were available to any and all who had the capital with which to make them productive, and there was an immediate relation between the granting of land and its seating, and accrual and lapse. Virginia's pioneer economy with its interests in manufactures and commerce had succeeded in establishing itself— the entrepreneur was beginning to become a social force: and her legislation throughout, especially during the Commonwealth, has the basic features of the capital society. Yet the Puritan economy had to forge ahead fighting—"the project (iron manufacture) would probably have succeeded if the king had not revoked the charter" [42]—and it was not destined to have sufficient time fully to develop.

A "complete break with the past" takes several generations to bring about: there was plenty of the past in the Puritans—they accepted and continued the system of vertical social organization that they had inherited from feudalism; and they were determined to maintain the class distinctions. Says Bruce:

> "From the hour when the voyagers disembarked at Jamestown ... all those social divisions which had existed immemorially in England, took root in the soil of the new country; the line of social separation between the gentleman and the common laborer was sharp ... under the influence of habit and feeling, and by the force of actual law, all Englishmen recognized and acted upon differences in social rank." [43]

The social disparity between the freemen was patent—the Puritans did produce the kind of people "who talk only to God." The classes were distinguished also by terms of address—in the Puritan world gentlefolk were referred to as "mister" and "mistress," while commoners answered to "goodman" and "goodwife." And punishment was "accordinge to ye quallitie of ye person offendinge." Bruce tells of an incident in 1640 in which a woman,

> "raised a cloud of scandal against Colonel Adam Thoroughgood's memory by publicly declaring that he had 'paid slowly or paid not at all'; complaint having been lodged against her by his widow, she was arrested and ordered by the court to beg Mrs. Thoroughgood's pardon on her knees in the court room; and also in the parish church." [44]

For a similar offense around 1654 Edward Hall was fined 5000 pounds of tobacco, but

> "Hall ... belonged to the social rank of a gentleman, and for this reason, the sentence was not accompanied by ignominious circumstances." [45]

Yet pre-Restoration Virginia's ruling group was based on capital, and this rendered the differences between the classes fundamentally quantitative: the gentleman was a rich man who had capital, while the commoner was usually a poor man who had hopes of acquiring capital; and the ethical standards of both—their ambitions, hopes, interests, pursuits—were the same. The fee simple independent title in land ownership precluded the owner-occupant relation from being feudal, and the estate was not a manor. Theoretically, membership in the upper class was predicated upon proof of having been born of "gentle blood" and of the right "to bear arms"; yet in the colony, as at home, capital could be the way to station; if a person had the capital he built himself a corporate farm estate and became a head of Hundreds, and nobody inquired about his "blood" as he was *ipso facto* accepted as of the governing group. Thus one of the members of the House of Burgesses of 1629, listed as Richard Tree, is also referred to as "Goodman Tree"—the list of Burgesses for 1632 mentions "Mr. Richard Tree"; this indicates a vertical fluidity as between the classes; commoners could become Burgesses, and they could rise to the station of "gentleman." The institution of "aristocracy," in the sense of the atmosphere of Versailles, can hardly obtain in a pioneer community. There was nothing "immemorial" in

America: the world was wide open, and the feeling of freedom was more natural than social; many masters were of the uncouth, artisan type not above personally supervising and helping in the fields; and the primitive conditions made for adventurism and leveling, life was rough and insecure for all, and habitations and furnishings were rudimentary.

> "While a few of the colonists were educated and able to educate their children in England, the great majority were not above the grade of laborers, and enjoyed but few of the comforts of life." [46]

The atmosphere of the forests, the economic fluidity and the rise of the entrepreneur bred a spirit of independence which encouraged an attitude of boldness among commoners towards the gentry—and the "force of tradition" had to be reinforced by legislation. Pre-Restoration Virginia found it necessary to introduce sumptuary laws: the Company instructed Governor Wyatt in 1621 "not to permit any but the council and heads of hundreds to wear gold in their cloaths"; [47] there was evidently sufficient affluence among commoners to enable them to emulate their betters. The owner of the corporate farm estate was a rich, powerful man who exercised leadership in founding and governing the colony: he had the makings of the modern capitalist, to whom a landed estate is fundamentally a business undertaking; and, although he tried to acquire all of the external habiliments of station, he remained essentially a "gentleman farmer."

The Puritans proved to be superb colonizers: in Virginia —the land without gold—work, trade and frugality were the primary values; and by 1660 the colony was a rich community. The commoner freeman was the chief beneficiary of this success—there were very few places in the seventeenth-century world where his equivalent was as well situated. The climate is mild, harmful wild life was never a serious problem, and the soil was rich: spaces were endless and people were few; the sense of private property was concentrated on the fenced-in arable area, surveyal was unimportant, and there was hardly any "trespass" sensitivity; the woods and the waters seasonably abounded in edible game, and there were no game laws and no such offense as poaching. Trade enabled the existence of the "landless freeman", and the commonalty farmers worked their farms with the help of their families and earned a living. Says an historian:

"during the seventeenth century a stout yeomanry developed before slavery got a hold . . . Sixty to sixty-five per cent of the landholders worked their plantations by their own efforts without the assistance of indentured servants or slaves." [48]

It is good and it is just that America was settled by people from other continents.

When the English came to America they found some native people whom they called "Indians". The aboriginals of the European continent were then the world's most highly advanced people in the artifices: they knew smelting, had developed the firearm, and were able to make water vessels that could traverse the biggest bodies of water in the world. The aboriginals of the American continent were wholly undeveloped in the artifices: they did not have the wheel, the ladder, and not knowing smelting they were without steel products; and their weapon for hunting and fighting, the bow and arrow, was crudely made and of very low efficiency. The naturalist Charles Darwin says:

"The difference between savage and civilized man is greater than between a wild and domesticated animal".

The natives of the European and of the American continents were totally different in their way of life, values and language. The Indian did not have the concept of "nationalism" with its hyper-sensitivity concerning rights of "sovereignty", and when strangers came from the water onto his habitat he did not resent it as "invasion". A "treaty" with Indians is per se fiction since it presupposes civilized values in the Indian: he did not understand what is meant by "real property", with all of its complications—title, conveyance, sale, purchase, payment; his habitat was wilderness without economic value per se, and it could mean little to him that the newcomers respected his "rights by prior possession" and "paid" him for his "land". The Indian way of life was based on the wilderness, while that of the European was based on land (arable): the Indian lost his wilderness; but the European was not thereby a gainer per se since he had to pay, with cash or labor, for every foot of land he got. There could be no rivalry between them since the bow and arrow are wholly ineffective against the firearm. The native weapon disappeared soon after the coming of the whites as the Indian learned how to use the firearm, but he never learned how to make or repair it. Thus the Indian power was always derived—it was never inherent: the Indian as a man is about the same as other men, but the Indian as an Indian is an historical nullity; he could never be a factor in his own right, or the primary cause of anything. The English could describe primitive life only in terms of their own values—Colonel Norwood refers to Indians as "the king, and . . . his nobles", "one of the royal blood"; and as late as 1705 Robert Beverly describes the identification of an Indian with the chieftainship as, "Accession . . . to the Imperial Crown"—and their application to the natives of such ideas as "grant" and "sale" of land, "marriage", "family", "parents", "wives", is fallacious.

The Indians contributed importantly in the struggle to found Virginia. A writing of around 1609 says of them:

"generally they are humane and peaceable, and enter
willingly into communication with our men and help
them with all that may be needed." [49]

The Indians—"this harmless people"—"were friendly to us in our great want," [50] and "by the Help of the Indian Provisions, the English chiefly subsisted till the Return of the Ships" in 1609.

The establishment of colonies north and south of Virginia accelerated her expansion westwards, which brought her into collision with the scattering of Indians in her neighborhood. The difficulty of arriving at mutual understanding; the gradual, inexorable destruction of the Indian way of life; and the eventual development by the English of a feeling of disdain for non-white "savage" races, which the natives were sensitive to and resented—brought Indian troubles. The Indian way of fighting—which was determined chiefly by their type of weapon—was without rationalization, and un-coordinated; although this could sometimes prevail against scatterings of frontiersmen, it was impotent for a large-scale massacre or war.

Virginia's first serious trouble with Indians occurred in March 1622.

"Within a few hours about four hundred English people, or nearly one-third of the entire population of the Colony, lay dead at the hands of those savages ... The massacre had been planned by a master mind and was executed with a thoroughness and precision which was little less than marvelous. . . . The iron works . . . were completely destroyed, fabric, machinery, and laborers together." [51]

The massacre of 1622 alarmed the colonists, definite steps were taken to control the menace from the forests, and the government permitted a good deal of autonomy of action for self-defense.

The settlers seem to have been in constant fear, especially in the earlier days, that disaffected whites would arm and incite the Indians to attack them; rampaging whites often used the ruse of disguising themselves as Indians*, and colonial defensive measures really aimed against internal

* As in the case of the Boston Tea Party.

or outside white enemies were often covered up by language
against Indians. The Assembly ordered in 1632,

"that no person or persons shall dare to speake or
parlie with any Indians either in the woods or in
any plantation . . . but . . . to give the commander
notice thereof".

It was also enacted that the giving of arms or ammunition
to Indians would be penalized with life imprisonment and
confiscation of property, and apprehended absconding servants who had brought weapons to the tribes were executed.
Nonetheless, in 1644—during the civil war in England—
another attack from the forests occurred in which about
three hundred whites were massacred. The author of "A
New Description Of Virginia" says:

"some of them (Indians) confessed, That their great
King was by some English Informed, that all was under the Sword in England . . . That now was his time
or never, to roote out all the English." [52]

The government promptly organized and armed the settlers,
a "warr" was waged on the Indians which was concluded
by a "treaty" of peace in 1646, and pre-Restoration Virginia
forever ended the large-scale Indian massacre.

In this treaty the tribes allegedly acknowledged the British Crown's preemptive right to the territory they inhabited, and hunted and fished in; the areas of Indian and
colonist habitation and ranging were segregated, with the
penalty for trespass the right to kill an Indian on sight;
the government pledged the Indians to its support when
it undertook "to protect them against any rebels or other
enemies whatsoever," for which protection they had to pay
tribute in furs and agricultural produce; and on their
chief's demise his successor was to be designated by the governor. It was further provided that,

"if any English do entertain . . . or conceale any Indians that shall come within the said limits, such
persons . . . shall suffer death". [53]

69

Contact with the European caused the Indian primitive economy to deteriorate: the white man's artifacts were so much more efficient that the native neglected his own handicrafts, and he became helplessly dependent upon the European; and Jamestown achieved economic control of the neighboring tribes. In 1676 the Assembly declared itself,

"sencible that such Indians as are amongst us in peace, if they be not supplyed with matchcoats, hoes and axes to tend their corne and fence their ground, must of necessity perish of famine or live on rapine."

Beverly says that "the Indians . . . (are) now depending chiefly upon the English for what they smoak", and "For their Strong drink, they are altogether beholding to us, and are so greedy for it."

But the efforts to keep the Indians unarmed were ineffectual. Some colonists were arming Indians on the claim of employing them as hunters and trappers; and the Commonwealth Assembly finally permitted its profit-minded traders to exchange firearms for furs on the allegation that other English colonies, as well as the Dutch and Swedes, were doing the same so that the Indians were armed while Virginia lost the fur trade. [54]

The continued taking up of the natives' lands— "our extreme pressures on them"; the killing of "trespassing" Indians on sight—"small account hath been of late made of shedding Indians' blood"; their subjugation to labor allegedly as debtors, their kidnapping for sale into servitude, and the inability to keep them disarmed, augured ill for the colonists—and the Assembly outlawed these abuses.

The competition of the Europeans for territory resulted in the development by the English of an Indian "policy." Under this policy the neighboring tribesmen were recognized as His Majesty's "subjects," whose territory was identified as British "dominion" but Indian "property"; this property could henceforth be acquired only by being "bought" from the Indians by treaty. The act of "buying" a tract as a substitute for outright seizure created a semblance of legality for the claim, which could be used as against rival white interests. This introduced the principle of respect for the Indians' right to the land by prior possession, as well as of their right to make treaties and to transfer title to land; and it gave the colony legal ground to extinguish their land title. But the Indians' right to transfer title rendered preemption defeasible: the pre-emptor had recognized a power outside of itself—the Indians—that could grant title to land, which anybody could then allegedly "purchase." The Assembly therefore instructed the Indians not to make grants to anyone without its consent, and it passed laws—ostensibly for the tribes' protection—predicating the acquisition of land on its own official act by forbidding unlicensed buying of land from or trading with the Indians. The pre-emptive right was thus legalized by local legislation, and whoever owned land in Virginia did so only by virtue of the Assembly's grant.

During the seventeenth century there began the development of trans-oceanic communications, which brought with it an inter-continental mass movement of people. The Puritans were primarily sea minded, and they made the English a sea-faring nation. To the Englishman of that day the world was a very big place, the greater part of it was a primitive state of nature inhabited by strange beings, and there was little hope that civilized man ever would contain it. The emigrant was leaving the civilized society—the garden spot of the earth—for primitivism, and there was no turning back. Civilization and primitivism are natural enemies—on contact one must in time give way to the other. America was an untamed wilderness, and its aboriginals were characterized by tribal values: the settlers had brought with them their civilized way of life, which they intended to transplant in the new world through the creation and expansion of a civil community; and the attempt of civilization to sink its roots in a state of nature meant constant struggle to overcome primitivism. Thus civilization in America was at stake—and the settlers were its pioneers, embattled in its cause. Virginia at this time comprised a number of small clearings on the continent's Atlantic coast: she was a microcosm of civilization on the edge of an infinity of wilderness on one side, and of water on the other; she was a lone outpost of western European culture and values for a full quarter century before the neighboring English colony Maryland came into being; in case of an attack from any source she had herself alone to rely on.

"The members of the early American settlements must have been men and women of most admirable versatility, endurance and courage."

The colonists were oppressed by a sense of space: the ship was a speck on the ocean, and the cabin was a speck in the wilderness—each was isolated, a tiny world in itself. Distance was a problem, usually a barrier, and there was frequent reference to "world's end"—the adventurers in colonization were located in the "middle of nowhere," which gave them a feeling of being lost. The abrupt change from a civilized to a primitive atmosphere had its effects on the mind: the dead weight of the primordial vastness about them took all their courage to resist—it could be overcome only by the invincibility of their values. Fear was a dominant emotion, which applied equally to all classes and conditions of men—they had a feeling of complete helplessness before nature. They had traveled across the ocean, which then took about six months—and they had a sense of accomplishment in having mastered it: but they knew nothing about the gloomy impenetrable forests which always everywhere towered over them, and pressed on the mind, and gave them a feeling of insignificance. Man has a tendency to fear the unknown, which he associates per se with evil: up to well into the following century the colonists imagined the interior of America inhabited by horrible monsters—

"Strange stories were current of marvellous and ab-
normal races of men beyond the mountains, which
were supposed to be washed on the other side by the
waves of the Indian Ocean.";[55]

westwards was "world's end"; they never knew what may
rush at them from the forests; a few did claim to have
ventured inland, but the reports they brought back were
vague and were not wholly credited. The most horrible
calamity that could befall the English settlers was the loss
of their values: their greatest dread was of the forbidding
interior which, as had happened in previous attempts at
colonization, could abduct them forever from the world of
civilization. They were very much concerned about "wild"
men, animals, lands—and they had to rely on civilized labor,
as they could not risk the introduction of a primitive force
in their midst. The home was a clearing in the forests:
farm animals could not be fully domesticated, and it happened often that a colonial awoke from sleep in a condition
of perspired terror, having had a "night-mare" about being
chased across an open field by a horse at night.

"They lived in comparative solitude, scattered along
the banks of rivers and isolated in the great forests,
holding little intercourse with each other or with the
outside world. Almost the only highways were the
great natural watercourses; and the annual ship from
England, laden with goods to pay for tobacco, was
the great event in their lives.... Alone on the edge
of the ocean, it seemed as if the wilderness behind
must, by the sheer force of its vast desolation, drive
the colonists into the sea."

They identified their salvation with what may come from
the direction of the ocean, and the first-century colonial
mind was concentrated towards the east. The Puritans were
more communicative on water than on land: they tended
to hug the coast, and there seems to have been more mari-
time and settlement activity in relation to the offshore isl-

73

ands than inner mainland penetration; their fear of European opposition—Spaniards, bond servants, Cavaliers—was secondary.

Virginia was established by the Puritans. The plans for the colony had to be made and carried out with great secrecy for fear of Spain; Puritan clergymen at home made earnest exhortations in its behalf through the printed and spoken word—"fortie yeeres were expired, before Israel could plant in Canaan." [56] "The paths to colonization are whitened by the bones of the colonist," and the hardships of the colony's "Starving Time" did not stop at cannibalism.[57] The venture swallowed up many thousands of pounds sterling but the London merchants, despite costly initial failures, unstintingly backed it. The Puritans inaugurated the British Empire by achieving for Virginia stability of existence—the first great prize wrung from the wilderness—and their success was due fundamentally to the fact that work and frugality were their supreme values. The Puritans set the precedent for modern colonization and empire.

References
CHAPTER TWO
FIRST PERIOD

[1] W. F. Craven, Dissolution Of The Virginia Company 124-5.
[2] Brown's Genesis 1; 15.
[3] A. B. Hart, American History As Told by Contemporaries 1; 279.
[4] Craven, 57.
[5] Hart, 1; 284.
[6] Brown's Genesis 1; 62.
[7] Wm. Z. Ripley, Financial History Of Va. 47.
[8] Ibid., 22.
[9] Chas. M. Andrews, Intro Beverly Bond's Quit Rent System in Amer. Col. 14.
[10] Craven, 283.
[11] Ibid., 71.
[12] Wm. W. Hening, Va. Statutes At Large 1; 403.

[13] *Ibid.*, 1; 210.
[14] *Ibid.*, 1; 115.
[15] Declaration Of The State Of Va. p. 17 in Peter Force's Tracts v3.
[16] Force's Tracts 3; 21.
[17] Hening's Statutes, 1; 115.
[18] Kathleen Bruce, Va. Iron Manufacture In The Slave Era p. 3.
[19] Edward D. Neill, Virginia Carolorum, 104.
[20] *Ibid.*, 93.
[21] P. A. Bruce, Social Life Of Va. In The 17th Century, 151.
[22] FT v3.
[23] Hen Stat 1; 307.
[24] *Ibid.*, 1; 413.
[25] *Ibid.*, 1; 208.
[26] E. I. Goodwin, The Colonial Church In Va., 35.
[27] Craven, 17.
[28] Robert Beverly, Hist Va. ed. 1705 Bk. 1, p. 50.
[29] Hart, 2; 136.
[30] HS 1; 277.
[31] *Ibid.*, 1; 369.
[32] Ripley, 111.
[33] HS 1; Intro vi.
[34] FT 3;3.
[35] J. E. Cooke, Virginia, 227.
[36] HS 1; 530.
[37] Neill, 89.
[38] Brown's Genesis, 1; 499.
[39] P. A. Bruce, Economic History Of Virginia, 1; 586.
[40] Ripley, 46.
[41] HS 2; 280.
[42] K. Bruce, p. 5.
[43] P. A. Bruce, Social Life, 102-3.
[44] P. A. Bruce, Institutional History Of Va., 1; 51.
[45] *Ibid.*, 1; 52.
[46] Neill, 276.
[47] HS 1; 114.
[48] Bean, 19.
[49] Brown's Genesis, 1; 265.
[50] *Ibid.*, 1; 585.
[51] Goodwin, 69.
[52] FT 2; 11.
[53] HS 1; 325.
[54] *Ibid.*, 1; 525.
[55] Henry Cabot Lodge, Hist English Colonies In America, 42-3.
[56] Brown's Genesis, 1; 582.
[57] Beverly, Bk. 1; 22.

Second Period: 1660-1705

PURITANS vs. CAVALIERS FOR POSSESSION OF VIRGINIA

The contemporary Beverly, who wrote in England about his native Virginia, says:
> "in the time of the Rebellion in England, several good Cavalier Families went thither with their Effects, to escape the Tyranny of the Usurper." [1]

The Cavalier, whose identifying marks were the horse and tresses, was a gentleman*—which the commoner could never be. Those who became emigres to Virginia, of whom some came directly from rural areas, were from the younger sons of England's lower gentry (not nobility)—a few were "titled Cavaliers." [2]

With the younger sons under feudalism disinherited of real property by primogeniture and entail places had to be found for them in the professions and in commerce. Thus the second son usually became an officer in the army or navy, the next one entered a profession such as the ministry or medicine, while those still younger were forced into mercantile pursuits. But the scions of tradition despised especially the latter calling, and they identified themselves ideologically with the aristocracy and supported the Stuarts in the civil war. Their sociology rested on their three traditional basic principles: no country without a king, no church without a bishop, no land without a lord. They were land bound: they were convinced that land is more capable than

---

* Thus in Spanish the word for horse is *caballo*, for hair *cabellos*, gentleman *caballero*, and in French the words are respectively *cheval, cheveux, chevalier.*

76

capital in managing the affairs of a country; aristocracy, to be genuine, had to be land based; and they dreaded the unknown, both in overseas exploration and in sociology. They believed in a static world, ruled by a blooded aristocracy; class distinctions between "gentleman" and "commoner" were clearly delineated, and each was strictly to keep his place—the commonalty had no claim to rule. Their economy was based on the autarchic agricultural unit such as the manor or the plantation; their politics were traditionally rooted in local autonomy, and they believed in uniformity or one Church because Non-conformity created tumult and jeopardized social stability; they were inspired by the Renaissance, which had taken hold in England—and their outlook on life was worldly, with religion taken lightly. Many of them were intelligent men with administrative experience. They regarded leisure as a primary value, which sometimes resulted in indolence: but they were not the sloths of Puritan tradition;* they could be militant, and never shrink the privations of military campaign and the risks of battle. Nor were they the swashbucklers of romance —this element came chiefly from the imported mercenaries, who were largely disliked by the native Cavaliers.

The historian Bruce declares:

"as the fortunes of the cavaliers grew darker, many of them emigrated to Virginia, where they found in the governor a sympathetic companion and a violent loyalist."

Governor Berkeley's

"influence was seconded by that of the large body of cavaliers who had found an asylum in Virginia, where their social accomplishments, experience in arms, and fidelity to the throne, had given their convictions and sentiments extraordinary weight." [3]

---

* The victor is articulate—his mind prevails: the Cavalier has come down in history largely as his conquerors painted him; and it becomes the doleful task of the student to exhume him.

Their revulsion to Oliverian rule drove them to the new world where—animated with all the passions natural to men recently engaged in a fierce and long-protracted civil war—they arrived as refugees, not as colonists. But the hopelessness of achieving their way of life at home due to the limited territory, the land laws and the additional restrictions imposed by the victorious capital people made them receptive to opportunities elsewhere.

When Sir William Berkeley left England in 1642 to become governor of Virginia the stage was set for the civil war that was to ravage the home country for the next decade. The Parliamentarian forces were then controlled by a relatively moderate leadership. But as the war raged on men's passions rose to insane fury, an extreme radical element came in control of the rebels, and the civil war brought results whose drasticness few had foreseen or intended. During this time Sir William was in Virginia, removed from the passions that were consuming his countrymen. The institutions of monarchy, aristocracy and church were sacrosanct to the seventeenth-century Anglo-Saxon traditionalist mind; the violation of these institutions by the Oliverian forces—their "complete break with the past," [4] left Sir William aghast. Thus the governor's first administration is no index to his second one: there was a profound difference in the state of mind of the royalist Berkeley who came to Virginia in 1642, and the Cavalier Berkeley who resumed his governorship in 1660.

The coast of Virginia is indented by four rivers running parallel to their heads in the interior, which is known as the "fall line." These rivers are called—respectively from south to north—the James, York, Rappahannock and Potomac. Between the rivers are three necks of land; this area, up to the fall line, came to be known as "tidewater" Virginia. The constant washing of the tidewater region by the tides of these rivers and their numerous tributaries made it among the most fertile areas in the world. The colony was originally established along the eastern tip of the James river, and it expanded chiefly in a northwesterly direction. During the earlier days expansion was very slow: the limitations of pioneering conditions—lack of sufficient capital, dearth of labor, fear of the interior and of the natives—as well as the plans to create other sources of wealth, made the land grants relatively small and numerous; the colony's basic activities on the mainland centered in the area between the James and York rivers, while the remaining tidewater region was unoccupied.

The emigre Cavaliers arrived "with their Effects"—and with a pattern of social organization that was totally different from the one prevailing in the colony. They were mostly of capital background—but they all had feudal values: what they wanted above all else was land—the life of the country gentleman; and they intended to use the capital they brought with them as a means towards an end—the achievement of their way of life. The picture that Virginia presented to the Cavalier—who had grown up in a land-starved atmosphere —left him fascinated: a vastness of virgin nature—beautiful, fertile, verdant soil; this was ideal for the feudal way of life—it was the Garden of Eden. Moreover, Virginia's first half century had proved that tobacco—a luxury product, hence to the Puritan mind a "useless commodity"—was the surest and quickest way to wealth. Its markets were rapidly growing. Its profits were higher than from any other crop because of its high yield per acre, its concentration of labor which enabled utmost exploitation, and its low weight and high keeping qualities. These were tremendous advantages where each acre had to be expensively reclaimed from forests, and where markets were thousands of miles away in a day of rudimentary shipping. All this Sir William Berkeley and the Cavalier expatriates around him had recognized as an opportunity to introduce in Virginia the sociology of Charles First, and with the return of their party to power they were enabled to act on it. In addition, they had neighborly encouragement: the proprietary system was restored in Maryland, and another such colony was established with the Carolina grant; Virginia was securely located between feudal colonies.

The principle of the Restoration was extended to Virginia: Sir William had never been deprived of his office by any government that tradition recognized as legal, and he regarded his accession to the governorship in 1660 as a restoration—not as a succession; the Commonwealth government of Virginia was a usurpation whose acts, including land grants, were per se illegal; he therefore ignored his election by the Assembly, and he traced his governorship to his original commission from the king.*

No sooner had Sir William resumed power than he and his group of emigres—actuated in all fervor by the values of which their "martyred king" was now the hallowed symbol—set out to abolish the principle of the Commonwealth or Virginia's people's capitalism, and to supplant it with the principle of the Restoration—without benefit of Breda—or the traditional feudal way of life. Feudalism is a hierarchy: the polity is the aristocracy, for whom it exists; and all its classes of men normally think, believe and act in terms of prerogative. Wrote an eye-witness in 1702:

"the proprietors (of Carolina, of whom Sir William had been one) attempted to establish a feudal system more perfect in its working than any in Europe. For the systems with which they were familiar were the results of development or accident, while this was to be carefully thought out and the results calculated beforehand with almost mathematical accuracy, and applied arbitrarily to a new state which was just forming." [5]

---

* The issuance of a second royal commission to Sir William could have been interpreted as a recognition of the legality of his deposition in 1652.

The first step was to take over the power of state in toto. The Cavaliers therefore immediately repudiated the principle of popular government, and they effected a *coup d'etat* and seized Virginia's government. The governor summarily replaced most of the incumbent state and county functionaries with his followers, and many of the names prominent in the colony up to 1660 abruptly give way to a set of new, chiefly non-artisan, ones. The legislative Assembly was retained, and Sir William filled the Council with his fellow Cavaliers. The Council, which was "composed of a few wealthy monopolists and their relatives," [6] soon acquired the status of an august body; each top Cavalier bore several official titles, all salaried, with no one to answer to; they voted themselves emoluments, exemptions and annuities; and they kept scanty fiscal records, and were above arrest. The House of Burgesses' popular base rendered it suspect, and the House was stripped of its powers. The basic power in Virginia—the pre-emptive right to the land, and the source of its conveyance and title—which had been vested in the Burgesses, was entirely taken over by the governor and Council. Sir William convoked a new House of Burgesses, but withheld another election; this House, known as the "Long Assembly,"* continued fourteen years and with vacancies appointed by the governor it became self-perpetuating. From 1680 the Councillors and Burgesses began to meet separately as respectively upper and lower House, and the "Grand" Assembly was succeeded by the "General" Assembly. The parishioners' right to choose their vestry was nullified, and the ecclesiastical and juridical systems were subordinated to the interests of the Cavaliers. An historian points to,

> "The concentration of all the offices and all the power in the hands of a few possessing no legal claim to such privileges." [7]

The machinery of state was securely in the grip of the new

* England's political language was paraphrased in Virginia.

masters.

The Cavaliers—acting with perfect sincerity according to the traditions of their way of life—now set out to create a transplanted aristocracy in Virginia. Aristocracy and land are inseparable, and they immediately took steps to bring about a union of property with state and church. They seized and used the accumulated resources and experiences of the colony's half-century start, and they introduced new principles in the attitude towards land, in the system of its distribution, and in the organization of the agricultural unit. The capitalistic quantitative mind, which regards the possession of empty wooded vastness as pointless—was replaced by the feudal qualitative mind, which regards land as the foundation of station and its acquisition as prerogative. Land acquired a sacredness: numerical expressions concerning acreage became indicative primarily of quality or station, not of capital value; the pre-emption and conveyance of land became a sacred trust that was the endowment of the elite few; the principle of public property in land was renounced as a "vulgar" concern; the fee simple independent title, or complete mastery in landowning, was abolished; and land could never be subject to the rialto. The land units known as "estate" and "plantation" were retained, but the social organization of the economic unit or the "corporate farm" estate—which as a system of farms covered a comparatively small area—was to be transformed into the vast feudal "proprietary" estate: the proprietary was fundamentally a quality of title, rather than a quantity of acreage; and the feudal forms of land tenure—primogeniture and entail and the right to sub-infeudate, as well as the payment of quit-rents to the king—were introduced.

During Sir William's first administration there had developed a number of vast estates. The security of those established required that the surrounding wilderness be settled and "the Assembly offered a fee simple title in ten thousand acres to any association of persons who would seat themselves in" [8] one of these frontier zones. In 1650 the founder of the tidewater Lewis family received a grant of over 33,000 acres, yet according to Bruce:

"From 1634 to 1650 inclusive, the average area ... acquired by patents ... did not exceed four hundred and forty-six acres." [9]

The Puritan ordinarily thought in terms of a farm or hundreds of acres, and the amount of arable in Virginia in 1660 probably did not exceed twenty thousand acres.

But from the Restoration a mania for land set in: feudalism is land minded—it thinks in terms of the proprietary estate or thousands of acres; and the penetration of the interior began in earnest with the Cavaliers. A measure of temerity towards the forbidding interior had developed: Virginia's more than half century and Maryland's over quarter century of existence constituted a record of constant growth, and triumph over obstacles; exploration westwards had broadened the area of comprehension; and the neighboring Indians were no longer a problem. The better part of the tidewater area was almost immediately engrossed as the governor and Councillors freely bestowed themselves grants [10] running into millions of acres of primeval loam; and land grants became relatively few and vast as the new masters began to lay out their proprietaries.

The Cavaliers became founders of families: while newcomers of station were admitted to landholdings, the expansion of the colonial elite was based largely on descent; the feudal law of primogeniture made many of their scions land heirs of the state, rather than of the family; the patrician began at the top as he was born into an estate, and this was provided for him as a matter of course through the principle of the "reservation." The men at the apex—acting in perfect good faith on the principle of privilege, as well as on the possession of sufficient capital with which to turn woods into arable—either themselves engrossed, in terms of proprietaries, vast portions of the inexhaustible forests or reserved them for their scions for future settlement. The head right system—with its requirements on seating, accrual and lapse—was supplanted by the reservation, under which grants of land existed, each amounting up to as many as fifty thousand acres, that had not actually materialized into occupied estates.

Governor Berkeley dispatched an expedition which explored the interior to the Blue Ridge mountains. In October 1660 the Assembly issued the following order:

"Whereas the acknowledgement of the land of (certain) Indians to Coll. Mathewes appeares upon record, but not how justly acquired ... It is ordered by that a consideration of fiftie pounds vallew, be proferred to the Indians for the said land ... the land to be confirmed by rights & pattents." [11]

By meeting the English legal requirement of "consideration" a landed estate could be protected against possible rival claimants. In 1679 the Assembly granted to Major Laurence Smith a proprietary estate—with "freedomes and priviledges and imunityes" which included the right to sub-infeudate—located at the head of the Rappahannock river, as follows:

"the said grounds to be priviledged as aforesaid shall continue for length upon the river ... two miles and one halfe below the fort built (there in) 1676, and three miles above the said fort being reduced into a straight line, and backwards into the woods fower miles, every way distant from such straight line ... all of which he presumes and accompts to be his owne land." [12]

This grant was made on the understanding that Major Smith would seat it with sufficient men and organize it with a view to protecting the colony's frontiers against invasion. In the same year a like proprietary estate for the same purpose, situated at the head of the James river, was granted to Captain William Byrd. Similar offers of such unsurveyed frontier areas were made to others.

> "It was no uncommon thing for councillors to obtain patents for twenty or thirty thousand acres, and sometimes they owned as much as sixty thousand acres." [13]

The polity existed pre-eminently for the good of aristocracy: official registration of patents for land acquisition and land reservation was unnecessary, as the Assembly followed the practice of periodically enacting blanket validations of status quo landholdings for which there was no deeding, recording or sealing "or wherein no valuable consideration hath been particularly set down and expressed." Thus the Assembly declared:

> "concerning the validity of patents for land ... not to be found amongst the records in the secretarys office, or for which no rights have been legally obtained, or have not been duly entered upon record, as they should have been ... be it enacted ... That all such patents for any lands within this colony ... shall be deemed ... valid." [14]

Yet despite their complete political power the conditions in the colony were such as to disable the new masters from immediately supplanting the capital economy with their own; and the social change implied by the Restoration's challenge to the principle of the Commonwealth, both institutional and ideological, took several decades to accomplish. The way of primitive accumulation is often usurpation, and considerations of force are weightier than those of ethics. After a propertied class becomes established it emphasizes its interests as "rights," and it prefers that its origins remain vague. Thus for the period from 1660 to 1682, which William W. Hening, the editor of the Virginia statutes, calls "a very obscure part of our history," the records on the land complex—acreage, occupancy, source and especially kind of title—seem unintelligible. The Cavaliers, however, knew what they wanted and how to go about getting it, and although surface events during the transition are confused and contradictory the underlying trend is clear and definite.

A number of grants to areas claimed by Virginia was also made by King Charles Second to favorites of his court. The Northern Neck,

> "situated between the Potomac and Rappahannock Rivers, extending as far towards the west as the heads of these important streams and towards the east as Chesapeake Bay, was in 1661 granted by the King to" [15]

seven of his favorites. Some years later one of the beneficiaries of this "magnificent gift," the second Lord Culpeper, became the sole proprietor. It was finally inherited by Thomas Lord Fairfax, and when surveyed was found to comprise over nine thousand square miles.[16] Yet the Northern Neck grant was not the conveyance of an individual estate: rather was it the grant of a proprietary jurisdiction, the same as with Maryland and Carolina. Virginia claimed the Neck, as she had the other two, as within her territory but her claim was not so conclusive that London had to desist. Having lost economic control Jamestown could, evidently through some shrewd maneuvering, retain at least political control, and the Northern Neck never developed a government of its own as it consistently sent its representation to the Virginia General Assembly.

> "The King, in 1671, bestowed the quit-rents on Colonel Henry Norwood, as some return for his fidelity to the royal cause in its darkest hours." [17]

The colonel was a kinsman of Sir William Berkeley.

In the same year the king,

> "Without for a moment consulting the wishes of his subjects oversea, by a few strokes of his pen transferred the whole of Virginia to the practical sovereignty of two members of his Court. In the grant to Arlington and Culpeper ...; so complete a gift of

the Colony, just as if it had been a mistress of whom
the royal fancy had tired." [7]
This grant was to last thirty-one years: it provided that the
proprietors be the sole source of land grants; that renewal
of title be made, under a new seal; that they could "give and
grant in fee simple"; and that they receive all the escheats,
quit-rents, duties and reservations. Virginia thus evidently
lost its status as a "royal" colony for the duration of the
proprietary.

In 1660 tidewater Virginia was occupied by the Puritan
landowner gentry, the commoner farmers and some Indians.
In making the proprietary grants to the Cavalier emigres
no cognizance was taken of the areas that were already
seated by the independent farmers and occupied by the
natives, and these tracts came within the limits of the
newly-created proprietary estates. The tractowners were
permitted to remain on and work their farms. But the original title under which they held was in process of liquidation,
and their legal status in relation to the land was changing:
they were losing the mastery of their fee simple title and
could no longer freely alienate, encumber or lease; it now
began to appear that they held their land by grace on a
sub-infeudated basis; and that they had to acknowledge the
overlordship of the emigre Cavalier aristocrat by paying
him rent, and obtaining his permission in making adjustments of possession on their tracts.
Sir William Berkeley was now definitely undertaking to
accomplish what Sir John Harvey had tried and failed. The
success of the Cavalier social revolution was predicated upon
the liquidation of the colony's powerful class of independent
family farmers: their political power had been broken when
the House of Burgesses was emasculated, and Sir William
knew that their economic subjugation could be consummated
basically through a change in the realty laws or the abolition
of the fee simple independent title. Harvey's purpose ap-

peared like an attempt from without, while Berkeley's seemed to come from within—and Sir William operated under circumstances that were much more favorable for imposing this method of covert expropriation. The powerful Puritan party in England was crushed.* Sir William's long residence in the colony had thoroughly familiarized him with it; he had his predecessor's experience to go by; and he had a strong, well-organized group of Cavaliers around him who knew what they wanted, and who were to constitute a class of resident landlords. Harvey's attitude seems to have been arrogant and overt, while Berkeley's was studied and shrewd. Thus was the governor covertly superimposing upon the people's agricultural economy a class of proprietors who tended towards the acquisition of all the rights and perquisites of England's manorial lords.

The Code of Virginia was revised in 1662, now the fourth time. The interpretation of "free and common socage" began to tend definitely away from fee simple and towards the feudal realty laws of primogeniture and entail; frequent use arose of such feudal terms as "freehold," "feoffee," "escheat," "tenant by the curtesy," "livery of seizin," "his majestyes leige people," and rights were granted to erect "mannors with courts leet, court baron, and view of franck pledge and other perquisites";[18] and a development took place which introduced the principle of *"nulle terre sans seigneur"* or no land without a lord, under which those occupying land "held'"—they did not "own"—and paid rent to the proprietor, and quit-rent to the king. Laws on descent and escheat were minutely drawn up, and the "escheator" and his deputies became important government officials.

All the land in Virginia came under the proprietary system. The Cavaliers continued the division of the freemen into gentry and commonalty, but the status of each in relation to landholding underwent a social change. The pre-Restoration status of the gentry—the "head of Hundreds,"

* By the Presbyterians.

was changed to "proprietor"; the former status of the commonalty—the "fee simple independent farmer" unencumbered, was changed to "sub-infeudated freeholder"; while the independent family farmer encumbered became a "tenant." Feudalism is a hierarchy: the proprietor held ultimately by royal grace, and he in turn had the power to sub-infeudate; he could make land grants subordinate to himself as within his own estate—such land grants being the "freehold" and the "tenancy." The freehold is defined by statute:

"every person who hath an estate real for his own life, or the life of another, or any estate of any greater dignity, shall be accounted a freeholder." [19]

The commonalty freehold was understood as being within and under the proprietary:

"colonial freeholders ... were under obligation to recognize in one form or another the higher title of some landed proprietor." [20]

Thus the king created the proprietary gentry, who in turn created the freehold commonalty and the tenants: the proprietor and the freeholder were freemen as each created and stocked his plantation on his own investment; the tenant was on a non-freeman status, as the few acres of arable and the log shelter he used were created by the proprietor's investment. The colony's Code says of the tenancy:

"no person being tenant under any other, shall be taken to be in possession of any lands, so as to claim a grant upon the escheat thereof." [21]

Each form of landholding was a quality of title rather than a quantity of acreage—it denoted a given social status. The freehold was the basis of the franchise, as it was held that those of inferior status or tenants could not "have interest enough to tye them to the endeavour of the publique good";[22] and there was no quantitative or minimum real-property franchise requirement.

The Cavaliers were very much opposed to the Arlington-

Culpeper proprietary because it sub-infeudated them—and it deprived them of the pre-emptive right, which eliminated them as a source of title to land: and in 1677 the Assembly declared;

> "The demise being for the terme of 31 yeares hath yett power of granting lands in fee simple, which being contrary to law may deceive those who shall sue out such grants since the foundation of their title, being illegally, they may be ousted of their possessions." [23]

The granting of fee simple estates is here declared "contrary to law" and "illegal." This is evidently a warning to the inhabitants not to take up fee simple estates from the proprietary since it is limited in time, which may subject them to expropriation.

Some of the estates of the landowner gentry—the leading figures of pre-Restoration days—were respected by Sir William, and a few of their owners were admitted into the aristocracy themselves to become overlords. It seems, however, that most of these estates were not omitted from the imposition of suzerainty, so that some were recognized as freeholds while the rest were reduced to the status of tenancies. The aggrieved Puritans took their complaints to the courts, and a contemporary writing tells of Mr. David Lawrence—a member of the House of Burgesses—"who ... had been partially treated at law, for a considerable estate on behalf of a corrupt favourite" [24] by the governor. It is also recorded that William Drummond, whom contemporaries describe as a "gentleman" and a "former governour of Carolina," was declared to have been a "tenant" [25] of Sir William Berkeley.

There was the consistent intention to continue the federal connective principle with London. Loyalty to royalty became pronounced—anti-monarchical utterances were declared treasonable. The Anglican Church became Virginia's Establishment as church and state continued united, and use of the Book of Common Prayer—the Cavalier Church-man's articles of faith—was declared mandatory. Noncon-formists, and Puritans as well, were identified as Oliverians per se; their congregations were regarded as political rather than religious, and these tenets were therefore outlawed and their adherents were expelled. Wrote a visitor to Virginia in 1724:

"This safe Receptacle enticed over several Cavalier Families, where they made many laws against Puri-tans." [26]

Beverly points to "the present (1663) Severities towards the Non-conformists." [27] With the expulsion of Dissenters evangelism and Biblical names disappeared.

Trading with the Indians for land and furs was organized, and required a government license; supplying them with arms or ammunition was again made a felony (non-English settlers had by this time been cleared from the Atlantic strip), and the law to kill trespassing Indians on sight was revived.[28] As early as 1651 Governor Berkeley declared: "The Indians, God be blessed, round about us are subdued." The organization, arming, supplying and undertaking of all military expeditions had to have government consent through the issuance of a commission, on pain of attainder of treason. Printing was made illegal, although everyone was presumed to know the law. The number of Burgesses from each county was reduced to two, and the county failing to send its representatives to a session of the Assembly was fined.

The Cavalier land policy submerged the heads of Hun-dreds: the commoner farmers lost their status as leasehold-ers, and they had the choice of remaining on their lands as tenants of the proprietary overlords or of leaving the juris-diction. In addition, the westward proprietary grants re-mained largely unoccupied for some time since it was very difficult to attract settlers on feudal terms, which retarded the colony's development. The government imposed a per capita tax on all males above the age of sixteen, and each paid the same amount regardless of the size of his estate. Loose ranging horses and cattle of the "haves" damaged the poor farmers' crops, who could not easily fence in. The governor and his camarilla monopolized the Indian skin and fur trade, which excluded those already engaged in it. The Indians were given arms and ammunition for their pelts— allegedly to enable them to kill fur-bearing animals, as well as pests that preyed on the settlers' livestock. The colony produced no arms, and since the government had established a monopoly on imports the interior settlers were helplessly dependent on it for protection. If the government's policies were inimical to the frontier farmers they received no arms, which left them at the mercy of the well-armed natives. As farmer westward penetration continued and brought Indian devastation of the frontier—and even of some of the inner— settlements, frantic appeals were sent to Governor Berkeley for a commission to outfit an expedition against the Indians. The governor had readily consented to such an expedition in 1644, but during his second administration he consistently ignored such appeals. A contemporary writing describes a meeting of disaffected colonists, whose leader:

> "Questions whether the Traders at the heads of the
> Rivers being his (Sir William's) Facters, do not buy
> and sell the blood of there brethren and country men,
> by furnishing the Indians with Pouder, shott and
> Fire Arms, contrary to the Laws of the Collony." [29]

Most of the outlying farmers had to abandon their tracts as they fled to the heart of the settlement for protection, which caused them the loss of their property and of sustenance. But Sir William remained obtuse to all pleas for help because the Cavaliers regarded farmer expansion as inimical to their social set-up, the Indians were considered allies in that they were clearing Virginia of border undesirables, a punitive expedition would arm a distrusted element, and the

Indian trade would be destroyed.

Meanwhile a conflict also had arisen between Berkeley's Cavaliers and the government in London. The granting away to royal favorites of the Maryland, Carolina and Northern Neck territories, which Virginia had always considered her own, created a fear that the process might continue to her extinction; and these fears seemed to be realized when the whole colony was handed over to Arlington and Culpeper. In addition, London's Navigation Act of 1660 stipulated that the colony must sell her tobacco only in the home country and transport it in English or colonial owned and manned ships. The British reciprocated by outlawing tobacco planting at home and decreeing that it be imported solely from Virginia, while their navy protected colonial shipping. But the Act destroyed competition and enabled the English merchants to set their own price on the product, and a sharp fall in tobacco prices at about that time brought an economic depression in the colony which further aggravated matters. These developments disheartened the Virginia aristocrats, and Sir William sent a committee to London to protest against them. When the efforts of the committee brought no immediate results ways were found to circumvent the obnoxious mandates. The inferior tractowners, however, got the worst effects of these decrees, which contributed towards their submergence. The historian Bruce declares:

"As in England, so in Virginia the restoration of the Stuarts was followed by a period during which the spirit of reaction revealed itself in nearly every department of public affairs; and the evils thus occasioned slowly accumulated until they brought about the most serious insurrection recorded in American history previous to the Revolution." [7]

Man's relation to land is three-fold: acreage and occupancy, which are corporeal; and ownership, rights in relation thereto, or "title." To the colonial mind (pre-technology), America was an infinity of forests that man never would contain. In view of the infinity and of the nakedness of the forests, and also of the fact that it was the grantee's responsibility to seat—acreage could mean little. The "estate" running into many thousands of acres had no economic meaning since it was a mass of natural land or wilderness. What did count was the reclaimed or social land, which even in the richest estate probably never reached five hundred acres at any given time. Thus the royal grant for the founding of a colony, as well as the royal or colonial grant for the establishment of an individual estate within the colony, was in itself innocuous. But title to land is one thing, and the *kind* of title to land is another. Regardless of government—capital investment was the foundation of title to land: registration of title in the land office was a formality, which was not strictly observed; title to land had to be, and was, always respected by all—in order to encourage investment. Trouble in relation to a land grant arose entirely from the problem of the kind of title*—which determined the social organization of the estate, and of the colony. The proprietary grant precluded those people who wanted to be masters of their own land—Puritans and Nonconformists—from settling within the area of the grant. They were not physically estopped from moving in but they would have to accept a sub-infeudated status. If some people had been previously settled and had made improvements within the granted area they had the choice to accept the same status or to leave. Thus no one in Virginia was ever physically dispossessed of land. There were land conflicts in the colony, but "land" was never understood in a corporeal sense.

Virginia had become the property of a few Cavalier families. The development of towns and trade was discouraged, expansion was becoming less intensive and more extensive,

* This is no problem in America today as the fee simple independent title is universal.

and social dynamism and class fluidity were giving way to stratification. The new masters were setting themselves up as a landed aristocracy: the territory within the jurisdiction was being taken up in terms of proprietaries solely for them, for newcomers of station, and for their descendants; and the feudal principle of no land without a lord—which rested on the laws of primogeniture and entail, and on the right to sub-infeudate—was being inwoven into the institutionalism and the values of the colony's social order.

This automatically closed Virginia to Puritans. Their charge of "favoritism" was never quantitative, or in relation to acreage (estate)—rather was it always qualitative, or in relation to the kind of title (proprietary). The feudal jurisdiction did not interfere with their occupancy, but they had to accept a sub-infeudated status. This was anathema: the Puritans were separatists of the land—their supreme ambition was to be masters of their own land, through the fee simple independent title. Here issue was joined: the people in Virginia had the choice to submit, leave or fight. The Puritans were the pioneers in the colonization of America, and also in sociology—they had left home and sailed uncharted seas to reach an untamed wilderness in order to build their world their way. Their primitive accumulation was wholly legitimate: they had come by their lands by virtue solely of capital investment—not through bestowal, corruption or seizure; they had wrested their farms from the forests with their cash savings, often enough also with their sweat, and sometimes even with their blood—and they were ready to protect their social order with their lives.

The Puritans' power rested on their kind of sociology. Sir William's first governorship had given them no cause for uneasiness; they were friendly to him during his retirement, and names afterwards identified with his ruling clique began to appear as members of the Assembly during the Commonwealth. But as the governor's second administration began to reveal his plans to abolish the prevailing social order the people began to give evidence that they had no intention to stand idly by and see themselves emasculated of power: the challenge of the Restoration made them conscious of their own way of life; and political differences within the colony became profound. There had been no feudalism in pre-Restoration Virginia: the Company's principles of social organization had sunk their roots in the colony to the extent that only violence could tear them up; the farming and trading gentry and commonalty were set in the ways of the capital economy, and they were a political and economic power to be reckoned with. Their protest at first was peaceful: they appealed to the courts—but Sir William's appointees ruled in terms of the feudal way; and the Puritans were left with but one alternative. Wrote Beverly in 1705:

> "the poor people becoming thereby very uneasy, their murmurings were watched and fed by several mutinous and rebellious Oliverian soldiers that were sent thither (Virginia) as servants. These, depending upon the discontented people of all sorts, formed a villainous plot (1663) to destroy their masters, and afterwards to set up for themselves." [30]

The conspiracy to rebel was instigated and supported by people in a position of influence, who wanted "the English Protectorate ... restored in the Colony." [31] The plot was aborted; the number of taverns in the colony was reduced as a measure against public gatherings, and a guard was organized to protect the governor and members of the Assembly. But an underlying bitterness continued intermittently expressing itself in isolated instances of "rebellion," which in 1676 finally flared into a general uprising. The uprising is known as Bacon's Rebellion.

Nathaniel Bacon was of the English gentry, whose forebears had been of the Puritan party.[32] A recent arrival in the colony, he was fresh from the commercial atmosphere in England. His social standing immediately elevated him to membership in the Assembly. He was young, impetuous and a good orator, and because of his local position and his family's influence in London the disaffected colonists readily accepted him as their leader. The people were with him— and he was also encouraged by some near the top who were not entirely averse to a capital based gentry, who did not want to see the erasure of towns and trade, and who were dismayed by the London decrees. William Byrd the Second wrote in 1718 that "several of the Council were suspected to be involved" with the rebels. Bacon demanded that the Declaration of Breda be extended to apply also to the colony;[33] he invoked the Puritan slogan, "the People," and issued a manifesto against the governor known as the "Declaration of the People." [34] The essence of Bacon's manifesto is a protest against Berkeley's seizure of the colony: his arbitrary "advancement of private favorites" and imposition of "great unjust taxes" to the ruin of "the people" or "the commonality"; the enabling of Indian depredation, and refusal to allow the colonists to defend themselves; the failure to advance "this hopefull Colony either by fortifications, Townes or Trade." The governor was doing as he wanted in complete contempt of the investments that were made and the rights that were exercised by the farming and trading folk from the founding days—"without acquainting the people ... even against the consent of the people." The manifesto concludes with the statement:

> "we the Comons of Virginia doe declare, desiering a
> firm union amongst our selves that we may joyntly
> & with one accord defend ourselves against the comon
> Enimy, and lett not ... the oppressors devide & sepa-
> rate us who have suferred by their oppressions." [35]

Here Nathaniel Bacon, although of the gentry, does not hesitate to identify himself with the commonalty—"we the Comons"—which had already established in the old country a tradition of self-assertiveness in terms of Commonwealth, commonweal, common law, House of Commons.

Sir William was evidently in hopes that the farmers would be goaded by Indian attacks into fleeing the jurisdiction, and—in view of man's inherent disinclination to rebel—had there been another colony with a capital economy nearby, this may have happened. Instead Bacon appeared with an armed force before the defenseless governor, whom he intimidated into the issuance of a commission for an expedition against the Indians. This brought forth the required arms and supplies, but Bacon no sooner left for the forests than Berkeley revoked the commission and proclaimed him a traitor. Meanwhile Bacon's men attacked the Indian base of operations, a "fort"—about whose erection and defense the Indians knew nothing—which withstood a siege for some time; a contemporary writing says, "twas suspected these Indians had received private messages from the Governor"; while another such writing, the loyalist-supporting "Burwell Papers," declares:

> "Bacon ... meets with the Indians ... killing a great
> many and blowing up their magazine of armes and
> powder, to a considerable quantity ... no less than
> 4000 wt." [36]

Bacon's attainder instantly branded him and his men as "rebels," and Sir William's act was tantamount to declaring Virginia in a state of civil war. On his return Bacon found the whole colony up and armed in his support. The few men the governor managed to assemble and arm could not stand up to the rebel show of force, and they retreated without a fight. Bacon seized Jamestown, deposed Berkeley from the governorship—the third forcible deposition of a royal governor—and dispersed the Long Assembly; and with the convocation of a new Assembly the rights the Cavaliers had destroyed were restored. Bacon's Assembly also passed laws predicating eligibility to office on at least three years' residence in the colony, and restricting office-holders to one salaried position at one time; and it enacted that Indian lands, "bee not granted away by pattent to any particular person or persons, but that the same be reserved, and by due form of law vested on the country, and dispose to the use of the publique." [37]

The beginning of hostilities immediately revealed the true state of affairs: sixteen years of Cavalier domination had aggravated, rather than strengthened, their control; the government in Jamestown was not representative; Virginia regarded the Cavaliers as an alien impinging force; the rebels had the people from the start—theirs was the mass base. The governor, like his predecessor Sir John Harvey, was an isolated figure: Beverly says "Sir William ... was ... abandon'd by all";[38] although efforts could be made to subvert some rebel leaders by promises of admittance into the aristocracy, the government was wholly without internal power. The governor and his few followers fled the mainland for the peninsula (the Eastern Shore, which juts out of Maryland), where the population was scanty and not friendly. Sir William was admittedly dependent upon external support: the Indians were his allies; and he organized the peninsula as a Cavalier rallying center, from where he dispatched an appeal to London for help. Virginia is flanked by Maryland and North Carolina, which were both proprietary colonies. Sir William was one of the proprietors in the Carolina grant, so that he had interests and authority in America outside of Virginia. At home the Stuarts were plotting to regain the traditional power of their throne, to which the colonial Cavaliers must have been privy, and which strengthened their community of interest. The governor spent several months on the peninsula gathering and organizing his forces, with which he finally invaded the mainland. The invasion now confronted the rebels with an irresistible force, before which they retreated into the interior and evidently dispersed in order to defend their homes in the individual counties. Sir William took over the government in Jamestown, and sent out detachments of his men to mop up the scattered rebels and to arrest their leaders. Soon Bacon died, and the rebellion abruptly evaporated.

The determination of both sides to fight is proved by the grim battle at the Indian fort—whose defense was not entirely manned, and certainly not directed, by Indians. But the war within the colony was primarily psychological: each followed the policy of confronting the other with a greatly superior force, there was comparatively little fighting, and the casualties were small.

Bacon's Rebellion—the only general uprising that occurred in colonial Virginia—was not a local affair. Sir William's governorship by virtue of the royal and the colonial commissions is the only factor that lends legality to his belligerent preparations, and creates the impression that the conflict was a "civil" war. The farming and trading kind of economy was caught between Cavalier proprietary colonies —and the war in Virginia was due to an act of invasion, which ended in the conquest and subjugation of the people by an ideologically alien force.

Thus the Restoration's attempt to substitute its way for that of the Commonwealth brought social strife in Virginia. The rebels wanted "the Ease and Liberty of Trade," [39] but land was still basic: the colonial understood the word "land" in a social, not simply in a corporeal, sense—"land" was a complex involving source and kind of title, investment, private and governmental income, quality of person or station, mastery, freedom; and sociology during pre-technology was determined by the kind of rights in land. Where the political differences between men are fundamentally quantitative there is usually no explosive condition: the cleavage in Virginia was qualitative—it was based on values, not on wealth. The farmer uprising was a protest against the Cavalier monopoly of the colony's territory and its distribution in feudal tenure: the feudal form of organization of the landed estate—the proprietary, in and of itself precludes the existence of a farmer class. The principle underlying Bacon's

Rebellion concerned the problem of the kind of title to realty: it was a conflict between the traditional fee tail proprietary title, and the developing fee simple independent title—and it was this that was fundamental in determining the sociology of colonial Virginia.

With the government now more than ever securely in their hands the Cavaliers threw aside all pretense: Bacon's Assembly with its legislation was wiped out, and was replaced by Berkeley's Assembly; the leading rebels were brought in for trial and punishment; and the gradually covert expropriation of the farming classes, both rich and poor, became sudden and overt. Meanwhile there arrived in Virginia a committee of royal commissioners, and a battalion of British troops (the first to be sent to America) commanded by Colonel Herbert Jeffryes. The colonel, who was also commissioned deputy-governor of the colony, brought a liberal pardon for the rebels from the king. Sir William Berkeley was intelligent and gentle, and remorseless: the royal pardon was ignored, and the feudal triumph introduced a reign of terror in Virginia; men were dragged from their homes, women were on their knees in vain pleas for their men's lives, and Sir William's satisfaction "was a revel of blood." The contemporary An. Cotton says that the governor executed "enough ... to out number those slane in the wholl war; on both sides." The leading Baconites who escaped the noose were punished by being humiliated, and mulcted virtually to expropriation. The Assembly enacted,

"that coll. Thomas Goodrich doe with a rope about his neck, on his knees, begg his life of the governour and councell, and in the like posture acknowledge his crimes of rebellion and treason in Rappahanock county court, and that he be fined to the king's majestie fifty thousand pounds of merchantable tobacco and caske ... and upon failer of such payment to be levyed by distresses ... and that he be committed to safe prison ... untill he procure good security for his future good behaviour ... and for payment of his said fine." [40]

Rebels were disqualified from holding office: measures were adopted severely punishing seditious propaganda, the defamation of men in authority, and the casting of doubt on the right of the new Assembly to govern; an unauthorized assemblage of five or more armed men was declared mutiny; and a day was appointed to "be solemnized ... for fasting and prayer to Almighty God" (the Puritan mind is here still evident), for having delivered Virginia from "the late horrid rebellion." Sir William used the uprising as an opportunity immediately to liquidate the capital economy. The eye-witness T. M. says, "rebels forfeitures would be loyall inheritances"; the domain owners, who had always been their own masters, found their legal status in relation to the land changed as they had to recognize an overlord; their property—some of which had been acquired from the founding days and was very desirably located—together with the commonalty farms, became absorbed into the Cavaliers' proprietary estates; and pardoned rebels were permitted to return to their lands, on the basis of the new order.

The contenders for mastery in seventeenth-century Britannia—traditional land and revolutionary capital—were conscious only of the worst in each other. The Puritan saw his opponents as indolent, pretentious and profligate. To the Cavalier the Puritans appeared stiff-necked, narrow-minded, prosaic and grasping—the trader can bicker interminably over matters that seem "mean" to the feudal mind. An enemy can inspire fear, or bring on nausea—the Cavalier was never afraid of the Puritan; a striking difference in their writings concerning each other is that the rebel statements are clean of lascivity. Moreover, the traditional mind is unable to associate the rebel with sincerity and competence. The two groups were mutually exclusive: they couldn't see each other rationally, and it was impossible for them to sit down and arbitrate their differences. The sentiment of the time in the Anglo-Saxon world was against total feudal-ism: during the eighteen years from Sir William's arrival in Virginia to the Restoration there took place in England what are among the profoundest social changes in her his-tory; the Arlington-Culpeper proprietary permitted the granting of land in fee simple independence; and when Sir William was in England during 1661-2 he was instructed strictly to enforce the Navigation Act, to promote towns and trade, and to tolerate Dissenters. Had there been a ten-dency to compromise a social arrangement like that in the colony of New York—which had vast feudal proprietary estates, and also towns and trade and commerce—could have been achieved. But both sides followed a policy of rule or ruin. At home the basic social changes had taken root, and the mind of the Cavaliers of Charles Second was in many respects importantly different from that of their prede-cessors. Sir William Berkeley, remote from these changes, had preserved the mind of Charles First: he and his emigres were enamoured of the life of the country gentleman; what they wanted above all else was to preserve, in all of its pris-tine purity, the world—the values and the institutions—of land-based feudalism. Sir William ignored even London in-structions when they seemed inimical to his plans: he was implacable—the embodiment of the vengeance of the Cava-lier; not a vestige of the way of the Commonwealth was to survive. The Puritans were the social revolutionary force of the time: they had a rebel tradition—they would rather fight than exercise their right to petition by sending a com-mittee to London to protest the governor's acts. The realm was in the hands of the Presbyterians, with whom Puritans at this time had no community of interest. The Puritans had been in complete control throughout pre-Restoration Virginia's half-century: and they were of a generation who knew nothing other than the capital way of life, which was expanding in wealth and power. Moreover, an arrangement such as that in New York would leave the jurisdiction pretty well in the hands of the feudal proprietors.

The royal commissioners and a committee headed by Governor Berkeley left for England to report on the troubles in the colony, but the governor died on arrival. The Cavaliers, evidently dubious of the legality of their rebel acquisitions, sought—and their committee in London obtained—the charter of 1677, which constituted royal sanction of their *coup d'etat* in Virginia. James First's original grant of the colony under the title of "free and common socage" was re-asserted; the Cavaliers' title to their tidewater engrossments and rebel seizures was confirmed, and the franchise was restricted to freeholders; the salary of Burgesses, however, was reduced. The king's pardon for former rebels was emphasized, and was exercised judiciously by the Assembly.

The sociology of colonial Virginia did not develop in terms of an underlying consistent continuity: a fundamental change in the social system took place; and it is this that "brought about the most serious insurrection recorded in American history previous to the Revolution." Seventeenth-century Virginia was an extension of England, and the colony—like the home country—was a scene of sociological conflict. The underlying principles involved in Bacon's Rebellion importantly coincided with those of Cromwell's Rebellion, and the upheaval was fundamentally a struggle between different ways of life.

With the crushing of Bacon's Rebellion the Puritan power disappeared, and Cavalier Virginia emerged: post-Restoration Virginia became politically rigidly monolithic, and socially serene; and the foundations from which rose the "First Families of Virginia" were laid to continue for nearly two centuries. Almost all the well-known names go no farther back than 1640. It is stated definitely that the Washingtons, Randolphs, Byrds, Beverlys, Masons, Pendletons and Carters were of Cavalier forebears, some of whom had fled Cromwell. Thomas Jefferson and John Marshall were

Randolphs on their mothers' side. The Fairfaxes* and Fitz-hughs [41] were of the English nobility. It is declared highly probable that the Lees, Ludwells, Pages, Madisons and Monroes were of Cavalier descent. There is nothing authentic in this respect concerning other leading families, although it is known that most of their founders were of gentle blood and that all arrived in the colony at the height of the Cavalier emigration, which took place from about 1642 when the civil war started in England to about 1670. Puritans were unwilling to go to Virginia after 1660.

In 1677 Virginia was referred to as "the most ancient and profitable of all the English plantations";[42] it was a rich prize, and three distinct groups—the Puritans, Berkeley's Cavaliers and Charles Second's courtiers—competed for its possession. The Cavaliers essentially won out. The Puritans were remorselessly erased. Berkeley's committee in London maneuvred skillfully against the king's courtiers, while in the colony the Cavaliers refused to recognize the Arlington-Culpeper proprietary as a source of land title. In 1684 London rescinded the proprietary, which restored the Cavaliers' power to grant title to land as well as the colony's royal status. The grant to the Northern Neck, however, continued as a courtier proprietary.

The Cavaliers now had a free hand: Sir William's successors faithfully followed his principles; and as the century neared its close their power took root, and the Berkeleyan program began to acquire reality. The feudal revolution erased the sociology of pre-Restoration Virginia root and branch: it abolished the economy of graduated wealth and income with its independent farmer class, commercial interests and entrepreneur values; supplanted it with a purely agricultural economy consisting of vast landed estates—which were organized as proprietaries patterned on the

---

* Thomas Lord Fairfax' paternal forebears were Parliamentarians during England's civil war, while his mother's family, the Culpepers, were Cavaliers.

English manor—and of wholesale numbers of slaves; and by the end of the century there were two classes in Virginia, namely, masters of different degrees of wealth and slaves of varying status. Says Wertenbaker:

> "Since they looked upon the life of the country squire as the ideal existence, as soon as they were settled upon the plantations, they imitated it as far as possible. With the possession of land they assumed the title of 'gentleman.' " [43]

The distinction between gentlemen and commoners was given stronger emphasis: there was much greater respect for "blood" ancestry than under the Puritans, and definite proof was required of a family's right "to bear arms" if it was to be recognized as of the gentry; and vertical fluidity among the classes virtually disappeared.

The colonial was conscious of himself as an Englishman—having a national, traditional, lingual affinity with the land of his origin: he identified his patriotism with England; the colony was simply a place where he resided and had invested his capital, and it had little meaning for its own sake. Up to 1689 Virginia's adherence and loyalty to the home country were fundamental in principle, but nominal in practice: there was no special agency in London for the strict regulation and control of Anglo-America; the communications were insufficiently developed, the colonies were not important enough to merit particular attention, and England was absorbed in her own problems. London had always asserted authority in the granting of land for the founding of a colony in America, but the acquisition and establishment of individual estates within the colony were the settlers' own autonomy. The federal governor was hardly more than a symbol of the Empire: Sir William Berkeley had been the only consequential royal governor in Virginia during this period; and there had been more than a community of interest between him and his Cavaliers—he was one of them.

THE SOCIOLOGY OF COLONIAL VIRGINIA

Thus Virginia had operated practically as an independent jurisdiction.

Meanwhile the Revolution of 1689 had taken place in England: the Stuarts were expelled and the Dutch House of Orange was installed as the royal family, and the people of capital through their Bill of Rights restricted the royal power. Parliament introduced the "oath of abjuration" and the "test act," which excluded from all offices of trust the supporters of the Stuart family claims to the British throne —who came to be known as Jacobites. These oaths were in conformity with the Toleration Act so that Dissenters, who could take them without violating their religious scruples, became eligible to office-holding. Stuart insouciance was supplanted by the use philosophy of commercialism, which developed into England's mercantilist policy. With exploitation a capital motif, organized steps were begun for the complete control of North America through the expulsion of the competing Bourbon imperialisms, regulation of the colonies' territorial expansion, enforcement of the Navigation Acts, suppression of piracy and smuggling, and emigration. Since wealth is based on population England denizated foreign Protestants* and helped extensively to finance their emigration to her colonies.

From the Revolution of 1689 Anglo-America began to be seen in a new light—it was to be subordinated to the interests of empire. London's imperial responsibilities necessitated the introduction of the revolutionary policy of nationalism, or centripetal political organization and control. This brought a fundamental change in the British-colonial connective principle—it meant the unilateral repudiation of the colonies' traditional federal political doctrine or local autonomy. London moved from passive to active domination of the colonies, as she took full direct charge: their management was lodged with the Board of Trade; and their strict,

* In 1685 France revoked the Edict of Nantes, which expelled her Huguenot population.

systematic regulation was introduced for the first time. The communications were improved, and external control became an ever-present reality in the life of the Virginians. The royal governor began to appear to them like a satrap, as it became his primary purpose to check on their every move. Insurance against enemies of the Revolution required that colonial clergymen be ordained in England by the Bishop of London, who appointed a local resident "Commissary" to check on their loyalty. Virginia was required to engage in England's wars, by contributing men and supplies, against forces with whom she had amicable relations —which could be disruptive of local plans. And she had to accept non-British settlers.

Agents of the Board of Trade were sent to investigate the colonies. The home country had no experts on the colonies—all she had were varying degrees of obtuseness: the royal official brought with him the thought patterns of a land-limited, farming, trading country; and her rules and regulations for Anglo-America, especially as in relation to navigation and land, were often impractical and sometimes even inapplicable. Thus for Virginia it was recommended that:

> "by requiring a strict survey of lands in every county, by demanding all arrears of quit rents, by giving strict orders that in the future no grant should exceed 500 acres"

it was believed that "100,000 acres (would) revert to the Crown." [44] The Briton had a feeling of constriction in relation to land—a hundred thousand acres, even of forests, was fabulous. Future land grants were to be carefully checked, and were complicated by requiring the governor's approval of the Assembly's recommendation with final sanction by the Board—every land patent to be valid had to bear the royal seal. Thus ultimate legality in the acquisition of title to land for the creation of private estates was taken out of local hands. The colonial was characterized by a sense of continentalism, which had become part of his sub-conscious being. A "strict survey of lands" or search of title; and the complication in the acquisition, and the reduction in the number and the size, of land grants—could have little practical value in an infinity of wilderness where the creation of arable is predicated upon the grantee's capital investment, and where the social organization is based on the vast proprietary estate. The "land" for reversion could hardly have been empty wilderness; and it certainly couldn't have been reclaimed as this meant expropriation, which the Crown had no intention to perpetrate.

Thus royal and colonial disagreement was never due to wilfulness on either side, but rather to differences in outlook and ways of doing things—the colonials were usually imposed upon as they were in a dependent position. They were very jealous of their local autonomy, and they resented the prying by royal investigators into their domestic affairs. But what was worst of all—the royal officials were attempting to introduce in Virginia the principles of 1689, which meant the restoration of the social order that had prevailed before Bacon's Rebellion. The contemporary Beverly says that in 1692 the new governor, Sir Edmund Andros:

> "caused all the Statutes of England, even those made since their last (1677) Charter ... (and) such as particularly related to Usages and Customs peculiar to England, to be Law in their (Virginia) Courts. ... they knew not what was Law, nor when they were secure in their Estates. He was likewise frequently pleased to say, they had no Title to their Lands." [45]

The writer then says that the succeeding governor, Nicholson:

> "has been heard to declare publickly to the Populace, That the Gentlemen imposed upon them"; [46]

which evidently referred to the foisting on the colony of a class of lords proprietor;

"and that the Servants had been all kidnapp'd, and
had a lawful Action against their Masters." [46]
This was alarming: revolts in several colonies had followed
the upheaval in England, and memories of rebellion in Virginia were fresh. The Cavaliers mobilized their power
against the governors, and they succeeded in getting help
from powerful places in England to overcome recommendations inimical to their way of life. Captains of incoming ships were enjoyned to bring information of political
changes at home to the authorities alone, and the populace
was cut off from events in the outside world. They also
wooed the support of the commoner freeholders: lowered
somewhat the social barriers to them, rendered the taxes
more equitable, and admitted a few to minor offices.

Virginia's aristocrats were pro-Stuart, and in view of the
Restoration of 1660 they hoped for a similar turn. Meanwhile, they maneuvred successfully to preserve their way of
life: the social struggles within the colony were conclusively
resolved; and for a full century—from the defeat of Bacon's
Rebellion to Independence—Virginia was a model of social
serenity. Thus Virginia was not forced to adopt the home
country's social order, but she had to submit to the invasion
of her local autonomy—taking orders from and answering
to London-appointed taskmasters was galling. From 1689
a new principle becomes apparent as the consciousness
dawned on them that they were something else besides Englishmen: as the Cavalier emigre began to give way to the
native-born aristocrat thoughts and actions became progressively less English and more colonial; and as their
thinking in terms of "the rights of Englishmen" receded,
the "Virginian" began to emerge. And the Virginian never
gave up his cherished tradition of local autonomy in principle and, to an important extent, also in practice. Thus the
resolution of the social contradictions within the colony was
succeeded, from 1689, by a political struggle of the colony
with the mother country—the struggle against royal offi-

ciousness became a constant primary concern of the Virginians. They did not mean to be contemptuous of London, but the inapplicability of many recommendations and instructions forced them to go right ahead their own way—which continued the tradition of independent colonial action. This put London in a position where she could charge violation of her instructions, but local initiative and investments in time often brought complications that could not very well be undone. The question was becoming paramount, whether the basic law governing Virginia emanated from England or from the General Assembly—and Virginians sometimes held that Parliamentary enactments, aside from incidentals concerning the colonies, were applicable to their country only up to the charter of 1677. The underlying question, however, was not one of law—it was whether a colony has to adopt the mother country's social order. The Virginians continued a close association with the English aristocracy, but they despised the alien Hanoverian kings and the people of capital who ruled the Empire. They began to regard the royal governor as the agent of an alien power against whom they had to defend themselves: the colony was given the necessary institutional adjustment to facilitate resistance; and all innovations emanating from London, such as the Toleration Act, were bitterly fought. One reason for their refusal to accept a Bishop for their Church in America was the fear that he would be another royal official to oppose. Complaints of their alleged rebellious and republican tendencies were made by Governor Nicholson before the end of the century, and by Governor Spotswood less than two decades later. The period's writings on Virginia—Hartwell 1697, Beverly 1705, Jones 1724—are all full of protestations against the idea of her ever seceding from the Empire.

Thus, just as the Cavaliers had coordinated Virginia to their way of life they were faced with a threat from abroad. The enemies of their social order had seized the British state and introduced profound changes. The General Assembly had to take an oath of loyalty to the Revolution of 1689, and since it was the established rule that colonial laws could not contravene the fundamental law of England—what were the prospects for Virginia? The Cavaliers were intoxicated by the way of life of the country gentleman: they had gone through the horrors of civil war, defeat, flight, and subsequent colonial rebellion—all in order to have their way. They had finally become convinced of the inexorable persistence of capital in its efforts to rule, and they became remorselessly calculating in their precautions against it. They concluded that the Charter of 1677 was insufficient to enable them to sink their roots in the colony, and they decided to reinforce it: and the plan of "the proprietors ... to establish a feudal system more perfect in its working than any in Europe" was consummated through the embodiment of these principles in the basic law of the land—the Virginia Code of Laws, which is a sociological, not simply a legislative, document. This necessitated a radical alteration of the existing Code, the fourth revision of 1662, which —together with the previous Codes—reveals evidences of groping; and in 1699 the Assembly appointed a committee for the fifth revision of the Virginia Code. The committee, headed by Edmund Jennings, went to London for information and guidance in its work, and it returned with the definitive Code of 1705. The Code of 1705 was fundamentally the de jure sanction of a de facto condition that had existed for some time: it constituted the liquidation of the sociology of pre-Restoration Virginia; and it became the base of eighteenth-century colonial Virginia's way of life.

The Virginian mind, both jurisdictional and individual, rested on land: the proprietary system was based on the vast landed estate, and tobacco was distressingly exhaustive of the soil—land was life. During the colony's first century there was plenty of room westward for expansion, and the attitude towards land was subjective—it was taken for granted. From around 1710 the tidewater area was all taken up: expansion into the region beyond—called the "piedmont"—was undertaken, but it does not have the tidewater's excellent river communications and time would be required for its development. This brought forth the consciousness of location advantage, and the tidewater landowners tended to acquire the status of a privileged group. In 1716 Governor Spotswood and a number of local notables viewed the Shenandoah Valley from atop the Blue Ridge mountains, and looming before them was the Allegheny chain: this meant the introduction of a new principle—land could no longer be taken for granted; future extensive expansion would be a problem. The Allegheny mountains were in earlier days feared as a highway for the invasion, and were now regarded as an opportunity for the expansion, of Virginia. The transmontane region was not clearly known, and was regarded with great fear as "back of beyond": Robert Beverly in his writing of 1705 has reference to the "Californien Sea," and in 1718 the governor sent a message home—concerning transmontane activities of the French—in which he mentions the "Misisippi" river; yet it was also thought that the "South Sea" was not far west of the mountains, and as late as 1724 Hugh Jones wrote "we don't know, but the Continent of America may be join'd to Tartary." To the colonial mind America was the Atlantic seaboard strip. The colonials had the confidence that they could get more land when they wanted it: yet the natural barriers brought into question the economic feasibility of further expansion, and there was some concern whether distension would not render the jurisdiction unwieldy for effective political control; and opposition was also beginning to be encountered from the other colonies—all of which gave the Virginians a tendency towards the development of a sense of land limitation, and a feeling of confinement in relation to the seaboard area.

The tidewater area had become fully occupied: the labor of the constantly increasing bondsmen had turned the wilderness into well-developed estates, and the quality of the tenements had improved;

> "we find many years before the close of the seven-teenth century, a succession of large plantations, on each of which there stood a substantial mansion, occupied by a family of social and political promi-nence, descended from the English gentry, and using coats-of-arms, to which they were legally entitled.";[47]

it had the advantages of communications, elimination of primitivism, remoteness from the frontiers; it began to be regarded as the area of "choice" tracts, and tidewater for-ests had evidently acquired a nominal sales value. With the overthrow of the Puritans the emphasis on manufactures and commerce was eliminated, and personalty as a source of taxes was becoming progressively insufficient. Thus realty in Virginia was beginning to acquire some intrinsic value: the primitivism of the pioneering days, which discouraged the introduction of feudal land tenure, had disappeared by the end of the century; and the conditions pre-requisite for the application of such laws had fully materialized.

The realization that continued extensive expansion could no longer be taken for granted, and the dawning apprecia-tion of realty as intrinsically valuable, began to make them land conscious—gave them something to prize and protect, and caused their mind to grip the land. But the Cavaliers' profound longing for the traditional way of life of the country gentleman; and their intention above all else to preserve it from the menace, whether from within or from without, of capital—to insure the rule of land, constituted the fundamental drive which induced them to embody the principles of feudal land tenure in the supreme law of their country.

Under the Code of 1705 a standard land-title form was drawn up in which land was granted to individuals in terms of the title by which the Assembly held of the king, as follows:

114

"to be held of us, our heirs and successors, as of our
manor of East Greenwich, in the county of Kent, in
free and common soccage, and not in capite or by
knight service ... paying unto us ... for every fifty
acres of land ... the fee rent of one shilling yearly." [48]

Thus the title to the colony as derived from London—despite
the changes in status from chartered to royal to proprietary
and back to royal—was throughout its history fundamentally consistent.

The practical interpretation of the king's title within the
colony, however, was evidently the Assembly's own power,
and the fifth revision established landholding definitely in
terms of the feudal realty laws. The following enactments
seem to establish the existence of primogeniture:

"if ... severall persons in equall degree shall claim
... the grant ... of any lands as next relation ... the
male relation shall be preferred, and if there be several male relations ... the eldest ... shall be preferred." [49]

"the heir at law, notwithstanding any land he shall
have by descent, or otherwise, from the intestate, is
to have an equal part in the distribution (of personalty) with the rest of the children, without any
consideration of the value of the land which he hath
by descent." [50]

But the language of the Code concerning the application of
entail is unmistakable:

"it shall not be lawfull ... for any ... persons whatsoever ... to cut off or defeat any estate in fee tail,
generall or speciall of or in any lands, tenements or
hereditaments ... such estates tail (may) be cut off
... only by an act of the general assembly of this
dominion." [51]

This law was subsequently re-enacted by the General
Assembly.

Colonial Virginia was the product of the distressed Cavaliers. The capital revolution had made the feudal way of life impossible for them in England, and taught them that a landed gentry cannot escape eventual economic subordination by merchants. They therefore organized their feudalism and "resumed" their way of life in Virginia, and they were very careful to preclude the development of a rival class to a challenging position.

The Puritan corporate farm estate and the Cavalier proprietary estate appear outwardly similar: the head of Hundreds and the feudal proprietor both owned and were masters of lands, tenements, labor; they constituted and controlled their respective governments; they were members of the top class—the gentry, who had prerogatives; and they both dominated commonalty freemen. But the one fundamental difference—the sociological difference—between them lies in the real property potential of the commonalty living within their respective estates. The independent farmers and the sub-infeudated freeholders may each be described as a class of small landholders, but the existence of such a class as a social force is a question primarily of the kind of laws under which its members held their lands.

The farmer, who is the capitalistic expression in agriculture, is enabled through the mortgage system to start from scratch towards the acquisition of a propertied estate—he pays back the capital advanced him, with interest, from the surplus of his labor. The Puritan leaseholder had the potential of full ownership of his land in terms of the fee simple independent title, which meant the emergence of the separate independent parcel—this rendered inherent the eventual disintegration of the corporate farm estate. The farmer's values are quantitative: success is measured in terms of wealth; and he is entirely on his own, which makes for self-reliance. Realty is subject to the rialto, and to foreclosure: property fluctuation in terms of gain and loss is rapid—which creates a dynamic world and renders social status fluid. To such a mind social stratification is stagnation. The farmer was the backbone of pre-Restoration Virginia's economy, and the propertied of all ranks owned their realty in full mastery. The Cavalier social revolution abolished this form of economic arrangement: the independent farmer owned by right, and he had the feeling of mastery inherent in such title—this created economic and political interests and a world view that were outside of and a menace to the feudal framework, for which reason he had to be liquidated. The farmers could hardly maintain themselves when slave labor, which farming cannot use profitably, became the measure of economic values; and they were disfranchised, subjected to confiscatory taxation, and exposed to Indian depredation. But the farmer class was liquidated fundamentally when the feudal realty laws achieved effectiveness and deprived them of the freedom of land ownership inherent in the fee simple title—there is no place for the farmer in an economy where land can be held only in terms of the feudal proprietary system. Some of the leasehold farmers settled to the new order as tenants, but most of them left the jurisdiction.

The feudal proprietary estate was qualitatively final—it existed in perpetuity: there was a fixity in social institutions and status; land, as the foundation of life, could never be the object of market turnover and changing ownership; there was a fear of change, which was associated with instability and insecurity—all of which resulted in a static society. The place of pre-Restoration Virginia's independent farmer was taken by the sub-infeudated freeholder, who lived within the proprietary estate: he never had the mastery potential; he possessed by grace, the traditional realty laws applied also to him, he had to pay rent in perpetuity, and he fitted neatly into the feudal pattern. The freehold became the foundation of the commoner freeman status. But the freeman status in Cavalier Virginia was predicated upon the ownership of slaves; and, while some of the freeholders

117

personally supervised in the fields, there remained no class of freemen in the colony living solely by the sweat of their own brow. With the rise in immigration the population and the settled area in Virginia rapidly increased: and there took place an absolute increase, but a sharp relative decrease, in the white population. The number of landowners —the freemen, also absolutely increased: however—the necessary vastness of the proprietary landed estate, and the general preference of emigrants for land mastery as well as their need for capital with which to acquire slaves, brought a drastic reduction in the number of landowners or freemen in proportion to the population and to the amount of land owned.

"Virginia in the Eighteenth century was to be the land of the slave holder, not of the little planter." [52]

The Cavaliers were not economy minded: they were alien to the complex investment having problematical long-term implications; and they preferred the simple economy with immediate results. They therefore confined their economy to agriculture, and based it on a single crop—the "useless commodity." The historian Conway refers to the colony as "Tobacconalia," and says that "A true history of tobacco would be the history of English and American liberty." Henry Cabot Lodge says:

"Just before the Revolution the exportation of tobacco ... had risen ... to one hundred thousand hogsheads, was worth nearly a million pounds sterling, and employed about three hundred vessels." [53]

Tobacco took the place of beaver skins as Virginia's medium of exchange, and in 1713 notes based on it at the rate of ten pounds to the shilling were issued as currency. The ever fluctuating output and market price of the weed made it a highly unstable currency base, yet it was used in payment of salaries, taxes, fines and debts; it acquired the character of "the root of all evil," and became a main interest of the commercial world; and it was tied up with the hopes and ambitions of the Virginia patricians, and with the cupidity of companies and kings.

Thus the prosperity of colonial Virginia depended entirely upon the size and price of the tobacco crop. Her mono-crop agricultural economy was helplessly tossed about by the caprices of nature and the market, and in 1681 a fall in tobacco prices caused enough hardship to fire Bacon's smouldering remnants into the aborted Plantcutters' Rebellion. This brought instructions from London and pressure from royal governors that the Virginians develop towns and trade. Nature in Virginia is kindly, and contemporary writers dilated on the colony's topographic features: fertile soil; abundance of edible game, fish and fruits, and of timber and minerals; capacious navigable rivers, warm water ports at all times, fresh water springs; and fine climate, salubrious temperature and wholesome air. The rivers wound deep into the interior, and were highways of exploration, discovery, expansion, and of trade. During depressions restrictions were placed on the raising of "our only comodity tobacco," and economic activities were attempted in other fields. There were some efforts to stimulate the building of ships. The colony's riparian communications had built up experience in making water craft, which coupled with the abundant forests offered the Virginians ample opportunity for commerce in shipbuilding, lumber and naval stores.

"in 1673 a paper published ... pointed out the immense, even unrivalled, advantages of Virginia for shipbuilding." [54]

"the presence of iron deposits was well known and their utilization frequently was urged upon the people by colonial writers." [54]

Laws also were passed to encourage the manufacture of silk, linen, yarn and other clothing materials; and in 1682 the exportation of wool and skins was prohibited, since they could

"be found profittable for the setting to work of many

men, women and children in this country which lye
idle for want of imployment, and some naked for
want of such necessaries as might be wrought out of
the same." [55]

The Assembly, chiefly in obedience to royal mandates, also
adopted several elaborate schemes for the artificial building
of towns. But the attempt to establish towns and trade is
fundamentally a problem in sociology—it is not simply a
matter of legislative enactment. The acts of the Virginia
General Assembly from 1660 towards towns and trade betray uncertainty—they were passed, revised, suspended, revived and repealed. The Cavaliers never planned their towns
and trade as an integral part of the colony's economy; these
plans, admittedly due to the "lownes of the price of tobacco,"
all came to nought, and they were little more than palliatives
for the relief of tobacco depressions.

The underlying trend was actually hostile to the ways of
the trading society:

"The Virginia colonists ... came more and more to
regard commercial and industrial pursuits as less
respectable." [56]

Laws were adopted tending towards the protection of the
landowner against the trader, and the pre-Restoration rights
and powers of traders and workers were erased. Thus the
tax exemptions that had been provided for merchants and
artificers were repealed; the rights of creditors to recover
debts, especially against the estates of deceased, were cir-
cumscribed; a law of 1679 against bringing tobacco into
Virginia was prejudicial to the merchants since their trade
with other colonies was largely thus paid for; in 1662, "by
reason of the unconscionable rates smiths do exact," the
county courts were empowered to regulate their charges;
and all disfranchised freemen, skilled workers and laborers,
were "pressed" for work and war at government dictated
pay.

The fur trade of early days was never large, and with

the rise of vast landed estates it practically disappeared. The failure of the local iron industry, and the restrictions imposed by the Navigation Acts, made Virginia wholly dependent upon England for firearms. Some of the proprietary landowners, who were located along the river shores and dealt directly with the British merchantmen which periodically sailed in, engaged in importing as a sideline and the interior planters bought their manufactured articles from them.

"The Governor and members of the Council in 1692 submitted a petition to the Lords of Trade in England encouraging importation in order to prevent the growth of manufacturing in the colony. . . . These men . . . continued to discourage manufacturing and other industry. Such communications as the petition of . . . 1692 were in the nature of State secrets." [57]

"These men realized that a strong industrial group would challenge their control of . . . Virginia." [57]

In 1696 all restrictions on tobacco planting were removed, and Virginia's "golden era" in tobacco prosperity set in. In 1708 Edmund Jennings, the only Virginian ever commissioned governor of the colony, wrote to London urging that its merchants,

"send in Continued supplys of Cloathing, which will be the only Effectual means to take off the Inhabitants of this Country from going on Woolen and Linnen Manufactures of their own. It was necessity that forced them at first upon this course; but the benefite they have found by it . . . seems to have confirmed in them too great an inclination to continue it in so much that . . . the planting of tobacco has been laid aside." [58]

London encouraged Virginia manufacture of naval stores,

"But you are not to suffer the people employed in the making of Tobacco, to be diverted from it, by this or any other undertaking." [59]

England's merchants disapproved of the act to establish towns in Virginia because,

"such settlements will encourage going on with the Woolen and other manufactures there, and should this Act be Confirmed, the Establishing of Towns and Incorporating of the Planters as intended thereby, will put them upon further Improvements of the said manufactures, and take them off from the Planting of Tobacco, which would be of Very Ill consequence, not only in respect to the Exports of our Woolen and other Goods and Consequently to the Dependence that Colony ought to have on this Kingdom, but likewise in respect to the Importation of Tobacco hither for the home and Foreign Consumption, Besides a further prejudice in relation to our shipping and navigation." [60]

Thus Virginian aristocrat and London merchant agreed on perpetuating the colony's plantation economy.

The proprietors regarded entail as a protection against capital domination, and the feudal realty laws were made so rigid that only a special legislative act could drop entails, while in England the courts had this power. Said Thomas Jefferson:

"In earlier times, when lands were to be obtained for little or nothing, some provident individuals procured large grants, and ... settled them on their descendants in fee tail. The transmission of this property ... raised up a distinct set of families, who ... were formed into a Patrician order, distinguished by the splendor and luxury of their establishments." [61]

By making realty the sole source of citizenship and wealth the rise of a finance class was precluded.

In this commitment to total agrarianism they were greatly helped by their geographic location, and by the policies of British mercantilism which preferred to keep the colonies dependent on it for manufactured articles. With the discouragement of the artisan and trader no towns could develop. The authors of the "Present State of Virginia" (1697), say:

"the bringing of the People of that Country to the improvements of Cohabitation, must be against their Will, by Virtue of the King's Prerogative, and not by expecting the Concurrence of their General Assemblies, the major Part of the Members whereof having never seen a Town, nor a well improv'd Country in their Lives, cannot therefore imagine the Benefit of it, and are afraid of any innovation that will put them to a present Charge, whatever may be the future Benefit." [62]

Virginia did not have a town worthy of the name for more than a century.

Virginia's continual readjustment to the political changes in England is reflected in the frequent revision of her Code of Laws. But the year 1705, when the fifth and final fundamental revision of colonial Virginia's Code was made, marks the end of an era. The writing of 1697 declares:

"the Government of Virginia, which before had been a Business of Care and Danger, came now to be a Business of Gain and Advantage." [63]

The struggle for existence was succeeded by the ambition for comfort.

The conditions tending towards the adventurism and leveling of the early days were gone: Virginia had acquired her mould and attained stability, and no political changes in England could now affect her basically; and her expansion henceforth was in degree. There was no longer any serious trouble with forces from within for the Puritans and frontiersmen as social factors were broken, the liquidation of the local Indians did not require concentrated settlement, and whatever quarreling took place was among the aristocrats themselves. Her struggles now were with forces from without such as pirates, Indians, neighboring colonies and his majesty's representatives.

Jamestown was abandoned, and the capital was moved to Williamsburg. In 1703 Virginia had twenty-five counties, and 60,000 population.

References
CHAPTER TWO
SECOND PERIOD

1 Beverly, Bk. 4; 52.
2 Bruce, Social Life, 61.
3 Bruce, Hist Va., 165, 6.
4 Oxford Hist Eng., 9; 148.
5 Graffenried-Founding Of New Bern, 67.
6 Neill, 321.
7 Bruce, IHV 2; 263.
8 Bruce, EHV 1; 510.
9 Ibid., 1; 531.
10 HS 2; 253.
11 Ibid., 2; 14.
12 Ibid., 2; 452.
13 T. J. Wertenbaker, Patrician & Plebeian In Va. 97.,
14 HS 3; 307.
15 Bruce, EHV 1; 567.
16 H. L. Osgood, Amer. Col. 18th Cent., 4; 99.
17 Bruce, IHV 2; 576.
18 HS 2; 575.
19 Ibid., 3; 240.
20 Chas. M. Andrews, Intro to Beverly Bond, 17.
21 HS 3; 317.
22 HS 2; 280.
23 HS 2; 428.
24 TM in FT, v1.
25 HS 2; 558.
26 Hugh Jones, Present State of Va., ed. 1724; 23.
27 Beverly, Bk. 1; 59.
28 HS 2; 237.
29 An. Cotton in FT, v1.
30 Beverly, 1; 60.
31 Bruce, EHV 2; 30.
32 Wertenbaker, Torchbearer Of The Revolution, 4.
33 Neill, 375.

THE SOCIOLOGY OF COLONIAL VIRGINIA

[34] *Ibid.*, 361.
[35] *Ibid.*, 364.
[36] FT v1.
[37] HS 2; 352.
[38] Beverly, 1; 74.
[39] *Ibid.*, 73.
[40] HS 2; 378.
[41] Conway, 197.
[42] HS 2; 534.
[43] Wertenbaker, Pat & Pleb, 25.
[44] Wertenbaker, Pl. Col. Va., 143.
[45] Beverly, 1; 95.
[46] *Ibid.*, 99.
[47] Bruce, Social Life, 157.
[48] HS 3; 309.
[49] HS 3; 318.
[50] HS 3; 372.
[51] HS 3; 320.
[52] Wertenbaker, Pl. Col. Va., 133.
[53] Lodge, 65.
[54] Va. Polytechnic Ins., Va. Economic & Civic, 5, 6.
[55] HS 2; 493.
[56] Va. Poly Ins., 10.
[57] G. L. Chumbley, Colonial Justice In Va., 136, 7, 8.
[58] Va. Cal. St. PPrs., 1; 124-5.
[59] *Ibid.*, 1; 90.
[60] *Ibid.*, 1; 138.
[61] Marie Kimball, Jefferson: The Road To Glory, 219.
[62] Hartwell, Present State Of Va., Wmsbg. ed., 5.
[63] *Ibid.*, 46.

Third Period: 1705-1776; CAVALIER ABSOLUTISM

Part One: INSTITUTIONS

The sociology of England had evolved but that of Virginia was planned, and the social engineer was Sir William Berkeley.

Sir William was of the English top gentry; his family was part of the royal household, and he was among the most powerfully placed persons ever to come to the colonies. As genuinely capable as he was traditional he was an Oxford graduate and a cultured man, and he had written a play that was staged in London. His training in the atmosphere of the court made him an aristocrat to the core. He was heart and soul for the Cavalier way: its society was to him the acme of human development, and he labored consistently and earnestly to duplicate it in the colony. He regarded self-assertive Dissenters as insolent upstarts who were to be mercilessly suppressed, but he showed respect for the traditional Anglo-Saxon civil liberties—no rebel was punished without a trial. Sir William—Britain's first efficient colonial administrator—was Virginia's governor for twenty-seven out of the thirty-five years he lived there: he remained an Englishman throughout—he was never a Virginian, yet he is easily colonial Virginia's most outstanding figure. He had the responsibilities of state at the height of the period of "Care and Danger": his was an uphill fight; he worked against the spirit of the time, and was opposed by almost everyone in the colony as well as by many in England; yet he met his tasks with courage and with remarkable ability, and he succeeded in re-creating in Virginia the sociology of the days of Hotspur. Wrote the eye-witness Jones in 1724:

"all the Laws and Statutes of England before Queen Elizabeth are there (Virginia) in Force, but none

made since." [1]
The settlers of Virginia established both a colony and a way
of life—it took much more time and trouble to establish the
second: in 1660 the colony's social organization was still
plastic; and the governor's efforts found their fruition in
the Virginia Code of 1705, which is the constitution of feudalism—an example of statutory sociology. The Stuart way
of life in England had undergone important modifications
because of the powerful capital influence: but in the Old
Dominion there were no such forces to mar the serenity of
feudal arrangement; and the outbreak of the War for Independence found the colony more traditional than the parent
country. Thus was Sir William Berkeley much more than
simply the governor of a province: eighteenth-century colonial Virginia was basically his brain-child; yet he built
bigger than he knew, for he transcends his time and place
as he acquires a stature that puts him among the leading
figures in all of American history—he was the progenitor of
what came to be known as "The Sociology of the South."

During the colony's second century her settled area had
about quintupled, and she stretched to the mountains—and
by Independence she had become divided into three sections
whose topographic variations created some economic differences. They were the "tidewater" area, which extends from
the Atlantic coast to the heads of the four important rivers
or the "fall line"; the "piedmont" area, from the fall line
to the Blue Ridge mountains; and the "valley" area or the
Shenandoah Valley, which lies between the Blue Ridge and
the Allegheny mountains. The social institutions, the values
and the laws prevailing in the tidewater area—where Virginia was founded and her way of life was determined—
fundamentally dominated the whole jurisdiction during the
colonial period. Beverly points to "the whole Country ...
having the same Tenures of Land, Usages and Customs";[2]
and Virginia was governed by "the common law of England,

and divers acts of parliament, which are binding upon the subjects of this colony," as well as by the enactments of her General Assembly.

Virginia pre-empted all the land within her jurisdiction as against everyone except the British Crown, and this empowered her to decide to whom and on what terms to make a land grant. Land was granted only in terms of private property, and there was no land in common. The king had the overall monopoly and he could at any time make a grant for the establishment of an individual estate within the colony. All land however granted was held ultimately by royal grace: an act of Parliament permitted the colonial governments to grant title to their unpatented lands, which were called "public domain"; yet the local legislative act making an individual land grant had to be approved by the Board of Trade—"the royal seal was necessary to the validity of every land patent." This predicated the growth of the colony on the consent of the Board, to which the colonials at first made no objection as they wanted utmost protection for their investments. During her first century the colony did not produce sufficient wealth to set aside a surplus for investment; her growth was based chiefly on the capital brought in by new settlers, and England was indeed the "mother" country. From about 1700 Virginia was beginning to accumulate native investment capital. The Cavaliers had developed the feeling that their way of life was definitively established. They had a base from which, and the capital with which, to operate westwards: this brought an emergence from a feeling of fear of trans-Allegheny towards one of aggressiveness, and from an attitude of submissiveness to London towards one of dignity and self-confidence; and the General Assembly began to re-assert its original power of granting land as its own right. Virginia's landed organization consisted of the "estate" which, whether a unit or in scattered parcels, constituted a man's total landholding; the "plantation"—the area in nature that had been altered by man through capital investment to suit his purposes—or the area of life and labor, which amounted usually to a very small part of the estate; and the "proprietary," which was the peculiar social organization of the estate. Land was granted officially almost exclusively in terms of the proprietary system—the grant in fee simple independent title was rare. The Cavaliers had introduced the principle of "quality of title" in the granting of individual estates; this created gradations of title—the proprietary, the commonalty freehold, and the tenancy. The proprietary grant was an act of state: with the Code of 1705 the Cavalier power had taken root, and the value of title was greatly enhanced; the acquisition of a proprietary estate was tantamount to the recipient's admittance into the aristocracy, and the most careful selectivity was exercised in its granting. The proprietor had the power himself to sub-infeudate within his estate to British subjects on the commonalty freehold title; this title was always open to those who had the capital with which to establish themselves; the commonalty freeholder had to pay rent to the proprietor—and rent was perpetual under feudalism, as there was no mortgage system. Virginia's social structure rested on a tripod which consisted of the plantation, the county and the parish: the plantation was the economic unit; the county was the legislative, judicial and military unit; and the parish was the ecclesiastical unit —these pillars of the Virginia society were securely in the hands of the proprietary aristocracy. Her economy was specialized agriculture, and consisted of a series of plantations scattered over a large area with the distance between them usually about twenty miles; a few were vast, stretching across as many as five hundred acres and having up to five hundred inhabitants, but the great majority were smaller. The plantations were mainly individually owned, but some were owned by lay (town) and ecclesiastical (church or college) corporations. The acreage of the plantation always had economic meaning and sales value since it was the area of investment, and of the production of wealth; and it used the maximum agricultural wealth-producing ability of the day. But Virginia's plantation economy was not a profit economy. The proprietary estate was not a business enterprise—it did not exist with a view to making profit: there was no engagement in the pursuit of gain, the primary purpose of the proprietary system being to maintain station; and there was no rationalization of land and labor, and they were not intensively worked. Occupancy was never a problem—there was no separation from the land: man's relation to land was universal, as it was the sole source of sustenance; everyone had to be definitely located, and there was no floating population. The plantation was the basic unit of Virginia's economy and wealth; there was very little wealth, and hardly any everyday life, off the plantation; with the towns little more than magnified market places along the wharves she was spared the age-old conflict between town and country or trader and landowner, and her inhabitants and wealth were diffused. Each of the larger plantations gave the impression of a village, and its population sometimes exceeded that of the smaller towns; it was autarchic in organization, which made it a self-sufficient unit—and there was no interdependence; and its location along a river shore gave it independent contact with the outside world. Thus Virginia was not strictly a society—rather was she a combination of plantations each of which was in itself a social organism. Says Bruce:

"the entire system of the Virginian life rested, not upon a civil division—the township as in New England, but on an economic division—the plantation. The community was simply a series of plantations." [3]

Her growth was entirely quantitative: the proprietary was the unit of her social organization, and expansion was simply an increase in the number of these units. The everpresent frontiers precluded fear of land shortage: the proprietaries never engaged in intrigues, and in inter-family feuds; and colonial Virginia politically was an association of these autonomous principalities, whose owners constituted the government.

The acquisition of proprietary title was coveted as the acme of human achievement: the grant of title was the grace of majesty—the grantee created his own patrimony; thus the grant of title to land was never the conveyance of material value per se—value lay in title, not in land. The direct royal grant was most precious and rare—it put the recipient at the peak of the social hierarchy: yet title—whether direct or colonial—was based on the royal seal, and was all-embracing or social in its significance; it was the key to life as it meant membership in the aristocracy—station, prerogative, exaltation of the personality; it was the foundation of freedom, of the freeman, and of the freehold—that the recipient of title had the capital with which to establish himself an estate on the frontiers by creating a plantation was understood. From towards the end of Virginia's first century her aristocracy acquired a power and prestige it had never before had—everything was subordinated to the good of the hierarchy. The Virginian's basic income was from "real" property, while personalty—as dissociated from land—was almost wholly non-productive; ownership in realty was virtually the sole origin of wealth, freedom, power and prestige; and the laws of primogeniture and entail, which by the eighteenth century had acquired reality, froze the colony in the grip of a few inter-related families. Bruce points to,

"the overshadowing importance of one or two families in directing the affairs of each county." [4]

Feudal land tenure is sociology, not legislation. The feudal land laws had much more than economic meaning: they created, protected and perpetuated the aristocracy, social station—as well as insuring its economic base; her proprietary social organization precluded the rise of a class of fee simple independent farmers, and enabled her to create a

131

fixed labor base. Land, in a corporeal sense—earth, trees, rocks—had no value per se: value lay in the pre-emption of the land—which gave the pre-emptor the power to grant title, with all the benefits that flowed therefrom. The aristocracy's monopoly of the land—through pre-emption, primogeniture and entail—is the key to the sociology of eighteenth-century Virginia.

The Virginians were beginning rapidly to change their labor system from the indentured servitude of the civilized European to the chattel slavery of the primitive African: says Fiske;

> "in 1700 there were probably 60,000 Englishmen and 6,000 Negroes in Virginia; by 1750 there were probably 250,000 whites and 250,000 blacks." [5]

Civilization in America during its first century wasn't sufficiently sure of itself in its struggle against primitivism: the Cavaliers were chary about planting a barbaric force in their midst; and Virginia's ideological atmosphere had been monolithic as the values of civilization were predominant. The coming of the African en masse introduced a new principle—he brought his mind with him, which created a duality in ideological atmosphere as the values of civilization and of primitivism both prevailed. By the turn of the century it was felt that the war with the wilderness was basically won: the Virginians had developed a sense of permanence and duration, and they had a subjective attitude concerning civilization in the new world—that its advance was irresistible was taken for granted. A century of existence had created a tradition of obstacles overcome; they had a record of consistent growth in area, population, and wealth; their polity had survived critical social strife; their economy had become self-sufficient, which gave them a feeling of power; the seaboard Indians were rendered harmless; and the interior had been explored to the mountains—to the other side of which the monsters, who were still a reality, had retreated. Virginia was geographically very favorably located, as other Anglo-Saxon colonies had sprung up all around her—and she was remote from alien settlements. There was plenty of force for civilization on the continent, and there had been a vast improvement in communications with Europe—the center and source of their values and culture. The Virginians—the pioneers in colonization and in sociology—had developed sufficient confidence to make the primitive an integral part of their milieu: and permanent preparation against the internal menace to civilization, which African aberration necessarily had to be, was a primary feature of their social organization.

Emigrants to Virginia either acquired land and bondsmen and organized their own plantations, or they came in as bondsmen. The overwhelming majority of her immigrants came in on a bonded status. Her inhabitants were therefore of two classes, namely, those who owned land and those who did not own land. The landholders were classed as freemen, who had legal being in the colony; they were "his majesty's subjects," which was a privileged status. The freemen were divided into the gentry, which category was predicated upon the right "to bear arms"; and the commonalty, whose members could not establish the right to bear arms. All freemen were classed as freeholders who, being enfranchised, were identified as "the People." Those who did not have title to land didn't count—they were without legal being in Virginia. They comprised two groups, namely, non-freemen and bondsmen. The non-freemen consisted of craftsmen under contract (not strictly indenture); and of tenants, who were discharged servants and their progeny who became hired workers, mean whites or frontiersmen. The freemen and the non-freemen—those of non-bonded status, had to be Caucasian. The bondsmen were Negroes, whites and Indians on various conditions of servitude. The landless were provided no right to property, no civil liberties, no religious, marriage or educational status; they were extra-social beings or outside the body politic, and they were not regarded as "people." Thus colonial Virginia's population consisted of the following classes: the freemen—proprietary gentry, and sub-infeudated freehold commonalty; the non-freemen—craftsmen under contract, and mean whites on a tenancy status; and bondsmen—indentured servants and entailed slaves.

The Cavalier emigres who seized control of Virginia had been succeeded, around the turn of the century, by a native-born generation of Virginian aristocrats. The state power of the aristocrats was the only centralized control in Virginia: everything else—economy, church, school, military—was decentralized, and subordinate to the state; no institution existed as a political, economic, ideological entity in its own right or to the extent of self-assertiveness towards the state. Her dispersed way of living and the primitive communications discouraged the central government from effectively extending its authority, and the principle of federalism or non-interference in the management of the units prevailed. The fourth revision of the Virginia Code in 1662 granted local autonomy to each county. Citizenship was predicated upon the freehold—which was a quality of title rather than a quantity of acreage—or an estate of greater dignity, while eligibility to office was the inherited prerogative of patricians; there was therefore no property qualification for office-holding nor, until 1736, for exercise of the franchise. The Council—which became the upper house—represented the interests of the most powerful proprietors, some of whom had received title directly from the Crown; the lower or House of Burgesses represented generally the landowners who had accumulated their property in the course of the colony's development, and as the only elected body it was associated with the principle of "popular rights."

Religion in Virginia was organized on the principle of the "Establishment": the Church of England was the Established Church; it alone was legal, state and church were united, citizenship in the one meant membership in the other, government officials and teachers had to be members, attendance was compulsory, and only its ministers could perform the baptismal, marriage and burial rites. Dissenters were taxed for the Establishment's maintenance and were persecuted, although Virginia's religious intolerance was political, not theological—Nonconformity jeopardized social stability. Thus the Establishment was an adjunct of the state, or essentially a political institution.

The proprietary estate was often scattered in variously sized tracts located in different counties of the colony. The tract best situated for fertility and health, and for proximity to neighbors, a harbor and a beautiful landscape, was chosen by the owner as the family seat. Such a place was identified by a special designation—"Mount Vernon," "Monticello," "Nomini Hall." Each tract consisted of cleared and wooded parts. The cleared part—the plantation or the area of life and labor—as a contiguous mass, could hardly have reached five hundred acres. The law of diminishing returns applied: reclamation was based on the axe; the primitive communications would have rendered too large a clearing unwieldy for effective control; and slave labor had to be kept under constant, direct and indirect, surveillance. The plantation comprised the arable part, which was at most about half the reclaimed area and of which less than half was under the plow at any one time; houses for shelter, work and storage; space for communications; meadow for livestock grazing; and parts abandoned for sterility. The plantation gradually receded into woods, which are necessary to its proper functioning—man can travel through the woods, which may also be used to some extent by work and food animals for grazing. The forest area in general was affected, although more remotely, by the interests of man, as predatory beasts and birds feeding on livestock and growing crops had to be controlled; and it was a medium for aristocratic equestrianism—riding, hunting and fox chasing. The number of laborers, which even on the richest plantation probably never reached five hundred, is the basic index to the productivity of the estate, since they were engaged predominantly in the creation of arable and in its cultivation. They had their division of labor based on race, sex and age; and—although there were instances of seasonal rushing—the underlying atmosphere was indifferent to efficiency and speed, and they were normally leisurely in going about their work.

The Virginian aristocrat, Robert Carter the Councillor, owned a tract in tidewater whose plantation was called "Nomini Hall." This tract was about twenty-five hundred acres in size, of which about ten percent made up the clearing. The inhabitants of the plantation consisted predominantly of bonded laborers, a scattering on the fringes of tenants, some imported European craftsmen, and the owner's family. The plantation was under the active management of a steward. The bonded laborers were unskilled: they consisted chiefly of entailed slaves—of whom the great majority were Negroes, and a few were Indians; and of a number of white indentured servants. The craftsmen were under contract; and the tenants were discharged servants of whom most were settled to the status of mean whites, while some were employed on the plantation especially as overseers. The slaves were divided into field hands and drudges in the master's household, some were apprenticed to the craftsmen, and a few supervised their fellows in the fields. The indentured servants were unskilled and they also labored in the fields. The proprietor had a clerk and a tutor who were under contract, and they lived in and were part of his household. According to one of George Mason's sons:

> "It was much the practice with gentlemen of land and slave estates ... so to organize them as to have considerable resources within themselves; to employ and pay but few tradesmen, and to buy little or none of the coarse stuffs and materials used by them

... Thus my father had among his slaves, carpenters, coopers, sawyers, blacksmiths, tanners, curriers, shoemakers, spinners, weavers, and knitters, and even a distiller." [6]

The mean whites would not work at all and lived as well as they could by hunting and fishing in the surrounding countryside.

The plantation's economy was overwhelmingly agricultural; the little manufacturing that was engaged in was incidental—it provided chiefly the laborers' necessaries. The agriculture was devoted almost entirely to tobacco. Being one of the larger plantations it also raised wheat, corn, cereals, cotton, flax and hemp. These were primarily for domestic use, although some was exported. Animal husbandry was an occupation of some significance. The aristocrat's plantation was well stocked with cattle, hogs and sheep. Poultry was also abundant. The horse was an animal of great importance in the Old Dominion of the eighteenth century, and was used in a variety of ways. Every rich planter had several well-filled stables.

The carpenter built and repaired barns, slave quarters, stables, fences, gates, wagons; the blacksmith shod horses, fixed ploughs, hinges, sickles, saws, and forged crude nails, chains and hoes; the cooper made hogsheads for the tobacco, barrels for flour and vats for effervescent beverages; the tanner prepared leather and the cobbler made it into shoes for the slaves; spinners, weavers and knitters made coarse cloth for clothing and bedding; the distiller made plenty of cider as well as apple, peach and persimmon brandy. And the plantation itself provided everything necessary for this manufacture. Glenn says that Councillor Carter,

"built and owned ships and mills, manufacturing ship-biscuit with which to supply schooners. He had a mill and bakery on the Nomini River." [7]

Some of the large estates also had small brick kilns, and salt and iron works. This manufacture was purely for the use of the particular plantation, with none for domestic or foreign sale. So scanty was this production, especially in cloth, that during a depression or war many of the slaves and mean whites went almost naked.

The planters had different systems of organizing their laborers. The Carters, according to Phillips, did as follows:

"These slaves, with small quotas of livestock, were distributed in a half hundred 'quarters' as working groups with a white overseer and a slave foreman at the head of each unit. In size the groups ranged from as few as six slaves to more than thirty." [8]

Many overseers had been indentured servants, and their number on a plantation varied with its size and the numerousness of the slaves. The overseer was on a tenant status: he had a small clearing with a log cabin on it; he was probably permitted to use a few slaves to work his land, as his duties disabled him from doing so himself; he was paid for his work in tobacco for which, together with the proceeds from his clearing, he could get goods at the master's store.

Each plantation had houses of various description. There were sheds for the blacksmith and other craftsmen, and sheds were used for the curing of tobacco; a storage house kept produce and goods, while barns and stables took care of animal life. The slave habitations were known as the "quarters." There were whipping posts and other instruments for the punishment of refractory slaves. There was also a large bell which was used to alarm the area in case of fire or trouble among the slaves.

"Many of the planters had on their estates general merchandise stores managed by salaried or indentured store-keepers, in which English and Virginia goods could be bought, and tobacco was currency." [9]

The mansion housing the master and his family was generally located on an elevation near the river. This enabled him and his assistants to take in at a glance a large part of the environs, such as the beauty of the landscape, the coming of visitors, and fighting, carelessness or, possibly, more serious trouble among the laborers. These mansions, sheltering an outdoor people, had large rooms and some had a secret room. Being prominently situated, they could be detected from quite a distance, which would be helpful in case of fire or some other calamity, while during inclement weather water could not form pools and interfere with freedom of movement.

The proprietary plantations were located along the banks of the main rivers, and were readily accessible by water to business and social calls. Places were set aside near various sections of the rivers where warehouses were built, to which the interior planters brought their hogsheads of tobacco by floating them down the tributaries in flat-bottomed scows. British merchantmen bringing manufactured articles and slaves sailed right up to the aristocrat's plantation or the warehouse location, unloaded their cargo and took on the tobacco and other produce used in payment. Virginia's exports were subject to the taxes and duties of England's Navigation Laws; sometimes a foreign merchantman stole in to trade with the planters, which enabled them to evade the duties and yielded them a much higher price for their produce—but this brought charges of smuggling.

In 1752 the Assembly spoke of "the planter, whose sole support depends on his (tobacco) crop," and the reliability of the weed's represented quality and quantity for the export trade was meticulously protected. English standards on weights and measures had been introduced as legal in Virginia by the Code of 1705. Each warehouse—at which the tobacco was received, inspected and storaged, and around which villages eventually arose—had a government inspector who checked on the contents of the hogsheads and, after deducting inspection fees, issued the planter a receipt for his goods. These tobacco receipts could be used in payment of quit-rents, taxes and fees. The government was very careful to insure the tobacco inspector's honesty. The sheriff could on reasonable suspicion, with a warrant issued by a county judge, break into a house in the day or night, and if any tobacco was found illegally packed or weighed, it was seized and burned and the owner was fined. Some offenses in the handling of tobacco for export drew a capital penalty.[10]

Virginia depended almost entirely on its many waterways for communications, and these were well organized. About 1700 wheeled vehicles came into use and trails or "horse-paths" were widened; but the virtual non-existence of domestic trade dispensed with the need for trading and shipping centers or towns, which discouraged the building of facilities for land travel such as roads and bridges. The colony's riparian communications seem to have been organized especially with a view to alarming the countryside in case of emergency; there were numerous privately owned boats and some public ferries, and the ferry-keepers were exempt from muster and other duties. Messengers to the governor had special traveling privileges. Colonial Virginia had more watercraft than wagons. The proprietor who built communications on his estate had the right to take toll.

The Virginians appeared to abuse their soil when compared to the painstaking care bestowed on it in land-limited England. Tobacco quickly exhausts fertility, but the period's agronomy was largely ignored chiefly because a fresh tract could at any time be secured by clearing some forest land. This situation was aggravated by the feudal land laws, and by slave labor—which had no hope of reward and was indifferent. The average planter worked only about one half of his arable at any one time; after around five years of tillage it was abandoned and another forest tract was cleared for use. After about twenty years the first tract was reclaimed for tillage. The tidewater area was predominantly forests. Thus each estate always contained both forest, cropped and abandoned tracts. There were no abandoned estates.

In an old established society man's ways of doing things are determined fundamentally by the "unwritten law"—by traditions and customs, whose origins are lost in antiquity. The primitive atmosphere is without tradition, it tends to weaken transplanted customs and habits, and unprecedented problems constantly come up. The pioneering condition is very much dependent upon legislation as the guide to ways of doing things, as they can be given integrity—emphasized, and introduced—only by the force of law: the "written law"—code, constitution, statute—which originates in legislation, is paramount; and the principle of the legislature was of much greater importance in Virginia than it was at home.

The Virginia Company, using England's Parliament as the model, had originally organized what eventually developed into the Virginia General Assembly—which constituted the colony's government. It comprised the Governor, the Council and the House of Burgesses. The two houses met separately. Specialization of governmental function as executive, legislative and judicial had emerged definitely in Virginia by 1680. The proprietors constituted the governmental personnel: there were no political parties, no professional office-holding class, and no politicians in the colony; there was therefore an absence of faction in the legislature, although the counties were so arranged that the tidewater always controlled the interior.

London had recognized the right of the Virginia General Assembly to govern the colony. In 1708 the following statement was issued:

"by Commission under the Great Seal of England, the Governour, Council and Assembly of Her Majestys Colony of Virginia, have been authorized and impowered to make Constitute and Ordain Laws, Statutes and Ordinances for the Public Peace, Welfare and Good Government of the said Colony— which are to be Transmitted to her Majesty for her

Royall Approbation or Disallowance of them." [11]
This order was subsequently re-asserted.

The executive function was performed by the governor, who was appointed by London. The governor represented the interests, and thought in terms, of the Empire. He had the veto power, and could convoke and prorogue the General Assembly, and dissolve the House of Burgesses. He was head of the Establishment, chief justice, and commander-in-chief of all armed forces; he appointed the colony, county and ecclesiastical functionaries, and he could remove church ministers and suspend Councillors. He had important perquisites, and his extensive appointive power brought him a huge patronage. His recommendation for a land grant or appointment to office was virtually equivalent to affirmation. He was generally absent from sessions of the Assembly.

The Council was the upper or "little house of lords," and it constituted the apex of colonial governmental power. Its membership, which numbered between nine and twelve, was for life and its members were from the peak of the Virginian aristocracy. They were appointed by the governor subject to London's approval; this predicated the councillorship upon a Crown commission, which was qualitatively superior to a colonial commission. The Council was thus a royal, rather than a colonial, governing body and it was referred to as "her Majesties Council here";[12] its membership's nativity and primary interests, however, were colonial. The Council examined and emended legislation, rather than originated it. Its deliberations were secret from the House of Burgesses; a demand by the Burgesses in 1749 for freedom of access to the Council Journals was rejected with the assertion that it is "inconsistent with the Constitution." [13] There was no law in the colony against a person holding several salaried positions at the same time; and the Council together with the governor also constituted the General Court, which was Virginia's court of last resort. Seniority of membership was a symbol of rank; the senior member was President of the Council, and he was acting-governor during the governor's absence and in the interim between gubernatorial succession. The Council was thus Virginia's supreme legislative and judicial power, and it exercised also executive authority during gubernatorial vacancies. The Councillors were tax exempt, and they had the places of greatest responsibility and profit; they had charge of revenue and quit-rent collections, and they acted as naval officers and county colonels.

The House of Burgesses originated legislation. It was elected by the freeholders of Virginia: its members were by nativity and mandate, as well as in their interests, wholly Virginian. It consisted of two representatives from each county and one from each corporation. The members had to be at least freeholders; they were paid fifteen shillings per day, by the unit they represented, for the session and travel time. In 1769 the House had 118 members. It was elected annually, although

"sometimes the General Assembly . . . was prorogued
from year to year, so that a new election might not
take place in seven, eight or ten years."

In 1762 a law was passed declaring that an Assembly had to be summoned at least once in three years; and that a House of Burgesses was to be elected at least once in seven years, unless it was sooner dissolved by the governor. As the only elected body the House continued to be regarded as "the voice of the People," and it began to regain some of its old powers. The right to choose state officials, such as the Treasurer, went down the gamut of governmental hierarchy until it lodged with the Burgesses; it elected its Speaker, and it gradually assumed control of taxation and appropriations. But it never fully regained its pre-Restoration powers.

The "members of both houses were men of large estates," whose economic interests were almost wholly in realty; and the General Assembly was little better than a family affair.

According to Lingley:

> "There was always a Cabell from Amherst, a Fleming from Cumberland, a Riddick from Nansemond, and a Randolph from Williamsburg or the College."

> "Of Richard Henry Lee's five brothers, one had long been in the council, two besides Richard Henry himself in the House of Burgesses, and a fourth, Arthur Lee, was abroad in the public service. Richard Lee who represented Westmoreland from 1757, Henry Lee who represented Prince William from 1758, and John Lee who represented Essex, 1761-1768, were all cousins of Richard Henry Lee. In other cases such a record could be approached even if not duplicated." [14]

The Assembly adopted strong measures to maintain its dignity before the public. An attack on a member was considered a reflection on the government; the members were therefore protected against slander and assault, and in 1763 it was enacted;

> "all and every member of the general-assembly is and ought to be, and forever hereafter shall be, in his and their persons, servants and estates, real and personal, free, exempted and privileged, from all arrests attachments executions, and all other process whatsoever, save only for treason, felony, or breach of the peace, during his or their attendance in general-assembly, and for the space of ten days before, and ten days after, every session." [15]

Members guilty of minor infractions were punished by the Assembly.

A local bill became a law after it had received the assent of both houses, the governor and the Board. Since London could veto a colonial act at any time a good deal of uncertainty and confusion prevailed in Virginia, and most of her legislation had to have a suspending clause pending approval. A "royal mandate" was per se law not subject to colonial amendment or repeal; but the Virginia General Assembly was jealous of its power, and it went through the formality of unanimously ratifying the decree in order to establish the right of local self-assertiveness. Thus the legislature's wording in accepting a royal mandate was, "Bee it enacted by the king's most excellent majesty by and with the consent of the generall assembly." In 1679 London ordered that the clerk of the Virginia General Assembly send it annually a copy of all laws enacted. The colony's officials were entrusted with the secrets of state and could be held for betrayal.

During Virginia's second century there seems to have been great fear, especially among the Councillors, that the recently-arrived utilitarian-minded royal governors would attempt to impose upon them the principles of the Revolution of 1689. After the failure of England's second Jacobite rebellion in 1745 the Virginians began to settle to her new order as permanent; they incorporated some of the new principles into their statutes, but their insistence on interpreting these principles in terms of local conditions virtually nullified their application in practice. The anti-Stuart oaths were finally fully adopted,[16] but with an important qualification: all office-holders were required to have,

"taken and subscribed the oath of abjuration, and repeated and subscribed the test, and also subscribed to be conformable to the doctrine and discipline of the Church of England." [17]

The last clause could not be accepted by Dissenters, which rendered them ineligible to office.

Appointments of officials for the colonies were made by the Board of Trade in the name of the Crown. Many of these officials were fortune hunters; the governorship was a sinecure furnished by the colony as the appointee sent over a deputy-governor to act for him. The General Assembly thought fundamentally in terms of Virginia, and it maintained a resident commissioner in London to represent her interests.

As the Board began to limit the colonies' territorial expansion the Virginians realized that their ambitions would have to be achieved largely through political maneuvering, and they developed a shrewdness for subtle domination of the governors. The changes in Virginia's Crown personnel were fairly rapid; the members of the Assembly had a good deal of contempt for the former's knowledge of the colonial hinterland, and without the cooperation of the local leadership the Crown officials were practically helpless. The colonials were in a position to let the Britons in on remunerative projects, partnerships were sometimes formed and there were clandestine understandings with their successes and jealousies. The Crown official soon caught the sense of remoteness from authority with its feeling of freedom, and the acquisition of colonial interests carried with it similar views. The governors were sometimes honored with special perquisites and gifts, and counties were named after them. They were also dependent upon the colonials for their salary, which could be withheld or paid in depreciated local currency. This gave rise to a powerful conciliar oligarchy, which during the eighteenth century served as the bastion of Cavalier absolutism and largely constituted Virginia's actual government.

Bitter quarrels sometimes arose between the colony's various ruling groups—governor, aristocracy, Council, Church —which had to be taken to London for settlement. The royal governors usually had their way when their proposals were not considered a threat to the domestic status quo. Governor Alexander Spotswood (1710-22), however, made an effort to reduce the conciliar power. He denounced the Council as a family affair, and he attempted to deprive its members of their judicial authority. A bitter fight ensued; William Byrd wrote of the governor's,

"endeavouring to take from them (Councillors) a Jurisdiction which they have held from the first Set-

tlement of that Colony";
and the case was taken to London. The Council evidently
had powerful backing in the home country for the governor
was removed from office, and Virginia's conciliar dictator-
ship thus received royal sanction. This was not without its
lesson to succeeding governors.

During the crisis leading to the secession from the Empire
the full governor came over. Virginia had made treaties with
Indians and with other colonies, as well as with Cromwell's
forces in 1652, the validity of which London never ques-
tioned. She had always exercised the right to extinguish
Indian title to land, but she was deprived of this right by
London's Declaration of 1763 which barred colonial trans-
Allegheny expansion.

Citizenship could be granted to aliens by London and by
the colonial legislature. Governor Berkeley's Assembly declared that naturalized persons shall have all the rights of
"a natural born Englishman," and shall be

"capable of free traffique and trading of takeing up
and purchasing, deviseing and inheriting of all lands
and tenements."

In 1680 the Virginia General Assembly adopted a royal mandate for the naturalization of foreigners.

Eligibility to franchise and office was predicated upon the
ownership of a freehold: the freeholder was one with a "visible" estate of at least £50 sterling; yet the exact meaning
of "freehold" de facto seems to have been unclear, and a
person was required to swear that "you are bona fide a freeholder ... to the best of your knowledge." In 1736 the
Assembly enfranchised those who had a freehold estate in
at least one hundred acres of uninhabited land (reduced to
fifty acres in 1763), or twenty-five acres with a house and
plantation on it, or a house and a lot in some town. The
freehold, even though uninhabited, had to pay taxes—and it
had to be invested to give it identity. The franchise was also
extended to the absentee owner of a freehold or greater es-

tate, of whom Virginia always had some; the Assembly refers to,

"the land of the right honourable the earl of Tanker-
ville, in Loudoun county, in the tenure and occupation
of John Farrow and Alexander Roane."

But there was a three-year residence requirement for eligibility to office; this law was first enacted by Bacon's Assembly to guard against emigre usurpers, and was later
adopted by the Cavaliers to protect themselves against emigre rebels. Notice of pending elections was read in church
by the minister, and the election was held at the county
court. Voting was by open ballot and compulsory; the citizen
voted, for two Burgesses, in each county in which he owned
a freehold, and elections were held on different days in the
various counties to allow travel time. In the election of a
Burgess in 1710 the winner received forty-four votes to the
loser's thirty-nine votes. No female, minor, convict, "recusant," or non-Caucasian, "although such persons be freeholders," could be a candidate for office or exercise the
franchise.

The county was thus the legislative unit; there were fifty-
seven counties in 1772. Says Howard:

"The government of the Virginia county ... was
highly centralized. All of its important officers were
appointed by the governor; while the inferior agents
of local administration were chosen by the nominees.
In the court was placed the entire government of the
county ... The principle of popular election appears
only in the choice of burgesses."

The counties of Virginia were organized, named, bounded,
adjusted and controlled by the General Assembly. Internal
improvements, or the building of communications, could be
forced on the counties on penalty by Williamsburg; they
were paid for by the county through a tax on its inhabitants
or by popular subscription. All tithable males in the colony were liable annually to contribute labor, in person or

in bondsmen, for the maintenance and improvement of communications.

A judicial system had developed, of which the county was the unit. The English common law, and English and Virginia statutory law, were followed. An act of 1667 provided law books for each county court. The county court had at least eight justices who were appointed by the governor on local hierarchical recommendation, thus keeping the judiciary securely in the control of the county proprietors. Great care was exercised to maintain the integrity of the judiciary, and there was a law for the removal of county judges who drank on court days. When inducted into office each judge had to swear that he,

"will do equal right to all manner of people, great and small, high and low, rich and poor, according to equity and good conscience, and the laws and usages of this colony."

The court met about once a month in the "county town" which consisted of the court house, a jail, whipping post, ducking stool, stocks, pillory, gibbet, and maybe a public inn (called "ordinary"). The county court had the power to probate wills and administrate estates; had final jurisdiction in all criminal cases not involving limb or life, and in civil suits up to £20 sterling; it punished vagrants, indentured orphan and bastard children and decided master vs. servant cases; and it had charge of tax collections, public roads, licensing ordinaries, and other local affairs. The county court was an index to the degree of local autonomy prevailing: from the Peace of 1763 some respect had to be shown for frontier self-assertiveness; and as the colony expanded and it became more difficult to reach the capital the powers of the county court were increased—it was given full jurisdiction over slaves, including capital crimes. The county court was also an important political body in that it recommended to the governor the candidates for appointment as local officials, and the county sheriff was chosen from among its judges; and as the repository of land records, marriage licenses, and other important papers it is the chief source of county history.

An appeal from the decision of the county court could be taken, on posting a bond of £20 sterling with good security, to the General Court, which consisted of the governor and Council and had jurisdiction over the whole colony. The General Court also adjudicated in admiralty and ecclesiastical cases; and it passed judgment on treason, rebellion, piracy and other capital crimes, on delinquent officials and church ministers, on inter-county disputes, and on involvements with Indians. When it was thought that frontier influences would preclude the county court from handing down a desired decision the case was ordered taken to the higher court. Trial by jury could be had under certain circumstances, and appeals from the General Court's decisions could be taken to London. British merchants and heirs to property in Virginia could sue in her courts for their rights. The juror had to be at least a freeholder; those qualified to sit in the General and in the county court each had to have, respectively, an estate worth at least £100 sterling and £50 sterling.

Law enforcement in colonial Virginia was predicated upon a well-organized spy system or on "the informer," who was rewarded with part of the culprit's fine. Itinerants were greatly feared in the colony: their traveling gave them an idea of the social organization as a whole, and they could act as go-betweens in conspiracies; and taxes could not be collected from floaters. The county was so organized that each inhabitant was known, and strangers were readily detected. Everyone had to have a definite residence; itinerants were discouraged to the extent that they could be held as "vagrants," who were sold into servitude for one year; and the laws against vagrants were strictly enforced. There was no underworld in Virginia, and no organized crime and vice. There was no prison system; absence of manufactures precluded work within restricted spaces, and imprisonment could not be a punishment for bondsmen. The county jail was used to hold over offenders for trial, escaped bondsmen for claimants, and condemned felons for execution. Offending freemen in non-capital cases were generally fined, for non-payment of which they were whipped or sold into servitude. Whippings were usually administered by the sheriff; the freeman thus punished had to pay the sheriff a fee of twenty pounds of tobacco. Since there was little domestic trading confinement for debt was uncommon. The fare of a confined debtor was charged to his estate at ten pounds of tobacco per day, while the fare of a criminal or runaway bondsman was charged to his owner at half the amount.

The right of "the People" to petition their government was introduced in Virginia by the Puritans—it supplemented commonalty representation in the House of Burgesses. The Cavaliers—under whom the commonalty had no representation in the General Assembly—permitted the right to petition to continue, although they restricted its use to freeholders. This right was much used, as it was the commonalty's only mode of articulation, and the petitions considered by the Assembly are an index to the mind of "the People." The right to petition was exercised through the county court, which was the clearing house for all public papers containing propositions and grievances, and claims for payments—as well as individual requests for land grants and county requests for improvements. Immediately after Bacon's Rebellion many people used this right to present "scandalous and seditious papers." It was therefore legislated that the county sheriff, before each session of the Assembly, was to receive all petitions, which were to be signed by the petitioners and attested by a clerk of the court, after which they were to be certified by the court for presentation to the General Assembly.

It is declared that in 1750 the white population of Virginia was around a quarter million, of whom between six and nine percent voted.[18] Only the freeholder, or the head of the family, could vote. It is reasonable to deduce from these figures that about 20,000 men voted. If their families averaged five persons each, then about 100,000 people were classed as freemen. Since a juror in the county court had to be a freeholder with a "visible estate" of at least £50 sterling, then there must have been many people with estates of less value who were classed as freeholders.

The county was also the military or defense unit. Virginia was subject to invasion from the sea and from the west, and since her social organization rendered a large part of the population inherently disaffected there was always danger of internal insurrection. Lighthouses were built and manned to guard against enemies from the sea. Under the Puritans defense rested on "the People" and every householder was required, on penalty, always to have a gun and some ammunition in his home. After Bacon's Rebellion, however, the government relieved the people of their arms which, together with the liquidation of the frontiersmen, necessitated a new system of defense; a military establishment, as an entity distinct from the people, was introduced. A standing army of mounted rangers was organized to patrol the frontiers, and proprietary estates were granted on the frontiers with a view to their organization for the defense of the settled areas. The capital had a complete monopoly on all arms and ammunition in the colony; all such equipment brought in had to be stored in specifically designated magazines, on pain of severe punishment; and arms distribution was predicated upon authoritative consent. During the eighteenth century the Negro slave became the chief menace; a county militia was organized as a safeguard and the governor, as commander-in-chief, appointed a "county lieutenant" to command the county militia. The county lieutenant could take the initiative during emergencies until he heard from his superiors, and his pay was seventy pounds of tobacco for each day of active service. A bounty of five pounds of tobacco was paid to volunteers for enlistment; but when enlistments were insufficient conscription was used, and all non-bondsmen from sixteen to sixty years old were listed in the militia and were subject to call. The common soldier's pay was one shilling or ten pounds of tobacco per day, but he was not paid at all if the muster ended within forty-eight hours. Armed resistance to the conscription authorities was punished by death, but the conscript could be released from duty if he paid £10 sterling or sent a substitute. The "soldiers ... frequently desert," and laws had to be passed against desertion and mutiny;[19] in these times "the informer" reaped a rich harvest. The conscripts had to return all arms when demobilized, on penalty. The military had the right to impress whatever it needed—men, food, horses, drayage—during emergencies. Virginia's armed forces were organized on the class system: the aristocrats, who were above impressment, were commissioned so they could "serve in such stations as are suitable for gentlemen." All military commissioned officers had to take the oath of abjuration and subscribe the test. The General Assembly pensioned the men who were disabled in the fighting campaigns, and the county had to care for those wounded. In 1715 Virginia's standing armed force numbered 14,000 and by 1755, when Braddock's defeat created fear of invasion from the west, its number had doubled.

The ecclesiastical unit in Virginia was the parish, which was always organized simultaneously with the county. The more populated counties each had several parishes of which some had several churches; each church had a minister, clerk and church-warden. Frontier parishes were as large as the county and had a lay reader or were vacant. The immediate affairs of the parish were entirely in the hands of the vestry, which consisted of twelve members of whom seven constituted a quorum. The vestrymen, each of whom had to be at least a freeholder, were originally elected by the freeholders and housekeepers of the parish; they were required to "take the oaths appointed by law"—abjuration and test—and to "subscribe to be conformable to the doctrines and discipline of the church of England." On the separation of a member the remaining vestrymen chose his successor, which made the vestry self-perpetuating and kept it securely in the hands of the parish's leading land and slave owners. The vestry made assessments for the building and maintenance of the church; and selected and dismissed the minister and other church personnel at will, and paid them their salaries. The churches were usually drab, but from around 1750 a few parishes began to show signs of wealth as they "purchased books, plate, and church ornaments of considerable value." The minister was assigned a "glebe" for his use, which comprised several hundred acres of land, a house and some slaves and livestock. The glebe was the property of the parish; the minister was liable for the proper maintenance and repair of all the realty assigned him, and in the event of his separation the assignment automatically terminated. Thus colonial Virginia's clergymen did not have the status of freeholders per se.[20] The minister's annual salary was usually sixteen hundred pounds of tobacco, whose quality was an index to his capabilities and to the wealth of his parish; and he had an income from the performance of baptismal, marriage and burial rites, while some also practiced medicine and taught school. The General Assembly had complete ultimate control of Virginia's Establishment; it formed, named, bounded and adjusted the parishes; and it ordered the election and dissolution of vestries, the establishment and abolition of glebes, and the building and demolition of churches. Canon law and ecclesiastical courts were not permitted in Virginia, and the clergy came within the jurisdiction of the common law and the secular courts. Her clergymen were all imported from the old country before the rise of native ministers, but whether British or native born they all had to be ordained in England by the Bishop of London. The resident Commissary did not have the power to ordain and confirm. Virginia's church of the eighteenth century was evidently also used as a military rendezvous; the county commander could order all members of the militia to assemble armed in church. It was also used as a publication center, as government proclamations were read from the pulpit. The vestry prosecuted immorality, compiled vital statistics, and it also administered the poor-law; the sick and crippled beneficiaries of the poor-law had to wear a badge of yellow color,[21] which marked them as paupers.

The Church of Virginia was an extension of the Church of England and, like everything else in the colony, the Church was decentralized or "really a collection of independent congregations." During the early eighteenth century the Commissary, James Blair, made an effort to put the Church in Virginia on a par with that in Europe. He wanted to make it a powerful body in its own right; an independent institution owning its own property, and exercising political and ideological influence. Blair was not lacking in determination and courage, but he failed. The aristocrats wanted everything in Virginia completely subordinate to their state; with the Church independent the clergy would hearken to London and thus introduce an alien sovereignty—a Church power within the secular power, or a state within a state; and the proprietors were most jealous of their sovereignty. Moreover, there was always the possibility of a social revolution resulting from a Church schism. London thought that the Virginia Church should be represented in the Council, to which it appointed Commissary Blair; but the Councillors kept him out. Thus while the Virginia clergy continued nominally subject to orders from the Bishop of London they were actually under lay control.

Governor Berkeley's statement,
"I thank God there are no free schools nor printing and I hope we shall not have them these hundred

years"
expresses the Cavalier attitude towards popular education,
which was faithfully followed by succeeding generations.
The records point to the existence of a school on the frontiers to Christianize Indians. Some contingent bequests for
the erection of free schools were made by testators, of which
three or four eventually materialized. In 1752 permission
was granted by the General Assembly—on the strength of a
private bequest—to build a free school in Norfolk town,

> "and to provide ... an able master ... capable to
> teach the Greek and Latin tongues, (who) before he
> be admitted ... shall undergo an examination before
> the masters of the College of William and Mary ...
> and produce a certificate of his capacity, and also a
> license from the governor ... agreeable to his majes-
> ty's instructions."

There were some private boarding schools one of which
George Mason attended and paid 1,845 pounds of tobacco a
year for board, books and tuition. But there were virtually
no free schools in Virginia. Most of the teaching was in the
patrician mansion houses—many of which had good sized
libraries—where hired and contracted tutors rendered elementary instruction to the scions of aristocracy. The plans
for the erection of William and Mary College, which was
designed primarily to train a native ministry, were made in
1693 but it wasn't until well into the eighteenth century
before it was built and began to function. Most of the time
it was poorly staffed.

The first printing press appeared in Virginia in 1682, but
it was suppressed. Printing finally became legal in 1733; an
edition of Virginia's statutes was immediately published,
and the colony's first newspaper, the weekly *Virginia Gazette*, appeared three years later. The "Purvis" edition of
the Virginia laws, published in England around 1685, had
circulated in the colony but it is held to be inaccurate. In
the early days the laws were promulgated orally by the

Burgesses when they came home, and sometimes there was a public gathering where they were read; afterwards copies of the latest enactments were distributed to the county courts for promulgation. Some laws and decrees were published in the *Gazette,* and they were also often publicly announced by authorities in church and at gatherings such as fairs and horse races.

The local and royal powers wanted to see Virginia expand, and she was enabled to do this with comparative rapidity when she began to produce her own surplus capital for investment. The nature and circumstances of her economy precluded intensive growth: her expansion was perforce fundamentally extensive, and was based on the taking up of frontier land—the turning of wilderness into arable, which required individual capital investment; and increase in population was predicated upon territorial accretion. During the seventeenth century the Virginian had a feeling of freedom: the world was open in almost all directions; the hills towards the west were far away, and between them and the settlements lay vast areas of rolling, virgin lands. As the century progressed colonies arose to the north and south with whom Virginia had to make boundary agreements, which precluded her further penetration in these directions. But she had no established western boundary, and her expansionist ambitions were henceforth confined to that region. By the end of her first century the area to the Blue Ridge mountains was well known: in 1716 the Shenandoah valley was explored, and Virginia was considered as comprising the area to the Allegheny mountains; and by Independence the tidewater, piedmont and valley areas had been carved into counties.

Around the beginning of Virginia's second century most of tidewater was settled, while the rest of the area westward was unsettled frontier wilderness or public domain. Her population was rapidly increasing: offers of denization brought Europeans for the first time in large numbers, settlers were arriving also from other colonies, and the tidewater landowners were prolific.

America had become the hope of distressed Europeans. Feudalism was crumbling in western Europe: members of the landed gentry were fleeing from the continent's Reformation upheavals, and some of these who preferred the feudal way came to the southern Anglo-American colonies. The organization of the feudal estate in Europe was essentially proprietary: the emigration was conducted on the group or household system, as the "baron" brought the families on his estate with him; the feudal relation was maintained intact through the emigration to the settlement in America; and in Virginia several communities of foreign Protestants arose—there were Frenchmen settled in Monacan Town and Germans at Germanna. But the British Isles continued to be the chief source of immigrants—and some of the landless scions of the lower gentry, as well as blooded fugitive Jacobites, came to Virginia to settle. All the immigrant elite were made proprietary grants to interior tracts and were admitted into the Establishment, which entitled them to membership in the aristocracy.

During the early part of the eighteenth century the westward expansion of proprietaries in Pennsylvania deprived thousands of Scotch-Irish and German Dissenters settled on her frontiers of the mastery of their lands. While they were not physically evicted their revulsion to sub-infeudation caused them to leave in search of open lands elsewhere. Since the Allegheny mountains barred the road west they moved southwards with the widening terrain and most of them settled in the Shenandoah valley, which Virginia claimed as within her jurisdiction. There the settlers—without requesting or receiving any land grants from Williamsburg—organized their society according to the principles that had obtained in pioneer Virginia, or in terms of the corporate farm system which tended towards the development of the fee simple independent farmer. They had no fully organized state of their own and no law and law-enforcement agencies, and their inter-relations were entirely democratic. Population being the basis of wealth Virginia made no objection to the settlements. By 1734 a fair-sized community had arisen in the valley: the General Assembly incorporated it into Virginia by laying it off as a county; and two years later the tidewater aristocrat Robert Beverly was made lord proprietor of over one hundred thousand acres of land located in the Shenandoah valley, which included the area settled by the Dissenters.[22] The Beverly grant liquidated the frontier social organization, and supplanted it with the sociology of the tidewater. Feudalism in Virginia was backed by the power of the organized state: the settlers were sub-infeudated—they were not dispossessed; and the Beverly proprietary introduced in the valley the principle of absentee landlordism.

But by far the most important source of the colony's population was the fecundity of the Virginians—the isolated life usually brings large families. The rigid enforcement of the feudal realty laws thoroughly entrenched the proprietors in the tidewater area, which was all taken up and well developed: they regarded it as "home" because it contained their family seats; and they used it as a base from which to operate for control of the undeveloped interior, which was viewed as an opportunity for family expansion and for investment. Primogeniture disinherited the younger sons, and they could each be provided with an estate within the interior's ample spaces. The landowner who wanted the grant of another tract filed a paper to this effect at the county court house: the court accumulated such and other pertinent papers, and dispatched them to the capital for submission to the Assembly when it was again in session; the petitions went through the regular colonial process of approval, after which they were signed by the governor; then they were submitted to London for confirmation, or the granting of the royal seal, by the Board of Trade. The securing of land grants through regular channels ordinarily took a long time: the General Assembly was usually prorogued, once for as long as seven years; and the time needed to process the grants through London also was procrastinated.

The frontier land grant under the Cavaliers took the form of the "reservation." The reservation gave the grantee or his heir the right to choose his own time and his own place on the frontiers, for actual occupancy: it was requested usually for the benefit of the succeeding generation, and the petitioner had plenty of time; there was no official stipulation concerning seating, accrual, lapse; the government bounded the grant in space in terms of acres, so as to give it identity; but there was no limitation in time, and no specified location—the longer the grantee waited the farther west he would be. No one thought anything of empty wooded vastness, and the phrase "land acreage" conveyed no sense of economic value per se: thus precision didn't matter, there was no surveying, and estates were never neatly delineated; and title to land had practical meaning in that it was governmental security for the investment necessary to turn woods into arable, and that it protected the grantee from the danger of being sub-infeudated. No one could object to the investment of capital for the expansion of the settled area: thus the confirmation of land reservations by the Assembly and then by the Board of Trade, especially if the request came from a well-established Virginian family, was a matter of course. Most of the reservations to the aristocracy's younger sons, and to the daughters for dowry, eventually materialized westwards to the mountains; some of these patents were obtained for the children before they were born—"and the same names can be traced from county to county and from generation to generation." The heir was secured by the grant and on reaching maturity he picked a desirable site on the frontiers, a good distance from the nearest occupied estates, for the setting up of his own plantation. The clearing had to be sufficiently spacious, and his residence elaborate enough, to comport with the dignity of aristocracy. The sending in of laborers, implements, materials, livestock—and the inevitable time required for the plantation to become self-sufficient—presupposed a good deal of investment capital. Sensitivity concerning trespass in Virginia was confined to the clearing: the newcomer's neighbors made no objection to him because they did not care to contest the occupancy of naked wilderness, one or more of them were his relatives, and he pushed the frontiers away from them.

From the penetration of the region beyond tidewater a new principle began to become apparent—the interior Virginian was beginning to adumbrate the "American." The local government with its royal commitments continued pretty well in the hands of the coastal proprietors: but the colonial of the interior found himself swallowed up in an immensity of forests—he was well isolated from the world of men and affairs, which caused him to develop a feeling of complete independence; his mind was turning from the trans-oceanic east to the transmontane west, and London—and everything associated with it—was becoming remote and strange. The identification of the validity of the land patent with the royal seal could never have been more than a symbol of London dominion: in acquiring land the Virginian was expanding the colony by turning naked wilderness into areas of life and labor on his own capital investment; he was actuated fundamentally by the dictates of the world immediately around him, rather than by concern about a dim and distant "authority"; and his attitude towards "regulations" in the acquisition of land tended less to comprehension and more towards impatience. The condition here is primarily natural, rather than social—and it was both logical and just for such a person to ignore "government," and to go off on his own and "take" land when he wanted it. Local legislative approval regardless of the Board of Trade could be taken for granted: the tidewater landowners were of one mind with those of the interior in this respect; and the General Assembly did periodically enact blanket validations of status quo landholdings. The Virginians based their right to local autonomy on tradition—their ancient charters: on principle —the federal political doctrine; but the conditions under which they lived, especially from the time they began to produce surplus capital for investment, rendered local autonomy the inexorable logic of the time and place; freedom of action was imperative, for the colonials could not adjust their local undertakings to conform with remote controls. The political Virginians—conscious of both the resident and the remote royal authority—were inclined to some measure of restraint, yet they too succumbed to the influence of the interior: about 1750 Virginia made the boldest move yet in her history—a group of piedmont proprietors led by Thomas Jefferson's father organized a land company called the "Loyal Company" to which the Assembly, without the Board's consent, granted 800,000 acres along her southwestern transmontane frontier. Virginia here declared herself the source of a grant for the establishment of an entire political jurisdiction—her colonial status did not discourage her from asserting imperial aspirations. The move was premature: such ambitions gave rise to serious involvements— quarrels between the home and local governments concerning the ultimate power to grant land, and competition from neighboring colonies. During the troubles that led to the secession from the Empire, London declared that lands acquired through patents issued solely by the authority of colonial legislatures were "allotments," not grants, which tended to render their title defective.

The land records in colonial Virginia are not a true index to land ownership: the absence of surveying caused overlapping; and the similarity, and sometimes the identity, of grantee names create confusion and uncertainty. Moreover, a good many colonials acquired acreage without concern about official permission; and sometimes—due especially to the demise of heirs—granted reservations never went beyond the land office entry, and since there was no allocation the transaction was nugatory.

The Virginians were under governmental fiscal obligation; they had to pay taxes to the colonial government, which were based chiefly on exports and on bondsmen; they also had to pay quit-rents to the royal treasury, which were based on the produce of the land; and during wars and other emergencies there were special levies. The quit-rent money was kept in Virginia, under royal authority, to cover expenses incident to Empire concerns, and "to be made use of upon any sudden and dangerous Emergency." The reclaimed area was the foundation of Virginia's economy and wealth: actual production is the measure of current wealth; since the maximum production of the largest single plantation could easily be achieved as within a ten-thousand acre estate then the estate several times that size was no richer, and acreage was no index to wealth. The governmental fiscal obligations were based on materialization and production: there had to be an actual existent estate; and, if such obligation was not confined to, it had at least to be concentrated on, the producing area. Thus the following conclusion seems unwarranted:

"The wealthy planters consistently avoided the payment of taxes. Their enormous power in the colonial government made this an easy matter . . . Estates of fifty and sixty thousand acres often yielded less in quit rents than plantations one-third their size." [23]

The charges of recently-arrived English-minded royal officials were not always based on a practical understanding of conditions in the colony:

"In 1717 the Governor complained that three million acres which should have paid £3000, did not in fact produce a half of it."

Corruption was never a social problem under total feudalism. The Virginian aristocrat was the state: he had a sense of identity with it, and was its heir; and feelings of tenderness were reciprocal. The landowners faithfully paid all their local taxes, and the colonial government was never in financial straits. There was a different attitude, however, concerning their fiscal obligations that were destined for royal coffers. The proprietors were very jealous of their colony and its wealth; they hated to see value leave their "country" for foreign emolument; and quit-rents were not paid without the feeling that they were an imposition. This attitude was not due, fundamentally, to Virginian cupidity: it flowed from their traditional political doctrine, and they proved their sincerity concerning it in the risks of war.

Legitimacy in the acquisition of arable land is determined by who created it. In 1632 Governor Harvey arrived with royal instructions to superimpose the proprietary system on Virginia, but his efforts failed. In 1676 Governor Berkeley tried to do the same and succeeded, which gave the Cavaliers their start and established them as a landed aristocracy. And in 1736 the Virginian patrician Robert Beverly was made lord proprietor of an area in the valley that had been settled, improved, and for some time established, by frontiersmen. Thus the Cavaliers took the tidewater away from the Puritans, and the valley from the Nonconformists. Are these instances of Cavalier arable acquisition legitimate? Where rival groups both have the same basic values the forcible seizure by one of the property created by the other is clearly immoral. But each of the contending forces in Virginia had a different view of life—the student is here confronted with the ideological *cul-de-sac*. The feudal proprietary regarded commonalty assertion of the right to mastery over land as insolence—the refusal to keep their place: the Cavaliers were perfectly sincere; and when the Assembly made Robert Beverly proprietor of the settlements in the valley it did so without a sense of arbitrariness or imposition—it was simply acting in terms of its own traditionally accepted way of doing things. The farmers were not dispossessed: they continued as before to live on and work the land; only a profound change had taken place in their legal status in relation to it, and in their social rights. While the legitimacy of the Cavaliers' start may be in question, that of their subsequent expansion is not. The allegation of corruption in terms of favoritism and discrimination presupposes equalitarian values, and the existence of economic value per se which is conveyed without any—or at least without adequate—consideration. Both these factors are entirely absent in Cavalier Virginia. A state of nature is not private property: being nugatory "land acreage" could have no intrinsic meaning, the legal requirement of consideration for conveyance could not apply, and all allegations of malfeasance—"great frauds were perpetrated by prominent men in securing patents for land" [23]—are untrue. These men were expanding and enriching the colony by endowing a state of nature with social value: for reasons of economy and class there could be no objection to their engrossment of forest areas; and legislative confirmation of their land acquisition was a matter of course.

Primogeniture and entail applied throughout the colony's jurisdiction; they comprehended lands and tenements, as well as hereditaments under which were included chattel slaves. The feudal law of "escheat" also prevailed; on the failure of lineal heirs realty reverted to the state, while personalty was inherited by collateral heirs.

The Virginia statutes never use the word "primogeniture", but the phrase "heir at law" occurs frequently. The General Assembly was determined to preserve each estate intact; yet the law couldn't allow the younger children of the aristocracy to be impoverished, while the contingencies of feudal inheritance often gave rise to complications that had to be adjudicated. The freeholder had the right to draw up a paper that he considered a will; its admission to probate gave it legal recognition. An act of inheritance represents the will of the state, of the testator, and sometimes also of the heirs. The testator of colonial Virginia had no say concerning entail: he was allowed some discretion in partitioning realty for descent; and he had a good deal of freedom in the distribution of personalty, which was always owned in fee simple. Where the testator ignored the rights of the heir at law in devising his realty the will was not *ab initio* binding in court; a certain period was allowed to the heir at law to contest the will, and if he did so the judiciary favored the application of the basic Virginia realty laws and give him the benefit of every doubt.[24] Thus the judiciary had some discretionary power concerning the application of primogeniture. If the owner died intestate primogeniture automatically prevailed—all the realty descended to the eldest son. The estates of the conciliar and other top Virginia families each comprised a vast acreage that was scattered in several counties. The family seat— which was often of more value than the other tracts combined because it was the most developed, and had the most laborers, the best location for communications and security, the mansion house—was willed to the eldest son. They were anxious,

> "to enhance the social importance of a family by
> concentrating the bulk of its property in the hands
> of the eldest son";[25]

while the younger sons received the outlying, less developed tracts. But primogeniture strictly applied in the descent of estates of the less wealthy gentry, who made up the bulk of the aristocracy. In a Remonstrance to the Crown, in 1752, the Assembly declared:

> "the chief end (of entailing slaves) was to give the
> heir of an intestate, to whom the lands descended, an

opportunity of keeping the slaves at their appraised
value as it would be advantageous to him in tilling
his lands, but not so valuable as money to the younger
children who had no lands".[26]

The enforcement of primogeniture was often necessary to
maintain an estate as such, since its division would have
destroyed it as an economic unit.

"in case partition shall be made of the said lands . . .
the value of the said lands will be considerably di-
minished".[27]

The estates of the aristocracy were rigidly entailed. In
1748 the Assembly declared:

"It shall not be lawful for any (one) . . . whatsoever,
at any time to levy any fine, or to suffer any recovery
to be had, whereby to cut off or defeat any estate in
fee tail, general or special, of or in any lands, tenements or hereditaments, within this colony, neither
shall any such estate tail be cut off, or defeated, by
any ways or means whatsoever, except only by act of
the General Assembly of this dominion . . . and all
and every . . . act or acts . . . whatsoever, which shall
be . . . for and towards the cutting off, or defeating
any estate tail whatsoever . . . otherwise than by act
of Assembly as aforesaid, shall be . . . null and
void".[28]

Cases necessitating freedom to adjust estates were infrequent, and there are 125 instances where the docking of entails was granted by special legislative act. Application to
dock entails with reasons therefor had to be submitted to
the General Assembly, and notice of this had to be published
in the parish church of the property's location for several
Sundays. Entail was docked on parts of estates to correct a
mistake, as where failure to survey had caused overlapping;
to integrate an estate through exchange of tracts, as when
marriage united two people whose property was widely
separated; to procure money or slaves for the benefit of

younger children; to enable a landowner much of whose lands were uncultivated for lack of sufficient labor to buy more slaves; and to enable him to satisfy British or domestic creditors after his personalty was exhausted. The docked lands were "vested" in state-appointed "trustees" to insure their handling as officially directed—provide for younger children, procure labor, pay debts. Entail in Virginia seems also to have been protected by London, which in 1723 directed that:

> "No private Act, affecting the property of any person, to be put in Execution without the Royal assent";[29]

and the docking of entail did not take effect until "royal assent" was received. The purchasers of the docked tracts held in feudal tenure.

The Code of 1705 also changed the slaves' status from "chattels" or personal property to "real-estate-entailed", so that they were annexed to the land. The "heir at law" therefore inherited all the slaves—with the exception of the widow's dower—as realty, but he was required to pay in money or tobacco to the rest of the children a proportionate share of the appraised value of the slaves. On his mother's passing he automatically inherited all the dower slaves. On the failure of lineal heirs the slaves did not escheat, but were inherited solely by the heir at law of the nearest collateral heirs.

Feudalism is a hierarchy: the king infeudated the proprietary, which in turn sub-infeudated the freehold. Rights in land distinguished the freeman—the freehold was the foundation of the freeman status. There is no "free soil"— arable has to be created: the freeholder had to create and to stock his own plantation which, although comparatively humble, means that he was a man of some economic substance. The freeholders, each of whom had his own separate clearing, were scattered over the proprietor's estate but off his plantation. The class of commoner freeholders originated from the domain owners of pre-Restoration, and it was constantly augmented by immigration. The immigrants were of two kinds: those who had the capital with which immediately to achieve the freehold status—they entered Virginia as freemen; and those who were to earn the status as freedom dues at the end of a working period as craftsmen—they entered as prospective freemen.

The man of that day was nowhere far removed from the soil, and most men yearned for life in nature. There were people in the old country who had accumulated some savings in the trades and manufactures, but who abominated the city: their work in the city was a stepping stone to life in the country; and they could best achieve this with their means in the feudalism of Virginia. It was also a custom at the time among English families of some substance to send a son—who was without prospects at home, or wayward—to America, where he was "apprenticed" to a wealthy colonial for a short time in order to learn the ways of the country. At the end of his probation his family provided him the funds with which to establish himself. The newcomers had paid their own transportation: they could create and stock their own plantations through their capital investment; and they entered the country as freemen. The proprietor sub-infeudated several hundred acres of wooded area within his estate to each of the immigrants on the status of commoner freeholder, and these grants could be entered into the county realty-office books in order to protect their investment.

The commoner freeholders had their origin also from the class of craftsmen, who had to be imported. The relation between master and craftsman was basically the same as in pre-Restoration: skill cannot be coerced; it was an indispensable part of the colonial economy, and it was respected. As time brought expansion more craftsmen were needed, and they were not easily available as those who emigrated

169

generally preferred the trading colonies. They were "under papers"—really a contractual relation, which was a privileged labor status; brute labor was wholly at the mercy of the masters. As Virginia began to become militarily active towards the west at least one "smith" was taken along on each expedition to shoe horses and to repair wagon wheels, "great guns", firearms. It is very significant that, despite the class—yes, the caste—system of the time, the pay of the smith was as high as that of an infantry colonel.[30] Each craftsman had several slave boys apprenticed to him, towards whom he was in a relation of "master". To repeat from George Mason's son:

> "my father had among his slaves, carpenters, coopers, sawyers, blacksmiths, tanners, curriers, shoemakers, spinners, weavers, and knitters, and even a distiller."

These slave craftsmen had been trained by the imported Europeans. Yet bona fide skill cannot be identified with forced labor and European skill had always to be imported. The craftsmen rendered the proprietor necessary services, gave him an income from their outside work, and trained slave apprentices. At the expiration of the contract the proprietor was to enable the craftsman to achieve the status of a freeman, which was based on the freehold: he had to create and to stock the freedman's clearing, and it was through the former master's capital investment that the craftsman was provided within the proprietary with the economic unit required for his establishment—several acres of arable within a granted forest tract, a log house, the necessary implements, and some livestock. Thus the voluntary servant became a freeholder through skill: there was never a fixed division in Virginia between white labor and the freeman status, and the craftsmen under the Cavaliers could achieve an important change in their social position.

The freeholders could not establish the right to "bear arms", which rendered them "commoner" freemen. They had their gradations of wealth, although the richest was quite humble by patrician standards. The average freeholder clearing was probably between about twenty and thirty acres in size, and each owned a few slaves and some livestock. Wertenbaker says that of the slave-owners in Gloucester county in 1783,

"156 had from one to five slaves, 66 from five to ten inclusive, (and) 41 from eleven to fifteen".[31]

They had a sufficiency of the best agricultural implements of the day, and of livestock—only animal labor was hitched to the plow. All this was accumulated commonalty capital—which most of them increased with the consistent growth of the colony and of its prosperity. But they had no craftsmen; they were dependent upon the big plantation for goods and services—manufactured articles, servicing implements, churning milk into butter and cheese, animal husbandry, shipping facilities—which were indispensable for the proper operation of the holding; for all of which they paid with produce, chiefly tobacco. The commoner freeholder was married, in the Established Church: he had a family, wife and children. Houses and furniture in his clearing were all log: many of them had each a comfortable log home of three or four rooms, while such shelters took care of laborers and animals; their simple furniture was improvised by themselves, more complex articles could be made by the local carpenter, and some could afford to purchase a few imports. Clothing was usually homespun. The freeman status was carefully protected—there was a severe penalty for misrepresenting a person as indentured. The commoner had legal being in the community—he had civil rights and was subject to legal liabilities. He lived under the rule of law, and of his betters: he had judicial rights as defendant in criminal and civil proceedings; he exercised the franchise, and could sit as a juror; and he was even endowed with local authority as he was admitted to county offices—sheriff, deputy-sheriff, clerk and judge of the county court and—from some time before Independence—he became eligible also to military commissions. The county officialdom was in the hands of the commonalty—on hierarchical approval: the sheriff, who was the active head of the county, was appointed by the governor with consent of the Council—a part of his duties was to collect the taxes and quit-rents. The commoner freeholder's economic circumstances could fluctuate quantitatively, depending upon conditions and on his own initiative—he could gain or lose in the amount of arable, labor, livestock, implements, he owned. As a delinquent debtor he was liable to imprisonment: he always owned his personalty in full mastery, which made it subject to distraint in satisfaction of creditors; he had to submit a sworn list of all his assets to the court, falsification could be held a capital offense, and he was released from "goal" after he was divested of all his personalty except family wearing apparel and occupational tools; but if satisfaction was not full he was liable for the balance from possible future acquisitions. But qualitatively his status remained fixed. The feudal land laws applied also to him: primogeniture had to apply, as the division of his estate could have ruined it as an economic entity —and the eldest son inherited all the realty; and entail protected him against realty distraint. This created a static world and gave him a sense of stability and security; and he was always a commoner freeholder, as he could go neither higher nor lower. He had to pay rent in perpetuity to the proprietor, whose person he could not put in the position of defendant but whose estate he could sue.

Pre- and post-Restoration Virginia were two different worlds. The Cavalier social revolution created a class of lords proprietor, and the fee simple independent farmers were supplanted by the commoner freeholders. In 1682 the House of Burgesses addressed a message to the governor "in behalfe of themselves and the whole commonality of ... Virginia": thus six years after the Rebellion the lower House, in the spirit of Nathaniel Bacon, still identifies itself with the commonalty: but with time, especially from the Code of 1705, the House of Burgesses became the monopoly of the gentry, and the commonalty was without representation in its own right. Under the Puritans everyone in Virginia was at least a prospective freeman: the Cavaliers introduced the principle of permanent bondage, within which was included eventually at least half of the population— and this created a hyper-sensitivity concerning the freeman status. The church in Virginia was also a school, as many ministers and their lay readers supplemented their income by conducting elementary classes: each of the well developed counties had several parishes; most of the clergy were on a social level with the commonalty, and some of the upper freeholders could send their children to the parish school— where they could sometimes board in the minister's home— for rudimentary instruction. The county officials and the proprietary stewards had responsible positions, and they were not without a good deal of literacy and alertness: a few had to have some learning in the law and in court procedure, and they all had to keep records and know figures; and they did get some respect from the upper class—practicing gentlemen attorneys had to plead before commoner judges in the county courts, and all the amenities of Anglo-Saxon jurisprudence had to be observed. The "master"— of crafts, school, fencing, dancing, music—had authority over his pupils, even though some of them were scions of aristocracy. But education within the commonalty as a class was on a low estate: their schooling was very limited, and book learning scanty; literacy was very poor, with most women and many men hardly able to write their names; and their knowledge was confined to what they picked up in experience. They were Anglican in religion, although not without a discernible strain of Puritanism—with time they began tending towards Nonconformity. Vital statistics were inscribed in the family Bible, and they had little sense of time and place and of events. The colonial planters of whatever class all accepted and were ready to defend the basic framework of their society with its agrarianism and slavery. The commoner freemen had the values and the interests of the aristocrat, and they were traditional in their world view: they wanted to preserve, not to abolish, the feudal sociology; and the crowning achievement of their life was to win commendation from the patricians, whose manners they aped;

> "Slavery developed in the small (planters) a spirit of pride and haughtiness that was unknown to them in the Seventeenth century".[32]

Says the Reverend Burnaby, who traveled through the colony in 1760:

> "Their authority over their slaves renders them vain and imperious, and entire strangers to that elegance of sentiment, which is so peculiarly characteristic of refined and polished nations. Their ignorance of mankind and of learning, exposes them to many errors and prejudices, especially in regard to Indians and negroes, whom they scarcely consider as of the human species; so that it is almost impossible, in cases of violence, or even murder, committed upon those unhappy people by any of the planters, to have the delinquents brought to justice." [33]

The commonalty masters had no overseers, and they had daily personal contact with their slaves in the field as supervisors. The ways of civilization had to prevail in Virginia: in the contact between civilization and primitivism the influence is not always entirely one sided; the Africans, who wanted to live according to their own ways, appeared to the European as stupid, dull-witted, obtuse; driving primitive labor can have dulling effects on the driver; it was not possible for the master entirely to resist the tendency to incline, and his European heritage deteriorated. The slave society has its imperatives—the master has to bend the slave to his will: a show of fear towards slaves is fatal, their relation is always at bottom one of struggle, the masters must always prevail, and they must constantly affect the iron mask; resort to swagger, alcohol, profanity, the whip, seemed to help them overcome resistance; and they became of overbearing mannerism and impatient of restraint, and they were given to abrupt outbursts of rage or, as the language of their country has it, "flying off the handle". They drank excessively: doctors and medicaments were practically unavailable; liquor could ease pain by deadening the sensibilities, and it was regarded as a medicine. They gambled at cards and dice and they brawled frequently, and they delighted in brutal sports such as bear-baiting, the cock-fight and the prize-fight. Life was hard under the best conditions: it was a brutal world, the participants and victims were from the lower classes, and the attitude of callousness to human suffering was not confined simply towards non-Caucasians. An act of 1752 declared the maiming of a Virginia subject a felony but it was evidently ineffective, and twenty years later the Assembly declared:

"Many disorderly and quarrelsome persons do frequently molest, disturb and ill treat many of his majesty's peaceable and quiet subjects, often wounding and doing them great injury".[34]

A law was therefore passed against,

"gouging, plucking or putting out an eye, biting, kicking, or stamping upon any of his majesty's subjects."[34]

Yet sometime later the contemporary resident Fithian saw a prize-fight, which he describes:

"By appointment is to be fought this Day near Mr. Lanes two fist Battles between four young Fellows. The Cause of the battles I have not yet known; I suppose... one has... call'd him a Lubber, or a thick-Skull, or a Buckskin, or a Scotchman . . . All these, & ten thousand more quite as triffling & ridiculous, are thought & accepted as just Causes

of immediate Quarrels, in which every diabolical
Strategem for Mastery is allowed & practised, of
Bruising, Kicking, Scratching, Pinching, Biting,
Butting, Tripping, Throtling, Gouging, Cursing, Dis-
membring, Howling, &c. This spectacle, (so loath-
some & horrible!) generally is attended by a crowd
of People!" [35]

The commonalty stood in awe, and often in dread, of "People
of Rank". Wrote a contemporary member of the class:

"For my part, I was quite shy of them, and kept off
at an humble distance. A periwig . . . was a distin-
guishing badge of gentlefolk; and when I saw a man
riding down the road, near our house, with a wig on,
it would so alarm my fears, and give me such a dis-
agreeable feeling, that, I dare say, I would run off,
as for my life." [36]

Colonial Virginia's class of commoner freeholders is an
historical nonentity as it exerted no distinct influence on its
social milieu. And there was no class of petty bourgeoisie,
or people whose economic interests are dissociated from
land, that made any impression.

With time it was realized that the tracts of the commoner
freeholders—the small plantations contained within the
estates of the gentry—could not for all practical purposes be
entailed. A "debtor" problem was arising in Virginia: and
these tracts had to be kept in a legal condition to enable
their confiscation in levying judgment for non-payment of
taxes and quit-rents, and of debt.[37] Entail complicated the
satisfaction of creditors, who were proprietors to whom the
commonalty had become indebted for rent, for use of their
craftsmen, and for the purchase of imported manufactured
articles from their stores. In considering the law restricting
the dropping of entails to legislative act, the Assembly declared:

"Which method has been found by experience, so

expensive to poor people seized in fee tail of small
and inconsiderable parcels of land . . . therefore the
docking intails by easier methods, will be a great
relief to such poor people and their families, who,
without it, must be confined to labour upon such small
parcels of land, when, by selling them, they might be
enabled to purchase slaves, and other lands more im-
provable." [38]

It is hardly likely that such parcels could have found purchasers.

Entail also tended to slow expansion: the aristocrats who
received grants to frontier estates had to organize them
on the feudal system, which discouraged many people from
settling there; and vast areas of the entailed lands remained uncultivated. In 1734 an area in the valley which
included the squatter settlements was incorporated into
Virginia as Augusta county. Williamsburg was well satisfied with the newcomers' decision to stay, but in view of
the intention to sub-infeudate them through the Beverly
grant there was fear that they would continue their tradition of fleeing from proprietary dominion. The tidewater
landlords therefore realized that total feudalism was a
barrier to effective frontier settlement: they were here
confronted with conditions that had obtained on the first
frontier—pioneer Virginia; land receded in value westwards, where many estates had to be small and cheap; and
it was concluded that the interior could not fully develop
without some freedom in land tenure and transfer.

The Assembly therefore began gradually, and very carefully, to yield bit by bit its powers over entail. The Code
of 1705 had originally permitted the ownership in fee simple
independence of up to one acre of land, located on the site
of towns that the Assembly planned to build, to the grantee
who agreed to erect a residence or warehouse on it within a
given period. Subsequently the Assembly declared that lots
in towns were to be sold so as "to convey the fee simple and
absolute estate and inheritance thereof to the purchasers".

The primitivism on Virginia's ever-present frontiers necessitated the introduction of some freedom in land ownership,
and a goodly number of settlers in the valley, outside and
west of the Beverly proprietary, were not sub-infeudated—
they were permitted to own moderate tracts as fee simple
independent farmers. A law of 1710 declared that debtors
up to £10 sterling whose personalty was insufficient to satisfy their creditors could have their realty sold—on permission of the county court—so as to meet their debts, which
released them from imprisonment. It was also declared that
estates of insufficient value to defray the administrator's
fees had to be sold. In 1734—the year Augusta county was
created in the valley—the Assembly empowered the Secretary of the colony to issue a writ at his office in Williamsburg, on request, which permitted the conversion of an
estate worth up to £200 sterling (quite an amount at the
time) from fee tail to fee simple. The buyer of this realty
took in fee simple title. Thus the General Assembly had
granted power to the county courts and the Secretary's
office to drop entails on estates of moderate value. With
time the operation where applicable of the Secretarial Writ
seems to have been accepted as a fact regardless of request.
By 1748 fee simple ownership of realty had attained sufficient importance to cause the Assembly to legislate in an attempt to clarify the rights of buyer, seller, lender, borrower,
heirs—and the Parliamentary act of 1692 "for the relief of
creditors against fraudulent devises" was first introduced in
Virginia. In the same year the freeholder won the right to
habeas corpus in actions for debt: the law declared that in
the case of an insolvent estate, where the debtor had been
imprisoned twenty days, all his realty "shall be vested in the
sheriff of the county" of its location, who was to alienate
it together with the personalty for the satisfaction of the
creditors and then free the debtor.[39] Thus *habeas corpus*
applied to those who had accumulated sufficient private
property, and was predicated upon the docking of entails.

178

By the inauguration of the Commonwealth the class of commoner freeholders owned their lands and slaves in fee simple title.

The Secretarial Writ of 1734 attached to the commonalty freehold the principle of fee simple, but not of independence; the freeholder could alienate whatever rights he had in a parcel of land within the proprietary on which he lived and worked—but not the land itself, for the use of which he or the new holder had to continue paying rent to the proprietor in perpetuity. Rent was the bond that held the proprietary estate together: the cessation of rent or the achievement of independence—the creation of the separate parcel of land owned in complete mastery, would have meant the disintegration of the proprietary estate or the dissolution of the feudal system—which no one then intended. Thus the principles of fee simple and of independence in land ownership do not necessarily go together: the freeholder had certain uses of or rights in the land which he could convey to a purchaser, but he had no rights to the land itself. Says Charles M. Andrews:

"colonial freeholders . . . were under obligation to recognize in one form or another the higher title of some landed proprietor. The payment (rent) in no way hampered the freeholder in the control of his land, for though actual ownership remained elsewhere, he was free to alienate or bequeath his real estate according to the laws of his colony and to exercise all the rights of possession, provided he conformed to the terms of his tenure." [40]

Entail meant the protection of realty and of social status: the docking of entails from the commonalty freehold, and its succession by the fee simple freehold, appears to have been prejudicial to the interests of the freeholders; they lost the protection of entail—their tracts were "freed" so that the proprietor could seize them in satisfaction of debt. The distrained freeholders were not evicted: they could continue to remain on and work their holdings, but on a declassed—on a tenant—status. The exposure of the moderate freehold tracts to distraint was an important stimulus to the subsequent commonalty transmontane surge.

The social consequences in colonial Virginia of the introduction of the fee simple planter and of the fee simple independent farmer were nil—the proprietary system continued unimpaired. The free tracts in the valley were devoted chiefly to farming: a farmer class with its individualist, entrepreneur values was again beginning to arise; but its numbers and wealth were insufficient to constitute an influence.

The Cavalier social revolution also introduced the "tenant" status in Virginia. The tenancy was a family agricultural unit that was created and stocked for the occupant by the proprietor's capital investment, which resulted in a master-tenant relation. The tenancy was a serf status: the tenant never had any property rights to anything in the economic unit that he worked; the tract and its produce were always the property of the master who, after leaving the occupant and his family a subsistence minimum of their produce, appropriated the rest as "rent"—which had to be paid in perpetuity. The class of tenants had arisen from the leaseholders of pre-Restoration—and it was constantly augmented from the ranks of the indentured servants, who had to be so provided at the end of their terms. Some tenants originated also from the commoner freeholders: a few of them may have had sufficient capital with which to provide another son with a freehold, but the younger sons generally had to settle as tenants. With the introduction of fee simple for the commonalty the distrained freeholders could remain on and work their holdings on the inferior status. The tenants were not freemen and they were not bondsmen—they could not be coerced into laboring, and they had freedom of movement. They may best be classified as "non-freemen", as they had no legal being in the com-

munity: they had none of the civil liberties—franchise, trial
by jury, habeas corpus; and they were without religious,
marriage or educational rights. Voluntary labor under the
feudal way of life is impractical, and the tenancy in Virginia
largely failed as a labor system: the tenants refused to
work, there being neither material reward nor corporal
punishment as a stimulus to labor; the climate created a
tendency to indolence, the servility of labor made it a disgrace, the master's rent was exacting, and they could never
acquire the capital or the skill with which to work their
way up to the freehold status; and they deteriorated to the
condition of "mean whites". There was little that could be
done with them: banishment from the colony was never
a penalty; and eviction was pointless. The master-tenant
relation appears just in principle, although fault may be
found in degree—the proprietor would have been amply
repaid had he taken appreciably less for rent. The economic
and social condition of the mean whites was very wretched:
they lived as best they could by hunting and fishing in the
surrounding forests, whose vastness dispensed with the need
for poaching laws; yet they were always undernourished
and they begged for alms from wayfarers. They were brutal:
they had no sense of sex morality as they mated promiscuously, and in 1730 the Assembly found it necessary to legislate against incestuous relations and copulation;[41] and
their offspring could be indentured as bastards. Their living
standards were probably below those of some of the slaves,
who looked down upon them as "po' white trash". The
contemporary Smyth says of them:

> "The third, or lower class of people . . . are in Vir-
> ginia more few in number . . . than perhaps in any
> other country in the universe. Even these are kind,
> hospitable, and generous; yet illiberal, noisy, and
> rude. They are much addicted to inebriety, and averse
> to labour . . . almost all of the lower class of people,
> are ignorant in the extreme." [42]

The mean whites were not laborers—but they were fighters: they could be used as an offset to the slaves, and during military expeditions they were impressed into the militia. The masters recognized their value: in 1727 the population of Middlesex county was three-quarters black, and as its low whites were developing a tendency to move westwards the authorities became concerned and spoke of, "The meaner sort of the people (in whom consists the strength of all Countrys)".

There were some peculiarly situated people in Virginia who were also on a tenant status in law. The overseer, the ordinary—store—ferry—keeper, each evidently had an agricultural unit near where he worked, and was considered a tenant. Special arrangements could be made to supply some slave help to work the clearing as part of their pay, while they were engaged in their several duties. It seems that the craftsman while under papers also had a tenancy, so that he was better situated while bound than was the freed common laborer.

In colonial Virginia land was life, and all its inhabitants had perforce a relation to land. Capital was scarce: reclamation was always based on the axe, and arable was hard to come by. The fundamental concern was one of title to land—the source, and the kind, of title. In view of the social upheavals in England, and their repercussions in the colony, there was often uncertainty as to the true source of valid title, and there was great fear that a political change at home would render defective the land titles granted by those previously in power. The kind of title to land determined a person's social status—proprietor, freeholder, tenant. During the eighteenth century Virginia had achieved stability concerning the source and kind of title to realty, and the "muniments of title" were sacredly regarded and carefully preserved in family strong-boxes. All changes in landholdings had to be judicially sanctioned and made in terms of a "deed" which carried the "royal seal", and the "recording every deed of feoffment" [43] in the county court was legally required. In 1766 all realty purchased or inherited from aliens was legislatively confirmed as valid in the holders. They were indifferent to precision concerning wilderness acreage, and there was little surveying. The boundaries between estates were indistinctly marked, and a "processioning" or remarking of bounds had to be made every four years. All controversies involving title and bounds to land were tried in the General Court, and the parties' pleas and the court's decisions were in writing and recorded in the court archives; and the Secretary's office kept all realty records. In 1748 another blanket validation of all lands held and claimed up to 1735 was made, even though "without any valuable consideration therein expressed"; and lands adjoining a patented parcel were permitted to be tacked on to the parcel and called one estate.

The General Assembly reserved the right of eminent domain over all realty: it could force alterations on private estates, such as the draining of marshes; and if part of an estate was needed for public purposes, especially in the building of communications, it was officially taken over and paid for. The erection of a town had to have the Assembly's permission: the town site, usually consisting of about one hundred acres, was granted by the owner and was officially vested in trustees who sold lots within it to reimburse the grantor. The conveyance of these areas was enabled by the legislative docking of entails.

Primogeniture and entail seem to have been considered a privilege, which was not extended to all: they were a safeguard against the absorption of estates by land speculators and monopolists, as they secured the aristocracy's economic foundation and guaranteed its perpetuation; and colonial Virginia exercised the greatest possible care for their basic preservation. These laws were rigidly, although not mechanically, enforced; no law suit ever occurred in which their validity in principle was brought into question; and there were probably fewer instances of exception from these laws allowed in Virginia than in any other Anglo-Saxon jurisdiction of the time. Thus the dropping of entails was permitted only through special legislative act and Secretarial Writ. The fee simple tracts were held down in number and value, and precautions were taken against the freeing of large estates bit by bit. An historian declares that "the majority of the entails were never docked in either fashion", and that "few of the old family seats were docked".[44] Thus the freeing of the commoner freeholds did not bring a social revolution to colonial Virginia—fee tail continued to be the basic realty law.

Expansion was solely extensive, and although each generation worked more land than the preceding one the number of landowners was relatively decreasing. With the aristocracy's economic grip secured in the state and inheritance automatic by law there was no stimulus to thrift. The owner was often well along in life when he inherited the estate; he had only a life interest in it, and a social position to maintain; and he lived entirely for the present. He was unable to get a cash loan because his property could not be used as security, and if he had the money he hated to sink it into the estate because his eldest son would be the sole beneficiary. He therefore wrung the most out of what he had while it lasted, which resulted in a minimum yield. The soil, slaves and livestock were abused while roads were neglected, swamps remained undrained and slave quarters sank into cesspools of filth and disease.

The effects of primogeniture in Virginia differed from those in England. The colony's vast spaces obviated the need for the younger sons to turn to professions and trades since they could secure themselves grants to land: the aristocracy was careful that its younger sons were sufficiently provided with the wherewithal for the creation of proprietaries, which were generally located towards the interior; but they had to start from scratch, time was required for the plantation to become economically self-sufficient, the communications were inferior, and there were no hereditaments. Thus in Virginia the eldest son did get the most valuable of the family possessions, but his social and economic position as compared to that of his brothers was not as exalted as in England.

Entail created a static society: there was no land speculation and turnover, and "there was no market in Virginia". They were without banking, and therefore without the *raison d'etre* of the commercial economy—a stable currency. The fiat paper money—issued to help finance war on the French—soon badly depreciated, the tobacco notes fluctuated, and no one knew the exact value of the circulating variety of "faran quoine". In 1769 a law was passed to bring in copper money. There were no corporations, stock companies, partnerships, and no laws for their regulation. While some alienation of realty occurred, there were none of the legal and financial complexities of encumbrance— trusts, mortgages, notes, negotiable instruments.

Virginia was dependent on England for manufactured articles.

"The colonists were even denied the privilege of making their own clothing . . . every effort was made to prevent the least independence of action, so that by complete economic subjection, the political supremacy of Great Britain might stand secure." [45]

"while practically all clothing for slaves was made on the plantations, the people of Virginia (in 1774) still were importing almost seven-eighths of their wearing apparel." [46]

All economic activities apart from agriculture had to have government consent through the license system. The few manufactories started, such as the iron works promoted by Governor Spotswood, were built and owned chiefly by English capital. Yet the arms needed to equip her military had to be imported. Spotswood improved Virginia's tobacco warehouse system, for the preservation abroad of her "Publick Credit"; and he tried to organize the Indian trade into a joint-stock company, but it seems not to have succeeded. The tax on exported skins and furs was set aside for support of the College, but was found insufficient for this purpose. The aristocrat's income from his "general merchandise store" was insignificant. The interior planters who bought manufactured articles from him were liable for interest if they defaulted in their payments; the Assembly called "usury" any interest exceeding five percent per annum. The constant conversion of forest tracts into cultivable land brought a super-abundance of timber; it was the sole fuel used, yet large amounts of it had to be destroyed by burning; and the simplest pieces of wooden household articles, as well as paper for printing and keeping records, were imported. The mechanical trades were regarded as "mistery"; there were a few itinerant "all-around" mechanics but the specialized workers—especially in the field of building construction—and the materials they needed, had to be imported. The available mechanics were at a premium, and skilled workers found among the British and Hessian prisoners of the Revolution were given employment. In 1772 plans were drawn up for the building of several canals, although the colony was entirely without engineers. Pedlars, who had to be licensed by posting a £100 sterling bond, also helped relieve the scarcity by visiting the plantations to sell their wares. Literates were in great demand as tutors and clerks, and they too had to be imported. With the little domestic trade based on barter money was unnecessary, and gentlemen could travel through the colony on hospitality. During extended gatherings such as horse races and fairs visitors had to bring their own provisions. Transportation was chiefly by river and on horse back.

In 1752 the Assembly referred to Virginia as "a trading country", and it was always very careful to protect "the credit of the country". But her trading and credit relations were entirely foreign. Some "sloops" and "brigantines" trading to the West Indies were owned by a few of the planters, yet Virginians seem to have had hardly any interests in the enormous ocean-going tobacco and slave carrying commerce. Virginia could import what she needed and didn't produce, and she probably had less domestic manufactures and trade and credit relations than any of the ancient Mediterranean countries. There was no spontaneity among the population towards manufactures: in 1759 a "committee for arts and manufactures" was appointed, but the Assembly despaired of results;

"The experiments of wine and silk are attended with
little expense . . . Small premiums have already been
offered by a society in England, and, the committee
of arts and manufactures in this colony; but such is
the force of habit that we have little reason to expect
any benefit from them. The prospect of future distant
advantage is not strong enough to engage our attention; and we shall find the planter continue, without
deviation, in the beaten track".[47]

The Virginians had no objection to manufacture provided it did not importantly affect their basic social structure—the plantation economy.

With the change in the colony's social organization Jamestown was abandoned, and the capital was moved to Williamsburg which was founded around 1700. In 1760 the capital consisted of some two hundred scattered houses with about a thousand people. It contained the governor's palace, the college buildings, the now historically famous Raleigh Tavern, a book shop kept by the publisher of the Virginia Gazette, a church, a theatre and a bowling alley. About a dozen patrician families permanently resided there. But Williamsburg was exposed to naval invasion. Richmond was founded in 1737, and being farther inland and removed from hostile war vessels it was made the capital in 1779.

187

Virginia's towns were very small compared to those of the other colonies. Says Bassett:

"in 1790 Richmond, the largest town in Virginia, numbered 3761; and Norfolk, Petersburg, and Alexandria were the only other towns in the State with a population of two thousand or more .... In South Carolina, Charleston had a population of about fifteen thousand ... Its (Baltimore) population in 1790 was thirteen thousand." [48]

Fiske says that by 1776,

"Philadelphia had some 35,000 inhabitants, and New York 25,000, though the population of their two states taken together scarcely equalled that of Virginia." [49]

This although Virginia had been founded before the other colonies.

Fear of fire was an important element in discouraging the rise of towns. The hot sun converted wooden houses to tinder; ovens for cooking and washing, fireplaces for heating, and candles for lighting were in constant use, and there was plenty of tobacco smoking. There was also fear of arsonists among the disaffected elements. The absence of proper firefighting equipment endangered the entire town, although the houses were widely separated. But the colony's plantation economy with its dispersed way of living was chiefly responsible for the non-development of towns; there was no popular spontaneity in that direction, and the legislative attempts to overcome this condition largely failed. Some of the towns that struggled into existence were allowed to stagnate, and in 1757 the Assembly declared:

"the streets and landings in the town of York are in so ruinous a condition that ... it (is) necessary ... to support them with a brick wall from being washed away by the showers of rain."

A small class of Scotch merchants had arisen in the towns who made their living chiefly by activities dissociated from land. In 1742 they were officially permitted to pay taxes,

debts, fees, in money instead of in tobacco, and later everyone was allowed to meet all obligations except quit-rents in
paper currency. But Virginia's merchant activities were incidental; the merchants were regarded as outside the social
framework, and they were disdained by the landowners.

The "ordinary" was a log cabin usually facing a path in
the woods, and some had sleeping accommodations for two.
The traveler's horse could be cared for in a rear shed which
sometimes had a blacksmith who shod horses, repaired guns,
and sharpened saws, axes and plows. Some sheds had a small
stock of agricultural tools for sale. The ordinary permitted
some gambling, but the main business was in serving liquor.
Its keeper was either a hired or contracted clerk, or a tenant
to whom the landowner had sub-infeudated. The workers
about the place were slaves. The ordinary was licensed on
the posting of a bond for 10,000 pounds of tobacco, and all
its doings—prices charged, credit extended, degree of tip-
pling, gaming—were regulated by law. It was illegal to serve
liquor to servants and slaves. Liquor debts for any one year
above twenty shillings were not recoverable in court. In
1668 the number of ordinaries was reduced for fear of public gatherings, but during the next century they became
centers of loyalty as keepers were required immediately to
report all strangers to the nearest constable. During military
campaigns soldiers were quartered in the ordinaries without
charge by government order. The ordinary as a social center
for news and gossip could never mean much in a world
where the hospitality of every aristocrat's mansion beckoned
the passing traveler.

The Virginians were much given to litigation; the lawyers
were generally ill-equipped for their work, and their fees
were fixed by law. The colony had no medical school, and
doctors were few and poorly trained. Many of them were
planters who engaged in the practice of medicine, surgery,
pharmacy and midwifery as a sideline;

"the dispenser of drugs, the rude village surgeon and

189

barber, or the unskilful apprentice, were the representatives of medicine in Virginia, and were not held in high esteem." [50]
There were a few doctors who had received training abroad, and they were in the service of the aristocrats. George Washington employed a physician regularly to look after his slaves, and in 1758 the Assembly paid £10 sterling to Dr. James Carter "for cutting off and curing a soldier's arm." But the bona fide doctor, and medical and surgical supplies, were scarce; the healing arts and the law were studied as apprentices of practitioners, and home remedies and Negro midwives and nurses were plentiful. In 1769 the Assembly restricted inoculation against small-pox.[51] A hospital was erected in 1773 for persons of disordered minds who "have been frequently found wandering" in the colony.

Surveying and map-making as exact professions began to become important from about 1745 in connection with transmontane activities. Expeditions were organized and equipped to fight Indians and help run the French out of America. Piracy around the colony's waters disappeared. Jefferson estimated the population of Virginia around 1780 at almost 300,000 white inhabitants and about 270,000 slaves.

Dissent in Virginia, especially Puritanism, had achieved great strength by 1660. But the Cavaliers considered Dissent inimical to their purposes, they set out to suppress it, and by the end of the century Nonconformity in the tidewater was insignificant while Puritanism was wholly eradicated. A number of Quaker* Nonconformists were permitted to reside in Virginia's settled areas, and with the Code of 1705 they began to win some rights. Their "affirmation," in place of the usually required oath, was legalized in court proceedings, which rendered their testimony valid and gave them some judicial rights. With time Quakers appear as commoner freeholders, and they exercise the franchise. The

* Quakers were held suspect by the English Revolution of 1689.

government also waived required oaths, that were repugnant to Nonconformists, for some minor offices and for the licensing of attorneys, which made Quakers eligible. From 1766 those having bona fide proof that they are Quakers were exempted from muster. But Nonconformists were not admitted to the aristocracy. Virginia also always had a number of Roman Catholics, some of whom seemed to have owned property. But they were held suspect and discriminated against, especially after 1689. They had no judicial rights as their testimony was per se invalid,[52] they were legally disabled from acting as guardians of infants and orphans,[53] and in 1693 "the extraction of the test oath from a prominent family of Papists" took place. There was a reign of terror against them during the trans-Allegheny war on the French, as it was thought that their sympathies were more religious than national. In 1756, during the hysteria that followed Braddock's defeat, the Assembly held that "it is dangerous at this time to permit Papists to be armed"; all arms of known and "reputed" Catholics were seized; and they were forced to take the oath of loyalty, on pain of forfeiting their property.

By around the middle of the eighteenth century the area east of the Alleghenies was pretty well absorbed, and the mind of the Virginian transcended domestic concerns as it turned definitely towards transmontane expansion. Several factors, however, arose to challenge these ambitions. The hills loomed as a formidable natural barrier. She began encroaching on the interests and ambitions of other colonies, who were exerting influences against her. This gave rise to a Virginia "foreign" policy. The Indians appeared as an opposing force; they had learned to differentiate between the various groups of whites, they feared the land-hungry Virginians, and they were well armed. And London began to follow a general policy of checking colonial westward expansion. Thus the Virginians' sense of land limitation was emphasized as they realized that future expansion would not come without trouble. But land was life to the planter economy: Williamsburg was very influential in London where, in addition to her own representative, she employed an Englishman as agent at an annual salary of £200 sterling; and around 1750 she organized the Ohio Company which succeeded in obtaining a royal grant to a half million acres of transmontane lands. Virginia had accumulated sufficient riches to undertake the highly expensive adventure of trans-Allegheny penetration, and organized steps were begun in this direction. The rivers flowing across the mountains—which had hitherto been feared as facilitating enemy invasion, and were now regarded as highways of empire— were to be cleared for passage, and roads also were to be hewn out of the wilderness.

The allegation that settlers transformed primordial America into a civilization with "their bare hands" is heroics: the ship, the pack horse, the conestoga wagon, the prairie schooner—each of these was a unit of capital, without which there could have been no settlement. Virginia had been always hitherto settled and expanded from the coast westward—from tidewater into piedmont—by the proprietary gentry: they were the prime movers—the dynamic element —in colonial life, as they were the only group that had a sufficiency of capital; and they had traditionally accepted views and attitudes concerning basic standards of social organization—state, church, property, labor. But the settlement of the valley introduced a new principle: the valley was settled from the early part of the eighteenth century by people coming from the interior of the continent; they were commonalty folk who had accumulated sufficient capital of their own to undertake the establishment of settlements of their own; and they had their own attitudes—different from those of the proprietaries—concerning the basic principles of social organization. The commonalty freeholders in Virginia had also accumulated some capital: they began to evince a restiveness concerning the fixity of their condition within the feudal framework; and, before the transmontane movement, there were some migrations of these people to the Shenandoah valley, where they joined the settlers already there. Since they were located on the fringes of the established colony, which were known as "the frontiers," the settlers came to be known as "frontiersmen."

The frontiersmen were Nonconformists: they wanted total independency, or separation of state, church and property —and they were hostile to the slave labor system; they had a positive practical program—they had something, which they were convinced was an improvement, to put in the place of what they sought to abolish; and the commonalty acquisition of capital identified it with the struggle for the fee simple independent title in land ownership. The people from Pennsylvania arrived in the valley as Nonconformists: the settlers from within Virginia were Anglicans, but their attachment to the Establishment had always been indifferent; and they easily came under the Independent influence. The frontiersmen, acting on their own, built their settlements with their own capital investment, and organized them in terms of complete mastery in land ownership or the fee simple independent title. Yet whatever the mind of the settlers, Williamsburg was the law—the validity of everything that happened in the valley flowed solely from the authority of the government: authority was entirely committed to the fee tail proprietary title in realty ownership; the law regarded the settlers as "squatters" or trespassers on the public domain, and their fee simple independent title therefore existed de facto but not de jure. When their settlements became sufficiently populated Williamsburg brought them under its authority: it established a lord proprietor over them, to whom they were sub-infeudated; and freedom in land ownership was automatically extinguished. Thus the social system of the tidewater was extended into the valley: it was considered that "wild" land, and the people settled on it, were given integrity by sub-infeudation as it brought them within the social milieu of Virginia; and as within the proprietary there was no squatter status—the people with capital were regarded as commoner freeholders, while the ordinary farmers became tenants.

The valley settlers had fled from proprietary sub-infeudation, but—like a curse, it followed them wherever they went. The freeholders yearned for land mastery—which brought with it mastery of state and church, or control of the settlement: the tenants had no recognition as "people" in a social sense, and they were without civil liberties; and they all had to pay rent to the proprietor, and taxes to the state and to the Establishment. Virginia's legislators had made a pretense at incorporating England's Toleration Act of 1689 into her statutes, but their insistence on interpreting the Act in terms of local conditions virtually nullified its application in practice.[54]

"Till the Revolution, only ministers of the established church were permitted to perform the (marriage) ceremony. Any 'pretended marriage,' made otherwise, was declared null and void, the offspring illegitimate and the parents liable to prosecution for unlawful cohabitation. The minister was subjected to a heavy penalty."[55]

Legal marriage required expensive fees—they added up to around 465 pounds of tobacco[56]—for a license issued at the county court, and for the minister. Many of the low whites did not know what "legal marriage" meant, and most of them were in no position to meet the expense of traveling to the county court and paying the fees. In 1734 ferriage across the Potomac river for a man or horse was two shillings and six pence, and toll had to be paid at bridges. The Assembly declared that in the county of Norfolk,

"there are five public ferries, over one of which most of the inhabitants are obliged to pass in order to go to church, court, and general musters, and that by the expense of ferriage many poor people are pre-

vented from bringing their small wares and commodities to the market." [57]
Bastards could not inherit property, and they were sold into servitude. In addition to paying taxes for the Establishment's maintenance Dissenters were required to pay its ministers, who were really officers of the state, for particular services rendered.

J. A. Waddell, the historian of Augusta county in the valley, says of the Beverly proprietorship of 1736—"we couldn't do anything about it at the time"; the frontiersmen had their own social program and the capital with which to achieve it, but Williamsburg wouldn't allow it; they again had the choice of remaining where they were at on a servile status or leaving; but this time a restiveness began to become discernible among them—they did not recognize their sub-infeudation to absentee landlords as final, and they developed an underlying disaffection that brought intermittent trouble. Their activities as soldiers—from which they acquired possession, and experience in the use, of firearms—gave them a sense of power, and the feeling that they count. Religion was the commonalty's only form of organized protest against politico-economic abuses: Dissent was the struggle of the commoners against proprietary sub-infeudation and for the acquisition of social rights, and it was persecuted fundamentally because of its social-revolutionary content. As Nonconformists they repudiated the principle of "supremacy" in religion, as they held that theological interpretation is a matter of individual conscience. Their scattered habitations made few churches possible, and their sects were illegal and largely unorganized. Most of their creeds were leveling, and they were feared because of their hatred of hierarchical organization and advocacy of the separation of church and state—with the two institutions united the one could not be attacked without involving the other.

Nonconformity had become rooted in the valley, and by 1740 it began to filter eastwards where it was sympathetically received by the commoner and tenant whites. A number of itinerant or unlicensed preachers arose who bitterly denounced the Establishment and caused it loss of respect, following and income. But the Church was a bulwark of the status quo, and it was jealous of its prerogatives. Several vestries of frontier parishes were dissolved when it was discovered that all or most of their members "are dissenters from the Church of England," and steps were taken against "influencing" the election and activities of vestrymen. Dissenters were required to have a license to preach: itinerant preachers could be sold into servitude as "vagrants," and there was a penalty for entertaining them. Virginia's Governor Gooch (1727-49), in condemning itinerant preachers, said:

> "Your missionaries producing proper testimonials, complying with the laws, and performing divine service in some certain place appropriated for that purpose, without disturbing the quiet and unity of our sacred and civil establishments, may be sure of my protection."

> "We should beseech our Christian brethren, of other denominations especially, to consider whether, when seeking to array the rich and the poor, the learned and unlearned, against each other, they are not committing a great sin against society and government, and against ... God." [58]

The power to grant license to preach was taken away from the county courts and lodged in the General Court as the Councillors became dubious of the sentiments entertained in the more western counties.

Thus Virginia was for the first time confronted with a "frontier" problem, but the underlying principle involved was familiar: it was the old question of the kind of title to land ownership—the conflict between the traditional feudal entailed proprietary system and the revolutionary fee simple independent title. The new way was persistent: yet it still couldn't achieve much against the entrenched tidewater interests; its protest was basic—it was aimed at the sociology of colonial Virginia. But the frontiersmen could not be entirely ignored: Virginia realized that her impending struggles for western empire would necessitate their good will, and she began carefully to make them limited concessions. The Assembly took cognizance of the fact that poor whites,

> "are subject to great oppression from the sheriffs and other collectors, who exact an unreasonable and exorbitant price for such levies in money." [59]

The oath of conformity to the Church of England was judiciously omitted as a few senior, and quite a number of junior, military commissions were bestowed on Nonconformists—Daniel Morgan, a frontiersman, was commissioned a general by Virginia during the War for Independence. Several commoner delegates from the western counties were admitted to the House of Burgesses. In 1754 Governor Dinwiddie offered two hundred thousand acres of trans-Allegheny lands to all volunteers for military service in that area, a large portion of which was to be distributed among the low whites. Yet the frontiersmen of Virginia were weak compared to those of Pennsylvania and North Carolina. Virginia's Nonconformity was an alien force which impinged itself upon the tidewater from without. The frontiersman eventually became a revolutionary factor as he developed his own way of life, but during the colonial period he was not an important modifying influence on the seaboard's social institutions.

As a result of Anglo-America's participation in the "French and Indian" War (1755-63) Virginia and several other colonies were maneuvering towards the acquisition of vast trans-Allegheny lands, and a competition for population was arising between them. But Virginia's statutory feudalism or the Code of 1705 had hampered the full settlement of her area east of the mountains. The leading immigrants from Europe who came to settle in the colonies were ambitious to make fortunes from land speculation, and they wanted ownership of realty in fee simple independence, religious toleration, naturalization or the right to participate in the political life of the colony, and opportunities for education. Most of the immigrants were settling in colonies having more liberal laws, and a tendency was developing among Virginia's commoners to emigrate to more hopeful places. Virginia had always led the other colonies in population, and her leaders feared that she would be outstripped. It was also realized that the assistance of the colony's numerous commoners and low whites would be necessary for the successful prosecution of the War for Independence. Moreover, there was a feeling that where land is unlimited an aristocracy can be maintained without primogeniture and entail. As Virginia was moving towards transmontane empire and secession the tendencies to freedom in realty ownership increased; and by the time Thomas Jefferson entered public life in 1769 there had developed among most of the landowners a good deal of impatience with the Code of 1705, as they yearned to be free in the disposal of their property.

The impact of the frontier was distintegrative; and the colony's westward expansion brought on a social revolution that culminated in the elimination of Cavalier absolutism. After Virginia's declaration of independence on May 15, 1776, and the adoption of her constitution, steps were taken which eventually led to the abolition of the feudal realty laws and of the Establishment, as well as to the facilitation of the naturalization of foreigners.

Part Two: SOCIAL ASPECTS

When Robert "King" Carter, of the peak of the Virginian aristocracy, died, in 1732, a publication in England declared: "He was President of the Council, and left among

his Children above 300,000 Acres of Land, about 1000 Negroes and 10,000£." [1]
There were none who owned more, although several could claim as much. Thomas Allen Glenn says:

"Four sons of 'King' Carter shared the family honors and estates in the succeeding generations. These were—John of 'Corotoman,' Robert of 'Nomini,' Charles of 'Cleve,' and Landon of 'Sabine Hall.' ... We find in the Virginia Land Office a number of grants to Robert Carter and his sons, and these of course do not represent all of their landed property. A cursory examination of these records shows Robert Carter, Jr., patenting over forty thousand acres, exclusive of the land that he took up with other persons, which on one occasion exceeded fifty thousand acres. Landon Carter received grants amounting to sixty-six thousand eight hundred acres, and once he and others patented over forty-one thousand acres. These numbers convey some idea of the magnificent estates the family became possessed of. ... In the early part of the eighteenth century the property of the planters was still largely in land, and they had now become, also, large slaveholders." [1]

In 1735 William Byrd the Second was granted 100,000 acres on the then frontiers, and on his demise in 1744:

"he owned no less than 179,440 acres of the best land in Virginia. Robert Carter, of Nomini Hall, owned 60,000 acres. The land of William Fitzhugh amounted to 54,000 acres at his death in 1701. Other prominent men were possessed of estates no less extensive." [2]

Mann Page, esquire, in 1730 owned over 30,000 acres of land, "a large number of slaves, and a considerable personal estate." An historian declares:

"the list of grants in Henrico (county), 1635-1755, shows the frequency ... of names such as Cocke, Randolph, Pleasants, Woodson, Fleming, Bolling, Ep-

pes, Branch, Ward and Byrd." [3]
The seats of the Randolphs on the James river consisted of
Tuckahoe, Chatsworth, Varina, Wilton, Curles, Bremo and
Turkey Island. There were other families similarly situated.
But Thomas Lord Fairfax, with a proprietary that exceeded
the state of New Hampshire in area, topped them all. Some
aristocrats also acquired interests in other colonies and in
England.

Robert Carter the Councillor, a grandson of Robert
"King" Carter, owned around six hundred Negroes in 1774.
George Washington worked over three hundred Negro
slaves on his estate at Mount Vernon; he had numerous
other tracts scattered in and outside of Virginia. His property in white indentured servants was insufficient, and he
wrote James Tilghman in 1774 saying:

"Interested, as well as political motives, render it
necessary for me to seat the lands which I have patented on the Ohio in the cheapest, most expeditious,
and effectual manner. Many expedients have been
proposed to accomplish this, and none, in my judgment, so likely as by importing of Palatines ... what
plan would be ... best to import a full freight, say
two or three hundred, or more." [4]

Washington's friend Robert Adam wrote him advising that
"the Scotch and Irish farmers would suit you as well ...
they are much distressed in their own country." [4] In 1772
Thomas Jefferson had "some two hundred slaves," and the
following year "Mrs. Jefferson inherited 142 slaves and
some forty thousand acres of land." [5] Just before Independence Washington paid £35 for a white craftsman, while
adult Negroes sold for as high as £90 each. The eye-witness
Fithian, who left his home in New Jersey to act as tutor at
Nomini Hall during 1773-4, declares: "The very Slaves in
some families here, could not be bought under 30,000£. Such
amazing property ... blows up the owners." [6] Says Wertenbaker:

"In Gloucester county in 1783, of 320 slaveholders ...
57 had sixteen or more. Of these one possessed 162,
one 138, one 93, one 86, one 63, one 58, two 57, one
56, one 43, and one 40." [7]
Thus eleven people owned 853 slaves.

When Thomas Jefferson embarked on his public career in
1769—that was to last almost sixty years—Virginia led the
other colonies in area, population and wealth. As the patrician families each acquired vast estates in scattered parcels
there arose the steward, under whom was a corps of overseers; and the labor of the constantly increasing number of
slaves was beginning to crystallize into the ease and splendor
with which the Virginian aristocracy is associated in history
and fiction.

"The enactment and enforcement of Governor Gooch's
tobacco inspection law of 1730 inaugurated in the
colony an era of prosperity and consequent extravagance, the like of which had never been known before.
It was in that period that the local magnates prepared to abandon their plantation houses ... and to
construct mansion houses in the English tradition,
such as Westover and Mount Airy; to import and use
'chariots' for occasions of ceremony; to drink madeira as well as bumbo; to ride formally to hounds;
and to keep horses for racing only." [8]
Thus Jefferson's youth and maturity were spent in an atmosphere exuberant with the consciousness of expansion.

As life and its interests broadened for the descendants of
the distressed Cavaliers shoddy homes and furnishings began giving way to mansions elaborately adorned.

"During the eighteenth century the most common
form of mansion, whether of brick or wood, on a
large plantation was the square building, two stories
high with or without an attic, and with a wide hall—
often called the 'great hall'—four spacious rooms on

each floor, and four chimneys. It was sometimes flanked by wings and sometimes by detached out-buildings used for office, schoolhouse, laundry and kitchen.... 'Rosewell' on the York, built by Mann Page in 1730 ... had ... a frontage of two hundred and thirty-two feet. The central building contained fourteen rooms twenty feet square and nine rooms fourteen by seven feet. There were nine passages, and the 'great hall' and hall over it were each large enough to have made three large rooms. Much of this space was occupied by the grand stairway, with its balustrade of mahogany richly carved in fruits and flowers, ascending by easy flights to the cupola, which commanded a wide view of the York River and the surrounding country.... The main building at 'Rose-well' had three full stories, besides garrets and cellars." [9]

The fireplace was an important spot, and "often there were seats within the chimney on either side."

"Carter's Creek" was the home of the Burwells, "Amp-thill" that of Archibald Cary, "Stratford" of the Lees, "Marmion" belonged to the Fitzhughs, "Mt. Zion" to the Thrustons, "Westover" to the Byrds, "Mt. Airy" to the Taylors, "Brandon" to the Harrisons, "Rosegill" to the Wormeleys; and there were many more.

Some aristocrats kept a park on their plantations where they raised deer, squirrels, pheasants and other harmless animals, and they amused themselves observing and feeding them.

"There were, in a formal sense, only a few gardens: commonly a rough lawn with great trees reached from the house to the river; irregular beds of herbs and wild flowers were tended by the women; a small burial ground was planted with myrtle and box."

The household furnishings had advanced from necessaries to the inclusion of luxuries:

"Russia leather chairs, Turkey-work chairs ... Turkey-work upholstery, imported from the Orient ... Turkey carpets, too, often reaching to and sweeping the floor—their weight and richness of color ... Japanned tables and cabinets ... looking glasses ... yellow silk and worsted damask hangings; window curtains to match ... vases ... two lions bronzed with copper after the antique Lyons in Italy ... large Wilton Persian carpet ... china began to appear." [10]

They were not to be outdone in dress:

"In 1761 Washington, in ordering clothes from London, wrote the merchant, 'I want neither lace nor embroidery. Plain clothes with gold or silver buttons if worn in genteel dress are all that I desire.' For Madam Washington he ordered a salmon colored tabby velvet with a pattern of satin flowers, to be made into a sack and coat; a cap, handkerchief, tucker and ruffles, to be made of Brussels or point lace, and to cost twenty pounds: two fine flowered lawn aprons, two double handkerchiefs, two pairs of white silk, six pairs of fine cotton and four pairs of thread hose, one pair of black and one pair of white satin shoes, 'of the smallest fives,' four pairs of callimanco shoes, one fashionable hat or bonnet, six pairs of best kid gloves, six pairs of mitts, one dozen knots and breast-knots, one dozen round silk stay-laces, one black mask, one dozen 'most fashionable' cambric pocket handkerchiefs, pins and hairpins, six pounds of perfumed powder, a 'puckered petticoat of fashionable color,' a silver velvet tabby petticoat, two handsome breast flowers, and some sugar candy.... The men were not behind the women in their love of gay apparel. Gold and silver laced hats and broadcloth coats with gold and silver buttons appear over and over again ... a sword mounted with silver." [11]

Children "dressed as their parents did and looked like

diminutive, quaint grown folk."

Most of the aristocrats had large, and a few even vast, amounts of English money in pounds sterling stored away in their strong boxes. Large quantities of silver plate were purchased in England as an investment, and Governor Spotswood's estate,

> "had two cabinets of plate, weighing one thousand and eighty-nine ounces of silver." [12]

Mary Newton Stanard tells of Virginia family possessions:

> "watches of gold and silver ... gilt cups and saucers ... silver tea and coffee pots ... In 1769 the silver plate at 'Westover' was valued at six-hundred and sixty-two pounds ... silver spoons ... owners of great estates whose silver was appraised at from one hundred to over six hundred pounds sterling." [10]

Inventories, wills and other contemporary documents point to the possession of great wealth in jewelry. In 1758 John Robinson, who was appointed Treasurer of Virginia, was required to put up £100,000 sterling as security. [13]

Virginian aristocrats sat for the best portrait painters in England and at home, and the family portraits which have survived are an important key to the period. In the year of George Washington's birth the Assembly legislated on ferry charges for "coach, chariot, chaise with four wheels," and anybody who was anything in the Old Dominion owned at least "a coach and pair." Those in the topmost circles owned a coach and four, and a few even used six horses. Thomas Jefferson, says a contemporary:

> "had a fine carriage built at Monticello from a model he planned himself. The woodwork, blacksmithing, and painting were all done by his own workmen. He had the plating done in Richmond. When he travelled in this carriage he always had five horses—four in the carriage, and the fifth for Burwell, who always rode behind him.... In his new carriage, with fine harness, those four horses made a splendid appear-

ance. He never trusted a driver with the lines. Two servants rode on horseback, and each guided his own pair." [14]

The aristocrats were epicures.

"Food for all courses appeared at the same time, and the bountiful table must have been heavily laden. They were particular about the carving of game, fowl, roast, and fish, and fine terms were used by the genteel and the well bred to describe the carving, but their mince and pumpkin pies arrived with the soup. Salads may have been slighted, white potatoes were conspicuous by their absence, and meat and fish were served in abundance, hot breads were in evidence at all meals, and all the recipes were lavish in butter, cream, and eggs." [15]

On the plantations cattle, hogs, sheep and fowl were plentiful. The surrounding forests abounded in a variety of game, and venison was as common as mutton. The numerous waters teemed with sea food, and vegetables and fruit trees were cultivated and they yielded abundantly. Spices, nuts and flavorings as well as chocolate, tea and coffee were imported. Nor did they neglect their cellars: the choicest wines, whiskeys and beer were brought from across the seas, while cider and certain brands of beer were domestic products.

References
CHAPTER TWO
THIRD PERIOD

Part One: INSTITUTIONS

[1] Hugh Jones, 63.
[2] Beverly Bk., 4 p. 23.
[3] P. A. Bruce, Hist Va., 273.
[4] Bruce, Social Life, 131.
[5] Fiske, 2; 191.

[6] Wertenbaker, Pat & Pleb, 50.
[7] Thomas Allen Glenn, Some Colonial Mansions, 1; 270.
[8] U. B. Phillips, Life & Labor In The Old South, 220.
[9] Mary Newton Stanard, Colonial Va., 154.
[10] HS 8; 73.
[11] VCSP 1; 119.
[12] HS 4; 559.
[13] VCSP 1; 243.
[14] C. R. Lingley, Transition In Va. From Colony To Commonwealth, 111, 2.
[15] HS 7; 526.
[16] Ibid., 6; 254.
[17] Ibid., 6; 503.
[18] A. E. McKinley, Suffrage Franchise In English Colonies, 46, 7.
[19] HS 7; 87.
[20] Beverly, Bk., 4, p. 30.
[21] HS 6; 478.
[22] J. A. Waddell, Annals Of Augusta County, Va., 28, 9.
[23] Wertenbaker, Pat & Pleb, 96, 7.
[24] HS 5; 231.
[25] Bruce, Social Life, 129.
[26] HS 5; 443.
[27] Ibid., 6; 415.
[28] Ibid., 5; 414.
[29] VCSP 1; 206.
[30] HS 6; 116, 7.
[31] Wertenbaker, Pl. Col. Va., 159.
[32] Ibid., 155.
[33] A. Burnaby, Travels Through No. America, 54.
[34] HS 8; 520.
[35] P. V. Fithian, Journal & Letters, 242, 3.
[36] D. Jarret, Autobiography, 14.
[37] HS 4; 423.
[38] Ibid., 4; 399, 400.
[39] Ibid., 5; 539 & 6; 342, 3.
[40] Intro to B. Bond, 17.
[41] HS 4; 246.
[42] J. F. D. Smyth, Tour In USA, 1; 68.
[43] HS 4; 497.
[44] C. R. Keim, Influence Of Primogeniture & Entail in The Development Of Virginia, 62, 195 (In Univ. of Chicago Library).
[45] Ripley, 121.
[46] Va. Polytechnic Ins., 10, 11.
[47] HS 7; 566.
[48] J. S. Bassett, Federalist System, 168, 9.
[49] Fiske, 2; 211.
[50] Lodge, 54.
[51] HS 8; 373.

52 *Ibid.*, 3; 298.
53 *Ibid.*, 5; 449.
54 JHUS v12, # 4; 223.
55 Waddell, 291.
56 HS 3; 445.
57 *Ibid.*, 7; 152.
58 Bishop Wm. Meade, Old Churches & Families Of Va., ed. 1878: 1; 433, 6.
59 HS 8; 382.

Part Two: SOCIAL ASPECTS

1 Glenn, 1; 235, 6.
2 Wertenbaker, Pat & Pleb, 34.
3 Keim, 151.
4 W. C. Ford, Washington As An Employer Of Labor.
5 Kimball, 173, 8.
6 Fithian, 285.
7 Wertenbaker, Pl. Col. Va., 157.
8 Va. Mag. Hist. & Biog., 35; 334.
9 Stanard, 64, 5.
10 *Ibid.*, Chap "Household Goods".
11 *Ibid.*, "Dress".
12 HS 7; 325.
13 *Ibid.*, 7; 178.
14 *Glenn*, 2; 221.
15 Gertrude I. Thomas, Foods Of Our Forefathers, 41.

CHAPTER THREE

THE MIND OF COLONIAL VIRGINIA'S
ARISTOCRACY

The members of colonial Virginia's ruling class considered themselves aristocrats—they claimed descent from
the English aristocracy, which they used as a model in
organizing their own class. It appears that their genealogical claims were largely valid: the great majority of
them were evidently collateral descendants of members of
the English lower gentry; a few were lineal descendants,
while some were no doubt of commoner origin who had
bought their way to social recognition. The position of
the lower gentry in England was none too exalted, although
in colonial America such descent meant a good deal. Aristocracy, however, is fundamentally a state of mind, not a
physiological condition—and the existence of a Virginian
aristocracy is therefore to be determined by their values,
rather than by their "blood". Whether Virginia's leading
immigrants after 1640 had all fought for the Stuart cause
or not and whatever their consanguinity, they were ideologically Cavalier and they organized their society accord-
ingly.

"These immigrants to Virginia, who had taken an
active part . . . or had openly sympathized with
the royal cause ... enjoyed an influence in the social
life of the Colony which was out of proportion to
their mere number. Some of these men ... were
persons of rank in England; others were untitled
officers in the royal armies, and, with few excep-
tions, all were sprung from the English gentry. They
brought with them to Virginia the tastes and habits

of the society in which they had moved, and to which they had belonged by birth as well as by association, the society of the English country gentlemen." [1]
The Virginians were aristocrats—definitely of land and of mind, not definitely of blood, and definitely not of capital.

The Cavaliers of Charles First were militant, while those of his son were leisurely. Leisure can produce instances of indolence, as thrift can of miserliness: but indolence is not creative—the time of Charles Second is among the most creative culturally in the history of the realm. The Cavaliers of the Restoration set the standard in Virginia, and an understanding of the seventeenth-century English aristocrats is a good index to their colonial imitators.

Feudalism was based on an agricultural economy. The laws of primogeniture and entail created a hierarchical world—the feudal society was severely vertical. They had a mania for the "quality person": there was sharp emphasis on the differences among men; distinction, which was based on personal characteristics rather than on achievement, was a virtue—everyone seemed determined to "be different or die"; everything, it seems—class, birth, blood, race, wealth, religion, education—was seized upon to create a claim for superiority; and Virginia was a scene of contrasts as her comparatively small population was compartmented into stratified classes or castes which differed qualitatively. Men were born into an hereditary condition in life—gentleman, commoner, slave—and they died in it. They were accustomed to rank, which was universal: everyone instinctively acted in terms of social space, and everyone knew and kept his place; and within each class there were gradations. Rank began in the family:

"In the family to which he belonged George (Washington), being two and a half years older than the second boy, was beyond the reach of competition. He remained so throughout life. Here we have one of the dominant features of his character—that he looked down from the heights upon his fellow creatures".[2]

The patricians were like another race of men: everything in their lives bespoke station, power, wealth, refinement; in every respect—appearance, dress, speech, mannerism— they were distinguished from the "common herd"; and they had the tone that is accustomed to command, and the bearing that expects implicit obedience.

In this society man's way of doing things was determined much more by tradition and custom than by law; they followed ways "the contrary to which the memory of man runneth not", and "social customs ... had all the force of a legal judgment". Law is comparatively superficial since it can easily be made and unmade, and the rule of law points to the existence of a dynamic, changing world in which people look chiefly to the future. In colonial Virginia the social system was accepted as qualitatively final: the future was not identified with such improvement; men responded to and acted from tradition and custom, and the ways of the past were sacred—which resulted in a static world. Slavery was a basic institution which had to be statutory because it was never a part of Anglo-Saxon common law or tradition, but law in the colony mainly provided for incidental problems as they arose.

At the peak of the social pyramid was the aristocracy, for whose being the polity existed: Virginia was the aristocracy, which constituted her mind—the repository of her values and culture; its members regarded the colony as their property, and they were very jealous of it. Membership in the caste presupposed the right to a proprietary estate, and was based on the "quality of the person": "quality" was determined, respectively, by birth, by the kind of title one had to his estate, by the antiquity of the family progenitor in the colony, and by the value of one's property.

The patricians were ideologically and institutionally united as a class. The fundamental bonds of their unity were ideological, and consisted of the aristocratic traditions and values. The institutional expression of their unity took the form of a political state for the enactment of law. Their rights and responsibilities emanating from their values were fundamental, while those due to law were incidental. Their class consciousness created the polity of colonial Virginia, which was an absolutism. Their association, known as the General Assembly, was a government which enacted law: but government and law existed for the maintenance of the status quo against enemies from within and without; they existed especially for the regulation and control of the "mean" and the "bestial"—for those not classified as "people", who constituted the base of the social pyramid. The Virginians knew the restraints of values, but not the restraints of law: they were subject to the rigid mental control of their class ideology, but they were free from the physical control of social institutions. As landholders and lawgivers they made laws for others; the "common" law, and fundamentally the statutory law as well, were for the commonalty. Since they were the government and the law—" 'The Colonial Cavaliers were little kings' " [3]—they were themselves above and beyond such restraints. The government was an instrument—a club in their hands, which they never used on themselves. They resented such subjection as an affront to their dignity as aristocrats. Their unity as a class enabled them to transcend the physical restrictions of social institutions and law, which immunity they identified with freedom and individuality.

Station is qualitative and static, while property is quantitative and changing: the social strata were determined fundamentally qualitatively, each category having varying degrees within itself; quantitative alterations—in lands, tenements, laborers, money—were secondary. There was a blend of land and social title; what counted was the quality of title rather than the quantity of acres held, although an inferior title generally implied fewer acres. The landed proprietors were exalted through prerogatives that distinguished them from other persons; their act in taking over vast estates, stepping into high political office, and voting themselves perquisites and exemptions, was not regarded as "corruption"—it was the inherent right of aristocracy. They were the source of lower class rights, and they could not grant away rights that were in any way prejudicial to themselves. They were above the "common" law: they were under the mental control of values, rather than the physical control of institutions and law, in their conduct in life; the commonalty could sue the patrician estate, but the persons of quality were sacred; no commoner could challenge them—whether to a duel, or in criminal or even in civil proceedings. There was no penal code for them: no powerful bourgeois class existed, as in England, which could incarcerate the quality person in the "common goal" for debt; and the law enforcement officials had no authority over the source of their powers. They could invoke the law against each other, but crime within the class was rare, and they generally preferred to rely on their traditional codes to settle serious quarrels among themselves. During the social serenity of the eighteenth century no patrician was arrested and tried, and imprisoned or condemned on criminal charges—to subject aristocracy to ordinary criminal procedure would have reflected on the class. They were convinced that their innate virtue and intelligence as "persons of quality" were sufficient guarantee of civil conduct, and they were controlled fundamentally by their own caste's unwritten codes of tradition, morality and honor.

> "Certain it is that a high sense of honor became
> eventually one of the most pronounced character-
> istics of the Virginians.";[4]

and there was far less uncivil conduct in Virginia among those under honor than among those under law. Their values set the standard for everything that was noble and good.

> "The humblest individual unconsciously imitated the
> habits and adopted the opinions of his social super-
> iors ... the latter became to him accepted standards

in all the relations in which fitness and character were to be considered, with regard to the affairs of public and private life. Thus influenced by a moral power he could not resist, even if he desired it, his social dependence upon those above him, was tacitly and cheerfully admitted." [5]

They fawned as they looked up:

"wee our most Dread and most gracious Soveraignes most humble and loyall Subjects";[6]

and they frowned as they looked down. They were characterized by "the Englishman's proverbial love of a lord": they patterned their lives in terms of the tastes and habits of the rural gentry at home, and the English gentleman who visited the colony hardly recognized in outward customs that he had made a change of habitation.

Admittance into the Virginian aristocracy evidently was predicated upon the right "to bear arms", and those thus entitled had the design of the family "coat-of-arms" ascertained in the old country; over the "great fireplaces . . . were sometimes carved the armorial bearings of the family", and they were stamped on the family silver plate and engraved on the tombstones. It was the way of their world (not a mark of pomposity) for social station to be based on terms of distinction, and they were always very careful to include the titles they claimed in all documents and legal papers.

"All the ceremonial terms indicating social superiority, all the badges and signs long adopted as marks of gentle descent, were in constant use in the Colony from its foundation." [7]

The Virginian's fondest hope was to receive an English aristocratic title, which could be bestowed only in London. There were several titled aristocrats resident in the colony some of whom had arrived so titled, while others were native Virginians who succeeded in achieving the coveted honor. The colony's records mention Thomas Lord Fairfax, Sir William Fairfax, "sir John Randolph, knight", "Sir

Marmaduke Beckwith, bart.", and "Sir William Skipwith".

The Virginian aristocrats were almost homogeneously English, their traditions revolved around family pride, and their religion was ancestor worship—whatever the validity of their genealogical claims, they had a "passion for illustrious ancestors", and "pride of ancestry" was a primary feature of their lives. The ancestral family and home in England were sacred: they were proudest of and considered most valuable everything associated with their origins; and they were nostalgic—they sighed for "the good old days" as they hearkened back to a golden era for inspiration and guidance. It seems that they felt themselves fallen from grace, and thought that there was little worthwhile in the status quo compared to their imagined origins in the home country. They did all they could to perpetuate the past; they prized heirlooms, and objects of special sentimental value such as pieces of jewelry, mirrors, books—things that endured, and made the past real and sacred to succeeding generations.

> "In the spacious halls of the mansions were hung
> the portraits of ancestors that were regarded with
> reverential pride",[8]

and various instruments of war allegedly used by them occupied conspicuous places; and the reputed noble extraction of remote forebears and their leadership in the service of England's monarchs, especially in that of "the martyred king", were drilled into the minds of the young. They were very careful about the "dignity of the calling"; to be descended from landowners was a matter of pride while to be descended from merchants was a disgrace, and the commercial activities of immediate sires were carefully concealed. They lived in the glory of the past and thought backwards, and the hearth, rather than the school and church, was their fundamental institution of learning. They always referred to England as "home"; regarded the English race as superior and its arms invincible; considered themselves an extension of the English aristocracy having all its privileges, and they imitated its sports, dress and mannerisms; studied maps of the country and of London, which they sometimes memorized; and the prospect of a trip home to visit relatives, study the genealogical tree, locate the family coat-of-arms, rub shoulders with the nobility, maybe attend traditionally royalist Oxford, and, possibly, receive an English title, was the hope of every aristocrat.

It was with great reluctance that the Virginians recognized William and Mary as the royal family. They always regarded as usurpers the alien Hanoverian kings and the people of capital who ruled the Empire, continued loyal to the Stuarts and prided themselves on having been the first to recognize Charles Second as king—Virginia had a king when England was a republic. In fact, during the Stuart rebellions in England of 1715 and 1745 a number of the visiting Virginians actively sided with the rebels. With the uprisings defeated some of the Stuart supporters continued the tradition of Commonwealth days by fleeing to Virginia where they were welcomed. Others came voluntarily, and there was always an important group among Virginia's planters who were born in England. English aristocrats had used their influence to get Virginians proprietary grants; some owned property in each other's country, and those related could reciprocally inherit. The English patricians' reaction to their idolizers was usually one of condescending disdain. One of William Thackeray's English characters in "The Virginians" refers to the future of the visiting young colonial as " heir to a swamp, a negro, a log cabin and a barrel of tobacco' ", while of the wealthy colonial in England who had married a count it was said, "The Countess's mother was a convict... sent out from England."

Every Virginian knew by heart his own genealogy, and those of his neighbors.

"The colonists clung to class consciousness and a sort of feudal system, and there was little talk of

215

the rights of man. In this transplanted aristocracy
the word gentleman had a distinct meaning." [9]
"Gentleman" was a term applied to all members of the
aristocracy or those who bore arms. But there were
gradations of rank within the class, which were distinguished by terms of address. The conciliar landowners—the
"little house of lords"—stood at the peak of the colonial
hierarchy. Their dignity was meticulously protected, and
their term of address, "esquire", was the most respectful
in the colony. According to Hugh Jones:

"the Governor and Council sit in very great State,
in Imitation of the King and Council, or the Lord
Chancellor and House of Lords."

The Councillors as lords proprietor were evidently acquiring
a status comparable to that of the English nobility. The term
"honorable" was applied to most government officials. And
among the Cavaliers the military title carried the highest
distinction. The women of the aristocracy were variously
addressed as "Mistress", "Madame", "Lady", "Dame".

The highest honor that could be bestowed on the Virginians was to be visited by a titled Englishman. Immigrants of gentle birth even if impoverished were socially
accepted, and some immediately became influential. But
people of lesser "quality", even though they had a good deal
of money, were frowned on. Says the contemporary Smyth:

"Many of them possess fortunes superior to those
of the first rank, but their families are not so ancient, nor respectable".[10]

They were chary about granting the proprietary title to
persons of doubtful social background. In 1741,

"the petition of Alexander Stinson for 1200 acres
in Goochland (county) was rejected 'as the petitioner
is not known to any of this Board (Council) and
therefore thought too much for so obscure a person' ".

Women boasted about their heredity and quarrelled with
one another over superiority in rank, despite some satirical

reaction to it. Those of higher station were specially attired, accorded precedence at the table, on the highway, on
entering a public building and in church, while "imposters"
were shown their place; marriage was strictly within the
caste; and there was no need for sumptuary laws as the
traditions and the social organization precluded the commonalty from ever achieving the appearance and the pleasures of their betters. Says the contemporary Fithian:

"if you should travel through this Colony, with a
well-confirmed testimonial of your having finished
with Credit a Course of studies at Nassau-Hall; you
would be rated, without any more questions asked,
either about your family, your Estate, your business, or your intention, 10,000£; and you might come,
& go, & converse, & keep company, according to this
value; and you would be despised and slighted if
you rated yourself a farthing cheaper." [11]

The greatest ambition of the commoner freeholders was
to climb into the upper brackets, and this sometimes happened. The aristocratic lady with doubtful marriage
prospects was an opportunity for some likely commoner,
and her family connections provided him with an estate on
the frontiers. Thomas Jefferson says that his parents were
among the earliest settlers in the area which two years
after his birth was set off as Albemarle county. There is
a letter preserved revealing the efforts of a minister of the
gospel to marry a lady of aristocratic birth, to whom he
wrote:

"I understand that you think it a diminution of your
honor and the Dignity of your Family to marry a
person in the Station of a Clergyman." [12]

He quoted ardently from the holy word to prove otherwise
and finally succeeded.

Nonetheless eighteenth-century Virginians married strictly within the caste, and economic alliance through marriage
of powerful Virginian families was the rule. While members of the ruling classes of other colonies made numerous
intercolonial marriages the Virginian's mating was both

aristocratic and—almost wholly—Virginian. It was the custom for an outsider who married a Virginia lady to settle in the colony and become a Virginian. But the Englishman was catered to; some members of the families of British officials sent to Virginia married into her aristocracy, and their spouses considered it an opportunity to go to and settle in England.

> "Those of the upper class were like one big, scattered family, for they were almost all related either by blood or marriage, and closely connected in all their interests." [13]

The following individuals, all with Virginian aristocratic names (the middle name was not yet in vogue) typify the condition: Nelson Page, Page Nelson, Carter Page, Page Carter, Mann Page, William Byrd Page, Carter Harrison, Harrison Carter, Shirley Harrison, Byrd Harrison, Shirley Carter, Carter Berkeley, Carter Braxton. This similarity in names often required the adding of the mansion house name for individual identification: the four sons of Robert "King" Carter are often listed as "John of Corotoman", "Robert of Nomini", "Charles of Cleve", and "Landon of Sabine Hall".

The feudal realty laws revolved around the family, which made it the nub of Virginian social institutions; "founding a family" was a duty, and bachelors were rare in the Old Dominion. The family was patriarchal: woman was regarded as mentally and physically inferior to man, and incapable of bearing responsibility; and the aristocrat as husband and father was absolute master.

Girls were taught dancing and the other amenities of the salon, but since their future was identified solely with marriage a smattering of the "three R's" was considered sufficient. During courtship a girl's role was that of "the clinging vine"; "chivalry"—the principle of woman worship—"was almost entirely a development in the colony", and "homage to the gentler sex was an important part of the social code". A girl's entrance into the conjugal state was the end of formal education, and her role became purely domestic: she was relegated to the home and her purpose in life was to please her husband, bear children and attend to household affairs. The spinster and widow were of necessity granted some legal rights*, but after marriage woman's personality was absorbed in her husband's. She was not a legal being, and could not vote; the property she had contributed towards the marriage—even her personal apparel, was subject to her master's jurisdiction. She had the legal right to complain against her husband's alleged mistreatment to the county court by petition or without the formal process of an action, but her fundamental protection lay in the chivalrous traditions of her class. Their ethics identified as feminine virtues: abject submission to the husband's will; no concern about his private affairs; suffering in silence if he gave her cause for pain—

"the women of the family knew that the handsome
quadroon was really the daughter of the head of
the house";[14]

no interference in political and economic problems; and the role of innocence, effeminacy, shining ornament and gracious hostess. Milady was not, however, always unhappy under this arrangement: she did not mind being relieved of worldly responsibilities, and she was not without a good deal of subtle influence. The marriage institution was respected, and the married lady was rarely approached with a view to an illicit relation. A marriage could be annulled but no court had the power to grant a divorce, and bigamy occurred. Virginian mothers knew nothing about sex hygiene, birth control, and proper care of infants and rearing of children, and a dearth of competent physicians necessitated grandmother remedies. The colony's need for population and the loneliness of life were important spurs

* There were a few instances where the Assembly recognized a widow as "executrix" of her husband's estate, and where it lodged title to property in the woman whose husband was an alien.

to procreation; they usually married in their teens and bore as many as twenty children, and sometimes more. It was therefore common for a mother and her daughter each to suckle her own infant at the same time, while uncles and aunts were often younger than their nephews and nieces. Families were large, men were proud of the fecundity of their women, infant mortality was high, the Negro wet nurse was indispensable, and mothers were chronically pregnant and weak. Boy babies were very much preferred, and mothers felt themselves reproached if they failed in this respect. Widows—who "were life-saving stations in colonial social economy"—and widowers, could always be had; they remarried hastily and often—

"General Washington's brother Samuel married five
times, and was under fifty when he died"—[15]
and half and step brothers and sisters were common.

Children were considered an asset: worship of the past ensconced the elders in the eyes of the new generation, and filial duty was stressed more than parental responsibility. Marriage was "arranged" or based on the parents' choice; but the children took for granted a measure of paternal indulgence in their choice of mates, and "duels about sweethearts were not infrequent". Yet the economics of the caste could not recognize a necessary connection between love and marriage; holy wedlock was a duty automatically determined by tradition and the property laws, and family pressure sometimes bore heavily upon those otherwise inclined. Thus the following item in the Virginia Gazette during 1769 was not thought strange:

"Yesterday was married in Henrico Mr. Wm. Carter,
third son of Mr. John Carter, aged 23, to Mrs.
Sarah Ellyson ... aged 85. A Sprightly old girl with
three thousand pounds fortune." [16]
The marriage of grandfathers and of profligates to immature girls was not unknown. Their ethics required the parents to determine the children's marital union; the fathers of the principals involved agreed on a settlement,

and the son and daughter were told to get ready for the nuptials.

In addition to tutors the children were provided with music, dancing and fencing instructors, with the latter becoming increasingly important. Every boy was assigned a darkey of the same age as body servant, which accustomed each from childhood to his respective place.

> "In childhood the young Virginian was brought up among the slaves and their offspring, which had the worst possible effect upon both speech and manners." [17]

Primogeniture created a class distinction within the family —the eldest son was the younger's natural enemy: the former was to exercise the franchise and continue the family name in public life, and he usually was sent abroad or to William and Mary for a college education. The "younger brother had but small honor at home" and, like his sisters, was economically, politically and socially on a level inferior to that of his fortunate brother.

The Virginians had high regard for the family as a social institution, but they cared little about the home and they neglected it. There is a relative frankness, and absence of self-consciousness, concerning sex in rural life: with matrimony simply the medium for the creation of heirs and milady chronically indisposed extra-marital indulgence by the husband was expected; and their ethics took for granted the double standard of morality. Some of those at the peak of the Virginian hierarchy kept mistresses: the mistress was often a beautiful, gifted woman; in the days before the Puritan ideology had rendered her of ill-repute her place in society was not only respectable but privileged; her lover's social standing did not suffer; and there were many "natural" children, of whom some were legitimized. Those less wealthy engaged in sex relations with their slaves, both black and white, an apparent motive here being slave breeding;[18] the miscegenation that occurred was largely due to them and was not thought immoral.

It has been shown that the plantation was the economic unit in Virginia, that each of the larger plantations gave the impression of a village, and that the colony was an association of these independent principalities. The aristocrat was absolute master of his plantation; he was there to command, and everyone else—slaves of all kinds, hired help, mean whites, his family—was there to obey. There was no back talk, no one on equal terms to converse with, everyone did him reverence and he was free to do anything he wished. Off his plantation he was similarly placed. There were many offices to be filled in the legislative, judicial, military and ecclesiastical spheres. Sometimes he held one post and, often enough, several. But wherever he was it was his to command.

Indolence was also a product of the plantation system, the traditions and the Mediterranean climate. Says the eye-witness Smyth:

"The gentleman of fortune rises about nine o'clock; he perhaps may take an excursion to walk as far as his stables to see his horses, which is seldom more than fifty yards from his house; he returns to breakfast, between nine and ten, which is generally tea or coffee, bread and butter, and very thin slices of venison-ham, or hung beef. He then lies down on a pallat, on the floor, in the coolest room in the house, in his shirt and trousers only, with a negro at his head, and another at his feet, to fan him, and keep off the flies; between twelve and one he takes a draught of bombo, or toddy, a liquor composed of water, sugar, rum, and nutmeg, which is made weak and kept cool: he dines between two and three, and at every table, whatever else there may be, a ham and greens or cabbage, is always a standing dish; at dinner he drinks cyder, toddy, punch, port, claret, and madeira, which is generally excellent here: having drunk some few glasses of wine after dinner, he returns to his pallat, with his two blacks to fan

him, and continues to drink toddy, or sangaree, all
the afternoon: he does not always drink tea; between
nine and ten in the evening, he eats a light supper of
milk and fruit, or wine; sugar, and fruit, &c. and
almost immediately retires to bed, for the night".[19]
Another characteristic of plantation life was loneliness.
There was no one in the vicinity with whom an aristocrat
could converse, while the members of his family had little
to say. Life in Virginia apart from the plantation—town
activities, and public places where equals could gather for
conviviality—was practically non-existent, and "in those
days and in those parts anyone was a neighbor within a
day's horseback ride". The plantations were widely scattered gaps in the forests, various natural obstructions separated them, and the absence of proper communications made
traveling always difficult and dangerous and sometimes
impossible. Travel was evidently regarded as a burden
rather than a pleasure, for it was referred to as "travail";
the rivers were often clogged with logs and other impedi-
menta; it was not uncommon for native wayfarers to get
lost in the forests, and it was evidently not safe to sally
forth unarmed.[20] During most of the bad weather season
they were confined to the mansion house, which virtually
cut them off from the outside world. Gentlemen travelers
in need of hospitality, pedlars and merchant vessels relieved
the monotony by bringing information, foreign newspapers
and correspondence, but this was infrequent. The Virginians were not a seafaring people, and a journey abroad
was a momentous undertaking. The conversation of ship
captains and travelers was eagerly sought after, and their
descriptions of Europe with its cities and buildings and
monuments made it appear like an enchanted fairy world
to the Virginians.

In normal weather this isolation was largely overcome,
but time hung heavy on tender hands especially during
inclement days. Most of them lolled their way through life,
but the more cultured made efforts to dispel ennui: they

read, wrote many letters, and kept diaries; experimented
with imported plants, and with mechanical contrivances—
such as the barometer, which was first coming into use;
whiled away the time fiddling, and noted with mathematical precision the petty details of some plantation job. Triv-
ialities were magnified, and posterity attributes logical
mindedness and accuracy to them. Theirs was a quiet,
static world: nature was always, everywhere; they were
alone—with God, primitivity, themselves; the simplicity
and the beauty of the life with nature was a reality, not
merely a poet's dream; the wilderness surrounding them
was compelling, and the imagination had free play. Their
isolation emphasized introversion: they developed a yearning for solitude; they were men of few words, produced no
conversationalists and were not given to levity and wit.
They preferred to be inaccessible: their persons were
sacred; their manner—they affected an air of sedateness
and cold formalism—was forbidding, and they had to be
approached with the utmost circumspection. They showed
no friendly warmth to anyone, including life long friends:
and they allowed no intimacy even as within the family—
George Washington in his letters to his mother addressed
her as "Honoured Madam," instead of "Dear Mother."
They were not misanthropic—they did not fear or hate
people: they were very much unused to people; they felt
pretty well at home among themselves, but outside of
Virginia they met with a forwardness that was embarras-
sing; and this gave them a tendency to self-consciousness.
They were uncomfortable in company—which discouraged
friendship, mutual trust, and confidence in and knowledge
of people; and they generally shrank from activities requiring association of men. Their tendency to self-consciousness has been often regarded as betraying a guilty
conscience. Says Claude Bowers in his "Portrait" of
Thomas Jefferson:

"But there is one unpleasant criticism of his manner
that cannot so easily be put aside—a shiftiness in

his glance, which bears out the charge of his enemies that he was lacking in frankness. The most democratic member of the first Senate, meeting him for the first time, was disappointed to find that 'he had a rambling vacant look.' Another found that 'when speaking he did not look at his auditor, but cast his eyes toward the ceiling or anywhere but at the eye of his auditor'. This weakness was possibly overemphasized, for he was notoriously shy." [21]

Fear was an underlying, ever-present reality in the life of the colonial Virginians:

"the extraordinary seclusion and monotony of the life in narrow clearings in the primeval forests seemed to emphasize the sombre side of human destiny".

Nature was ubiquitous: the mind of pre-technology was oppressed by the towering vastness within which it felt alone and insignificant; there was no confidence in man's ability to cope with it; and colonial life was pervaded by a feeling of complete helplessness towards nature. The countryside was full of disease-breeding swamps; there was no sewage system, and insect vermin abounded; various endemic ailments were prevalent, and competent medical attention was practically unavailable; happiness was thought of as a state of being "out" of this world—the water for drinking was often unclean, distillation has its purifying effects, and liquor was regarded as a medicine; infant mortality, especially among the slaves, was frightful; and the average life span was short. They had stood beside the beds of dying loved ones, and tended their last wishes; and then trailed silently after the pall-bearers to the "small burial ground planted with myrtle and box" where, with bowed heads, they saw the mortal remains laid in the final resting place. They brooded on the purpose of life, and many of them even in youth suffered from despondency. The Sage of Monticello was hardly twenty when he wrote:

"I verily believe that I shall die soon . . . I am tired

of living." [22]

James Madison was twenty-one when he wrote to a friend:
"I think my sensations for many months have intimated to me not to expect a long or healthy life:
I . . . therefore have little spirit . . . to set about
anything that is . . . useless in possessing after one
has exchanged time for eternity." [23]

Jefferson had to dissuade his daughter Martha from becoming a nun when they were in Paris.

" 'hypochondriac complaints' . . . were among the
chief ailments." [24]

The misery of the slaves all about them, their cries as they
were being beaten, and the heads of those executed impaled along the roadside [25]—had their effects on the mind.
They lived dangerously. They were in fear of the night,
although in Virginia it is short: the night created a baleful
atmosphere, and gave them a feeling of weakness and resignation; the plantation had no lighting system, candle lights
cast lurid shadows across the large rooms of the mansion
house, there was no night life—and the stillness all about
them was awful. The vast majority of the plantation inhabitants were enslaved. They were in great fear of "slaves
. . . abroad in the night", and the "bell in the night" brought
pounding hearts and chilled spines. Although slave revolts
were infrequent, individual acts of sabotage, arson and murder were common; and the nearest neighbor was miles away.
Wrote a contemporary resident, "I sleep in fear too, though
my Door and Windows are all secured." [26] The few who
could afford a home in town fled thither to find relief from
the despondency of some tragedy, while some who visited
London declared life in Virginia dismal and hated to return.

The monotony, the loneliness, and the underlying melancholy of plantation life led the colonial Virginians to excessive indulgence in sociability. "It was the most leisured
and pleasure-loving society America has ever known", for

they took advantage of every oportunity to gather in groups. Most of their amusements were active, dynamic and exciting and they found little enjoyment as passive onlookers at others' skill. The arena and forum were nonexistent and the concert was little known, but they loved the theatre and between the long intervals when traveling companies visited them they staged amateur plays with themselves participating as actors.

They loved the great outdoors. They were adept at use of the firearm, for as late as near the end of the seventeenth century predatory beasts were still being found in the oldest settled areas, and there was constant need for protection against the primitive inhabitants. Deer hunting, fowling and fishing occupied a good deal of their time, and they engaged in competitive sports such as boat racing. But they found their greatest pleasure in horseback riding, and in the fox hunt and horse-race, and the animals incident to these sports, the hound and the horse, were meticulously bred and cared for.

"the planters rode to hounds in the lush countryside of Virginia and Maryland in blue coats and scarlet waistcoats; they went to horse-races and cock-fights, betting heavily in so many pounds of tobacco or so many slaves."

Equestrianism was introduced in England by James First, it became the tradition and symbol of the Cavalier, and in Virginia regard for the horse—"man's best friend"—approached that for the cat in ancient Egypt. Fox-hunting in colonial America indicates superlative horsemanship, for the insufficiently farmed terrain was full of natural obstructions. The aristocrats had several race tracks built that became popular and were always kept in good condition. They imported special breeds of horses from England, and they took great pride in the ownership of several thoroughbreds whose pedigrees were carefully kept. There was "extreme jealousy in preserving the reputation of his horse", for the owner of the champion race-horse was the most renowned man in the county. Slaves were often used as jockeys. Every scheduled horse-race was eagerly looked forward to, they traveled long distances to be present, the betting was heavy, the jealousy keen and the finale sometimes bloody. The court records of the period are full of litigation over race-track disputes. The meet lasted several days and was consummated with "the invariable ball", which sometimes took the form of a masquerade. Fairs were often held at which there were sack races and bear baiting, and competition for prizes: men "cudgeled" for a valuable hat, wrestled for a pair of silver buckles, danced for a pair of handsome shoes, and fiddled for a violin; and a pair of silk stockings went to the handsomest maid. They also made merry at picnics and barbecues in the woods, and on river festivities.

Their indoor pleasures were also active, and every unusual event such as the coronation of a king or the arrival of a new governor and the ordinary national and religious holidays, birthdays, engagements, weddings, births—often even burials, were made the occasion for eating and drinking and dancing. Music was an essential part of the aristocrat's education, the "music master" was a frequent visitor to the mansion houses, and musical instruments—the piano forte, virginal, violin, harpsichord, hand lyre, harmonica, guitar, flageolet, flute, hautboy—were abundant in Virginia; and there were also servants and slaves who could play some of them. They despised the abstemiousness and other-worldliness of the Puritans; and they believed in good fellowship, and were boon companions and hospitable. There was an atmosphere of freedom in Virginia; the traveler of rank had no sense of intrusion as he entered any home, where he was welcomely received, fed and given sleeping accommodations, while his horse was cared for by the servants. As early as 1650 the Cavalier emigre, Colonel Norwood, wrote:

"using the common freedom of the country, I thrust myself amongst Captain Wormly's guests".

They were ostentatious, and their entertainment was magnificent and appearance resplendent.

"The great event was the annual visit . . . to Williamsburg. Once a year, when the House of Burgesses met, and the Supreme Court was in session, the great coaches were brought out on the plantations, the six horses were harnessed, and the leading families drove in state to the capital. There the fashionable world of Virginia assembled. They spoke of their annual gathering with all the simple and ludicrous pride of a provincial aristocracy as rivalling the Court of St. James and the society of London." [27]

"Peyton Randolph . . . gave a dinner (in 1768) that was the talk of the whole Province."

They constantly visited one another and it was the custom for an entire family with their Negro attendants, often numbering up to twenty people and more, to drop in at "the cousin's" and stay three or four or more days. There was always company:

"Washington . . . said that for twenty years his family never once dined alone."

According to Fithian life in Virginia seemed one gay round of visiting, carousing and entertaining and, says he:

"Mrs. Carter informed me last evening that this Family one year with another consumes 27,000 Lb. of Pork; & twenty Beeves. 550 Bushels of Wheat, besides corn—4 Hogsheads of Rum & 150 Gallons of Brandy." [28]

This display of opulence and the over-indulgence sometimes dissipated their wealth, and often their health.

The church in Virginia was fundamentally a rendezvous for sociability; before and after the sermon, which seldom exceeded fifteen minutes, women displayed their finery, gossiped and exchanged invitations while the men discussed sports, amours and politics.

During the sixteenth century there began to develop from within the Christian world in Europe a movement known as the "Renaissance". This was a reaction against the doctrine of divinely revealed eternal truth upon which the knowledge of the world, of life, of man, was based: it was held that man's worship of God is not tantamount to self-effacement, that an understanding of the universe is a subject of continuing development, and that it is within the competence of man to achieve this understanding through his own investigation. This brought a resuscitation of the work and the mind of ancient Hellas and Rome—which had been interred for more than a millennium. Hellenism predicated its ways of knowing—of apprehending the world, on man's own rational and empirical faculties. It was concluded that there is truth in the world outside of religion: the house of worship began to appear like a flight—like a separation of God, from nature; the attempt to discover truth was thus taken out of the atmosphere of supernaturalism, and brought into the open—into the world of nature. There followed the exhumation, appreciation, and emulation of the classics of antiquity—which restored confidence in man's own mental faculties: the responsibility for fathoming and explaining the world was thrown upon man, who was ready to follow wherever his own thinking would lead him; the reliance on rationalism emphasized the contemplative, speculative life—which brought a revival of learning; and the great thinkers of antiquity began to displace the saints of religion as the inspiration of men. The resurrection of the classics—the eternal monuments to the mental power of universal man, emancipated human intelligence; learning was no longer confined to the recluse, as it became a part of life; it made this life—the only life man knows, worth living for its own sake; and there was exultation in the rediscovery of the value of nature and of man. Thus the Renaissance is associated with naturalism—the appreciation of, and curiosity about, nature; with humanism, the exaltation of man; and with rationalism, the confidence in the ability of the mind of man to achieve an understanding of the world.

Cultural freedom—the right of access to the classics, the humanities, science, philosophy; the right freely to drink at the fountain of human goodness, beauty, wisdom— became a supreme value in the life of western man. Supernaturalism was regarded as inimical to cultural freedom, and the Renaissance developed as an endeavor against the authoritarian church.

The Renaissance reached England, and profoundly influenced the life of the country. It had its political implications—the international principle in religion was supplanted by the native expression in church and faith. Henry Eighth's quarrel with Rome was economic and political; the Church of England was therefore theologically Catholic and politically Protestant; and the introduction in England of the principle that the secular authorities are the final arbiters of theological disputes subserved the Church. Contemporary philosophers had postulated the superiority of reason to supernaturalism, and the mind of the English aristocrats on religion may be described as deistic. They were worldly, and when the Stuart Restoration took place,

"The Cavaliers were in a frenzy of joy. A formal, political, and hence unlovely, type of Puritanism had succumbed to the noisy, jeering, and pleasure-loving sycophants of the Court. Taverns, brothels, and theaters had rapidly increased since the Coronation day." [29]

The Church of England symbolized social stability, was primarily an instrument for the perpetuation of the status quo, and represented the religion of the "gentleman" or of the ruling class. It emphasized ritual and art, not theology; its preachments were devoid of spiritual and ethical content and salvation was by faith, not works. Religion as an emotional experience and moral guide characterized the lower classes, and the aristocrats therefore identified it with baseness and held aloof.

The Cavaliers brought with them to Virginia the spirit of the Renaissance—the appreciation of naturalism, hu-

manism, rationalism—essentially in terms of its English
expression; they are the pioneers of culture in America.*
Their descendants were animated by a consciousness of
debt to the ancient European civilizations, and it was a
matter of principle with them never to lose intellectual
contact with home. The Hebraic teachings in Virginia
were institutionalized, while the values of Hellenism were
purely ideological—the spirit of the Renaissance pervaded
the atmosphere of the colonial aristocracy throughout its
history.

This was the heritage of the Virginians. Their ethics
and morals came from their traditions, not from the church.
Christianity and the clergy were taken lightly: the Bible
was not regarded as divinely inspired and was read, if at
all, as just another book; and it sems to have been considered an alien influence, as it savored too strongly of
Oliverianism. Sunday school and the catechism were no
part of their upbringing, and there were no family prayers.
With the founding of William and Mary College Virginians
could study for the ministry: but they were men of the
world, and it was never an aristocrat's ambition to affect
the vestments; and colonial Virginia produced no spiritual
leaders of note. They regarded the church as a menace to
cultural freedom: theocracy, ecclesiastical authoritarian-
ism, the priest—were anathema. Theology was no part of
their lives. They did not stress the relation of the soul to
God nor believed in the efficacy of prayer: had no sense
of sin, and no need for repentance and grace; and they
were singularly free from witchcraft, superstition and hell-
fire terrors. They believed in class religion, and stood in
contempt of the Nonconformist sects which identified religion as an emotional experience in which one feels himself transported; and they had vague notions of a hierarchical after life. They preferred one Church: they persecuted,

---

* The other settlers in America—the Puritans and Nonconformists, and the Latins—brought religion.

but never executed, Dissenters.*

As early as the middle of the seventeenth century there was a Captain Mitchell in Virginia who is said to have,

"wondered that the world has been deluded, so many hundred years, with a man and a pigeon, referring to Christ and the Holy Spirit." [30]

Robert Beverly's discussion of the Indian worship shows some insight into the philosophical aspects of religion. He seems very suspicious of the motives of priests, and he alleges a difference between religion as the worship of a universal intelligence and as priestcraft:

"In this state of Nature, one would think that they (Indians) should be as pure from Superstition, and overdoing matters in Religion, as they are in other things: but I find it is quite the contrary; for this Simplicity gives the cunning Priest a greater advantage over them, according to the Romish Maxim, Ignorance is the Mother of Devotion. For, no bigotted Pilgrim appears more zealous, or strains his Devotion more at the Shrine, than these believing Indians do, in their Idolatrous Adorations. Neither do the most refin'd Catholicks undergo this pennance with so much submission as these poor Pagans do the severities, which their Priests inflict upon them."

"the Fathers of the Romish Church tell us, that our Lord left the print of his Feet in the Stone, whereon he stood while he talkt with St. Peter; which Stone was afterwards preserv'd as a very Sacred Relique . . . it is kept, and visited with great expressions of Devotion . . . the Indians, as well . . . are not without their pious frauds." [31]

Moncure D. Conway says:

"the tendency of Virginians was much more towards rationalism than superstition. Deistical opinions

---

* The Quaker William Robinson was imprisoned in Virginia for six months; on his release he went to Massachusetts where he was hanged.

were widely prevalent in the colony during the eighteenth century. Two professors at William and Mary College, albeit clergymen, were deists, and distributed the works of English deists among the students. Peyton Randolph probably, certainly his brother John, the King's Attorney, Chancellor Wythe, and Jefferson were deists, and the first bishop, Madison, was a rationalist." [32]

"Robert Carter of Nomony,—Councilor Carter,— ... has the distinction of being the earliest Swedenborgian in America, and (he) liberated his slaves during his life because of religious principles." [33]

Of George Washington's father, the writer says:

"Captain Washington was a deist. . . . Freethinker though he was, Captain Washington was active in parish affairs." [34]

It was said of William Byrd the Second:

"He is sceptical, but not militant. He feels himself too much the superior of the parson to enter into any controversy." [35]

The Virginians' indifference to church and faith does not indicate a void: it flowed from a positive foundation— from their background in the principles of the Renaissance. They were convinced that there is truth—and they sought it—outside of religion, and their education was secular. They believed that science and scripture are inherently conflicting: they preferred to study the Work, rather than the Word, of God; and their supreme purpose in life was to live in harmony with nature, rather than in harmony with "the Book". They regarded as mental stagnation the fact that it is easier to believe than to think: they repudiated the principle of finality in relation to the knowledge of the world, as they realized that such understanding is an eternal developmental process—man's persistence can force nature gradually to reveal her secrets. They regarded reason as superior to intuition, believed in a rational explanation for everything in nature, and were great enthusiasts for science; and they were convinced that an understanding of ultimate causation could be attained through "thinking" or the metaphysics of the Greeks, rather than through "feeling" or the ethics of the Jews.

They were in love with life, youth and love and they contemplated old age, sickness and death with dread. Their skepticism in religion created some interest in philosophical problems, especially teleology; their way and condition of life lacked purpose and gave them a morbid turn; and this, together with the frontier influences and their reaction against Puritanism, caused the abandon and hedonism for which they are known. There seemed to be an absence of genuine religious emotion at their burial rites and in their mourning.

"the persons attending a funeral (had) . . . the amplest provision that the house could afford made for their entertainment. The eating and drinking were often preceded by a furious fusillade."

"At the funeral of Mrs. Elizabeth Eppes . . . five gallons of wine and two gallons of brandy were drunk by the persons in attendance; and, in addition, a steer and three sheep were consumed." [36]

Some thought that merry-making at funerals was "very unseasonable and inconsistent with the occasion," but

"the funeral had some aspects of a festive event, however decorously conducted." [37]

Their minds seemed to revolve around the grave, their writing was importantly devoted to epitaphs chiseled on elaborate tombstones imported from England, and Virginia cemeteries are repositories of her history. The following epitaph, dated 1763, is dedicated to a boy of nine:

"Beneath this humble stone a youth doth lie
Almost too good to live, too young to die:
Count his few years, how short the scanty span!
But count his virtues, and he died a man."

And here is one of the early nineteenth century:

"Though wars have ceased, the hero claims renown:

With choicest myrtle let his tomb be crown'd;
And ye, sweet nine, your plaintive tribute pay,
And o'er his virtues shed a milder ray.
In scenes domestic man is truly known;
In scenes domestic Meade forever shone.
His soul, unconscious of one narrow thought,
Of self regardless, did the thing he ought.
Where'er his form benignant bent its way,
Grim care soon vanished and each heart was gay.
At mercy's call he ever foremost press'd;
For meek-eyed pity sway'd his manly breast.
Hasten, fair nymphs of Frederick's peaceful plains;
Attend, fond youths, to breathe your mournful
strains
Votaries of hymen, follow to deplore
That Meade, your pride and father, is no more.
But why, blest shade, should friends lament thy
doom?
Joys celestial hover o'er thy tomb;
Thy Mary, purer than the snowdrop white,
Shall guide thine offspring to the realms of light." [38]

These epitaphs are devoid of Christian content. The statement that "Meade . . . is no more" seems to despair of an after life; the only consolation offered the departed is the care to be bestowed on his offspring; and the references to "myrtle", "fair nymphs" and "Votaries of hymen" are plainly from ancient mythology. Some tombstones, however, do have Christian references. The following one is dedicated to Mary Page, who died in 1690:

"A good Christian, ready at God's call
Thou lived and died, upon Christ relying;
Thou died to rise, and now livest by dying.
Thy faith doth yield, thy piety doth give,
Restoratives to make thee ever live.
Thrice blessed friend, this epitaph is thy due;
When saints arise, thy Lord will say, 'tis true' ".

The inscriptions on many tombstones are in Latin, and

some are in Greek.

Colonial Virginia is the nearest approach to a freethinking civilization in the new world. Her Establishment was organizationally Christian, and ideologically Renaissance: it was fundamentally an adjunct of the state, rather than a religious institution; it had no political or economic power and influence in its own right; and it could be used as an instrument against Puritan merchants and Nonconformist frontiersmen. The Church of Virginia was without even the pretense to spiritual and ethical content: it was simply a bulwark of property; it was needed to legalize and sanctify the family through baptism—"the heirs of his body, lawfully begotten". The clergymen were under lay control and subject to the common rather than the canon law, and instead of being respected as spiritual leaders they were regarded as subservient hirelings and were often treated with contumely. The living standards in the colony were set by the ruling class; to conduct one's self in such terms was an achievement, and the mind of the clergymen was fundamentally a reflection of the values and ethics of the aristocracy. They therefore took religion lightly and were ignorant of theology, which rendered the Hebraic influence in Virginia insignificant. The glebe was not their property, and parishes paid poorly: their chief ambition was to accumulate enough capital with which to create a freehold estate—to acquire lands and slaves, and to grow tobacco; they were fundamentally planters, and only incidentally ministers of the gospel—"The Establishment is indeed Tobacco". [39] They did not perform the ministerial rites without fees; and the arrogance and condescension of Anglicanism as a class religion caused them to disdain the plain folk, which discouraged missionary work. Infidelity to the accepted teachings of the Church was evidently rampant: laws had to be passed punishing disturbers of divine services; and the Code of 1705 had to make provisions against atheism, deism and polytheism, as well as to allow no work and make church attendance compulsory on "the Lord's day, commonly called Sunday". But this was rather with a view to protecting the Establishment, which was prized primarily as an instrument for the maintenance of social stability. The parish covered a huge territory of scattered habitations, and the Virginians' church attendance was infrequent and perfunctory. Their life and mind did not center on the church, and they were bereft of religious fervor: the church was without an atmosphere all its own, in which the worshiper finds himself immersed in another world; and their family burial place was located near the mansion house rather than in the church yard.*

A study of the world may be made from the standpoint of the laws of God, supernaturalism; the laws of Nature, naturalism; and the laws of Man, artifice or sociology.

The Virginians loved nature: it was the foundation of their life and thought, and they drew from it their emotional inspiration and rational conclusions. The Maytime beauty of their surroundings was intoxicating, the boundlessness of the world—*their* world—created a feeling of mastery and freedom, the tang of the fresh spring air brought rejuvenation; here was beauty, mastery, freedom—life. Thomas Jefferson, who was chiefly instrumental in reducing to rational expression the Virginian world view, wrote:

"And our own dear Monticello, where has nature spread so rich a mantle under the eye? Mountains, forests, rocks, rivers. With what majesty do we ride above the storms! How sublime to look down into the workhouse of nature, to see her clouds, hail, snow, thunder, all fabricated at our feet! and the glorious sun when rising as if out of a distant water, just gilding the tops of the mountains and giving life to all nature." [40]

---

* This custom was strengthened by the fact that the church was far away, the communications were poor, and bodies could not be kept in the great heat.

They drew life from "the many-breasted earth", and they exalted it—and they formed from it their world view.

They never posed their naturalism as against super-naturalism: this contrast had been thoroughly studied and developed by the European, especially by the British, thinkers; and the colonials accepted the Europeans' fundamental conclusions, and saw no need to improve on them. Rather did the Virginians pose their natural law as against artifice or social law—the complex of human relations which flows from towns, industrialism, machinery, division of labor, and brings the principles of nationalism, interdependence, and individualism. Pioneering—the early days of industrialism, the transition from tradition—had its immediate unfortunate implications: there was abundant good reason for the exhortation, "back to nature"—which really meant back to feudalism.

The Virginians were horrified by—they recoiled from, the machine: its concentrating power was non-existent in the colony; the visitor was impressed by their love of rural life—most of them had never seen as many as a dozen houses together until their late teens, when they first came to Williamsburg. They couldn't endure noise, and the thought of crowds and congestion gave them a sensation of smothering. A contemporary writing quotes a Virginian as saying:

> "it would be impossible for us to live, when a matter of a hundred Families are coop'd up within the Compass of half a Mile of Ground." [41]

Like the English poets, who crystallized the feudal values—the loveliness, peace and quiet of country life—into song, the Virginians preferred to be "Far from the madding crowd's ignoble strife," and "remote from the noise of city street and the busy haunts of men." Their strength was earth-given: they knew good land when they saw it, they loved the open spaces and always needed elbow room, and they were aggressively determined on Virginia's territorial expansion. They were characterized by claustrophobia: they

239

seemed in fear of the fence, they tended to shrink from the enclosure, and they were uncomfortable in a tent, and in a building—cabin, church, shop, factory; their own mansion houses were quite spacious. Their agrarian economy, scattered population and nature environment precluded the society concept: they believed with the ancients that "God made the country, and man made the town"; the life of man apart from nature was inconceivable; they thought in terms of the natural—not the social—man, and the theory of "natural rights" fitted beautifully. Land was a hereditary possession associated with station and family pride: with land went the perquisites of a social class, and the undisturbed control of the life of an entire area; dominion was identified with ownership of everything within sight of the mansion house—as the proprietor surveyed the vista before him in all directions he wanted to see nothing but his own domain. It was his purpose,

> "to fence his slaves in from all contact with the great world, to create his own petty and tyrannical kingdom on his own plantation, and keep it for his exclusive reign."

The feudal agricultural unit was a social microcosm—a world in itself: it was not an "economic enterprise"—a business or money-making endeavor, and land was never an object of speculation; the proprietary was not primarily a symbol of economic power—rather was it a symbol of social status. Thus the patrician prized his entire estate, although material values were confined to the plantation.

Their society being based on "birth" vertical fluidity among the classes was precluded: with their property and social position assured by the state there was no need for individual initiative and efficiency; the plantations were thus largely haphazardly directed, and with the constant price fluctuations and the absence of definite money standards and of specie most of the proprietors were hazy on what they owned and owed. Land ruled over finance, entail precluded speculation and turnover, and trade was out-

side their milieu. They were not money conscious: money
is confined to the market place; the market place—with
its people, values, ways—was unknown to the Virginians.
They eschewed the state of mind which could not see life
beyond dividends, and they regarded the exploitation of
people by one another—the mind to use, as petty and anti-
social. Their relations were always social, never economic;
they did not live off one another, were not out to "make
money," had nothing to sell, never thought in terms of
"driving a bargain," and they never viewed their fellows
as customers. The tendency to cupidity was non-existent:
the habits of thrift and close-fistedness were unknown;
the Virginians never produced a miser, and they created
the tradition of "southern" hospitality. The absence of
money values had its influence on the mind—and they
seem like Homer's Odysseus, who was "bitten to the quick"
when he was accused of being,

> "such an one as comes and goes in a benched ship,
> a master of sailors that are merchantmen, one with
> a memory for his freight, or that hath the charge
> of a cargo homeward bound, and of greedily gotten
> gains."

Wrote Governor Spotswood early in the eighteenth century:

> "I think it below the dignity of one of her Majestys
> Governors, to be a Trader." [42]

Henry Cabot Lodge points to Virginia's,

> "trading portion of the middle class, who were re-
> garded with great contempt by the owners of lands
> and slaves,who esteemed trade a mark of inferiority,
> and an occupation unsuited to a man of birth and
> position." [43]

> "It was esteemed a disgrace for a young man to
> enter the counting-house of the first merchant in
> Virginia." [44]

Thus were the Virginians innocent of the mysteries of
high finance: their way of life precluded them from ap-

preciating the importance of, and developing an interest in, the subject; and when they found themselves confronted with it they tended to derangement. Their governmental fiscal measures were based on simple mathematics. Colonial Virginia produced no financiers.

Their identification of life and freedom with the open spaces caused them to recoil from the artificialities of urban existence; they shuddered at the thought of confining one's physical being to the mustiness of the tradesman's shop, and narrowing one's mind to profits and percentages in terms of pennies; and their claustrophobia brought revulsion to city congestion. They were very careful of their economic base, but they never engaged in the pursuit of gain. No one thought of questioning their right to their exalted position in the world, and they were ordinarily unconscious of the "rights of private property"*—they simply took their estates for granted. Their main interest in life was quality, not gain—and theirs was a government of gentlemen, not of tradesmen.

The Virginian aristocracy was a leisure class. The sense of time is created by things moving: the absence of change in colonial Virginia—yesterday, today and tomorrow seemed to blend into an eternal sameness—brought a relative unconsciousness of time. The grandfather clock at the foot of the stairs in the mansion house was wholly ornamental; the days passed very slowly, and life seemed longer. Time did not enter into their calculations: the idea that "time is money" was unknown; no one looked forward in hopes that "things will pick up," and there was no anxiety for time to pass. "The leisurely tradition of Virginia" created a state of mind where everyone always had plenty of time— in eating, playing, traveling, keeping engagements; punctuality was not a value. The Reverend John Clayton, who

---

* London's insistence on its right to tax the colonials, to quarter troops on their plantations and to requisition supplies, brought forth a consciousness of the rights of private property among the Virginians.

visited the colony in 1688, says:

> "a Planter's Pace is a Proverb, which is a good
> sharp hand-Gallop." [45]

The financial integrity on which the credit of the trading
society rests was unknown, and the Virginians were leisurely in the payment of debts. They had no sense of economy:
a London merchant wrote to a creditor in 1768 saying
that the planters,

> "over value their incomes, & live up to their sup-
> positions without providing against Calamities . . .
> From your account & indeed from every ones ac-
> count Virginia is at this time greatly distressed,
> but as the distress has arose from the cause, I have
> assigned, I hope the present Generation will take
> warning & not be the means of reducing their
> Familys to such Extremitys." [46]

Virginia's British visitors—who had been brought up in
the ways of mercantile utilitarianism, and who thought of
the countryside in terms of their own neat, well-trimmed,
cultivated fields—are unanimous in their indictment of the
Virginians as wasteful, and as indifferent to making the
most economically of what they had. Andrew Burnaby,
an English clergyman who traveled through the colony in
1760, was surprised when he found them lacking a "spirit
of enterprise," disinclined to "expose themselves willingly
to fatigue" and displaying "extravagance, ostentation, and
a disregard of economy." "The Virginians," he says, "out-
run their incomes . . . There are but few of them that have
a turn for business." Visitors from the northern colonies
were similarly impressed.

They were without the restless ambition, the feverish
hurry, and the calculating connivance of the commercial
world—sincerity was never the virtue of a fool. The impact of the materialistic ethics of capitalism on the insouciance of the feudal landowners left them bewildered;
the "tricks of the trade"—"the arts and contrivances of
designing people"—were beyond their ken; and they could

243

easily be victimized by merchants. British commercial life
was rife with venality; there were questionable practices
by British merchants in their handling of Virginia's tobacco, and they advanced credits to the colonials at extortionate rates. Says Ripley:

"The system of keeping open accounts in London
was calculated to encourage extravagance; and these
accounts were habitually overdrawn. Many of the
merchants even made it a rule to encourage this
indebtedness, so as to assure the continuance of
their customers. It gave them a certain advantage
in all their dealings with the planters . . . Once
firmly in the grasp of the merchants, extortionate
prices were charged for everything." [47]

According to Harrell:

"In 1791 a group of merchants in Great Britain submitted to their government a statement of amounts
due them from American customers in 1775. The
total, with fourteen years interest, amounted to
£4,930,656; £4,137,944, over five-sixths of the total,
was due from states south of Pennsylvania; £2,305,-
408, or over half of this amount, was due from Virginia.... the planters were in an almost inextricable
position in 1775; it seemed that nothing less than
virtual repudiation could relieve them."

"Kippen and Company, of Glasgow, and Jones and
Farrell, of London, held bonds against Thomas Jefferson for approximately ten thousand pounds." [48]

British exploitation was largely covert: for fully a half
century before Independence Virginia's plantations each
year sent enormous quantities of tobacco—as well as a good
deal of corn, wheat and rye—to England, yet it seems that
the more produce they shipped the more money they owed;
Virginia—the southern colonies' biggest single shipper,
was also by far the biggest single debtor. Exploitation was
also overt: Britain was "sucking the vitals of (colonial)
trade to herself;" the colonials were being mulcted by the

Navigation Acts. Thus by 1776 the Virginian proprietaries were virtually bankrupt: their lands, homes and laborers were mortgaged to a few British merchants, and the colony was in a state of vassalage; and the feudal realty laws could not protect her landowners from British creditors, since London exercised the right to transcend all colonial law. Flight did not save the Cavaliers from eventual merchant domination.

Among the Virginians' primary values was freedom: they associated it with the totality of life; and it was theirs both in nature, and in society. Freedom in nature was open-spacedness, the medium for ranging—in forests, mountains, streams. Freedom in society was government-al—politics; ecclesiastical—faith, morals, learning; economic—property; social—race, nationality, sex. The conditions of their day caused them to feel that their political freedom was menaced: this became a problem of supreme importance to them, and brought an interest in and emphasis on theories of politics and government—which could create the impression that they identified freedom simply with the mechanics of governmental organization. They regarded the problem of political freedom as an endeavor against the state: organization and freedom were mutually exclusive—the one was per se the enemy of the other. Virginia from her inception had been a member of a world-wide political organization—the British Empire, and their relations were based on reciprocal rights and responsibilities. The principle of political liberty therefore presented itself to the Virginians in terms of two problems: the relation of the individual to the state, which was internal; and the relation of the political unit (the colony) to the whole (the Empire), which was external.

The Virginians knew government over men only as an instrument of repression: their polity was an ordered inequality—the liberty of a few was predicated upon the slavery of the many, and a minority of masters was saddled on a dehumanized population; and they eschewed government over themselves even as a "necessary evil." They identified freedom of the individual with proprietary mastery and seclusion, or no outside interference: they had a yearning for inaccessibility, to be alone with one's own way—and they stood squarely on their immemorial tradition that "a man's home is his castle;" their resentment against intrusion—on person, property, polity, ran far deeper than rational conviction or political doctrine—it was a psychological condition; and it was an unwritten law of colonial life among all classes, from log cabin to mansion house, that intrusion could be a fatal offense. Their traditions, values, way of life—and the fact of slavery, rendered them hypersensitive concerning their own rights as freemen. They evidently distinguished between government over men and administration over things, and they did not regard as intrusive the administrative requirements concerning the registration of land patents and the handling of produce for export. Since Virginia was the aristocracy no fundamental conflict could arise between them: there was no threat to the social status quo from any quarter; and the problem of the relation of the individual to the state was viewed as domestic, and was never in issue. Their way of life with its freedom from institutional control was a practical approach to anarchism, and this resulted in individual inefficiency: but they were collectively the acme of efficiency, and their polity was thoroughly organized; "eternal vigilance" was the price also of life, social problems did not arise, and the General Assembly was a model of smooth functioning and absence of fraction.

Their fear of intrusion as a deep-seated emotion was extended to the polity, and it eventually acquired rational expression as it developed into a political doctrine. They were very much concerned about the freedom *of* Virginia, not about freedom *in* Virginia: they felt assured of civil peace and personal liberty; they never charged anyone with the intention to intrude on their individual estates, but the collective of proprietaries that constituted their polity was alleged an object of foreign dominion. They were conscious of government over themselves only as an external force, and—although all outsiders were suspect— the Virginians' fundamental concern respecting political freedom was confined to their colony's Empire relations. This rendered paramount the problem of the relation of the political part to the whole, which resolved itself into three doctrines: particularism or local sovereignty, federalism or local autonomy (union of States), and nationalism or local subordination (union of people). The doctrine of federalism occupies an intermediary position, and it creates the problem of jurisdictional conflict: the local and central governments both have rights as within the political part — but where the power of the one ends and that of the other begins has never been definitively determined; this ambiguity gives rise to wrangling, which encourages tendencies to one or the other political extreme. The Anglo-American colonies had inherited the political doctrine of particularism or sovereignty as in relation to one another, and of federalism or local autonomy as in relation to the parent country. The federal principle found expression as within each jurisdiction both in the attitude of the county towards the colony, and of the colony towards the Empire. They had no tradition in nationalism, which was an alien doctrine.

What the ancient Greek and Roman thinkers had said about political tyrants was a much greater inspiration in the life of the Virginians than the wisdom of the Hebrew prophets—yet their fundamental influence in this respect was Anglo-Saxon. The ideological struggles at home—of which Virginia herself was originally a product, and which directly shaped the history of her first century—were still live issues. The identification of political liberty with separation from an external central authority, and the substitution therefor of local independence, were inherited from their immemorial nativity, and were given emphasis by the spirit of the Renaissance—the theories of John Locke "framed the principles afterwards embodied in the American War of Independence." This was Virginia's political heritage: her patricians were seventeenth-century Englishmen; and like their Cavalier forebears—who sometimes refused to fight for "the martyred king" outside their own shires, the Virginians expected the delegates to the House of Burgesses to represent first the interests of their particular county, then the interests of the colony, and last—if at all—those of the Empire.

> "Virginia ... was a place of nativities; men were born and died and elected to honours from particular neighborhoods, localities they knew, land they owned. The trees and lanes and fish in the streams were familiar ... They fought for a village, a single field, it might be, or a mere clearing on the side of a mountain."

Thus the Virginians' political thinking was from the part to the whole: they did not have the "nation" concept, and the centripetalism and the monolithic loyalty of nationalism were unknown; the tendencies under federalism were centrifugal, and loyalty was divided as it tapered in emphasis from the province, to the section, to the federation.

As the patrician families each acquired holdings scattered in several counties their minds broadened from the locale to the colony. Their fortunes became bound up with those of the colony—they rose with their class, and individual ambitions and rivalries were secondary. They regarded Virginia as one does his private estate, and their sense of proprietorship was concentrated fundamentally on the colony, not on their personal estates. Thus "real" estate was not strictly regarded as "private property"—rather was it the property of a class to be handled in terms of the basic interests of the class, not of those of the individual. Citizenship was like membership in the family; in accepting the

feudal realty laws they surrendered to the polity the liberty
to control their property, and they attained the acme of
their individuality in the state. The development of Anglo-
America forced them into more numerous and involved contacts with alien men and ways, which brought forth a clear
consciousness of patriotism; they began to refer to Virginia
as "our country" (which later became "my native State") ;
their love of their "land"—which was not entirely confined
to idealism—acquired the fervor of religion, and it probably
transcended their devotion to the family; they felt with
Oliver Goldsmith,

> "Where'er I Roam,
> Whatever Realms To See,
> My Heart, Untravelled,
> Fondly Turns To Thee" ;

and the statement, "I'm a Virginian," became a mark of
distinction uttered with pride.

The move from federalism to particularism, or the enunciation of the right of secession, inhered in the existence of
Virginia to the extent that its peopling was due to flight.
The Cavaliers had brought with them the Anglo-Saxon in-
sular mind, which found expression in the autarchic plantation and was emphasized by the sense of seclusion and
freedom that remoteness from authority created. Stuart
federalism allowed and isolation necessitated unusual independence of action, and judgment and responsibility in the
operation of government, which created ability and self-
confidence. Virginia often found herself ignored because of
the chaos in England and her early economic unimportance,
and she was sometimes for more than a year without a
royal governor or instructions. Thus the traditions together
with the conditions of the Virginians' life had attenuated
their federalism virtually to particularism, and this created
what may appear like a "narrow provincialism."

The Virginians identified individuality with mastery and
isolation or no outside interference, and political liberty

with a local autonomy that verged on sovereignty—these were their fundamental values. Nationalism—with its centralizing tendencies and destruction of the independent unit, and its introduction of division of labor and of the complexities of interdependence—was regarded as subjugation.

It was the infancy of civilization in America. Virginia was in her springtime—she was a simple society in a natural world. Her own political organization was simple: she had one sole external political relation—membership in the British Empire, which compromised her independence but assured her a maximum state of peace and security. It was in the days of the economy of scarcity, or before technology had solved the problem of production—which is the relation of man to nature: expansion could not be intensive—it had to be entirely extensive; the iron machine was yet to be—which necessitated the human machine, who had to be regarded as machine rather than as human; "wealth"—family possession of the goods of life—was a primary value, as it was a mark of success, power and distinction; and the conical system of civil society—the glaring contrasts in economic condition, the great wealth of the few and the abject poverty of the many—was universal, and it was accepted by all classes as normal. The principle of aristocracy, the "quality" person—the person of virtue, culture, freedom—could not be extended to include the entire population. Virginia was a snug little world: the slave, the commoner, the gentleman—each fitted neatly in his place, and God was in his heaven; her society was like the poet's "painted ship upon a painted ocean." Social relations within "the unconscious simplicity of traditional feudalism" were elementary: there were no cross currents creating complexities, there was a profound homogeneity of mind, and disagreements were superficial; men could not be diverted from underlying principle by incidentals—and demagoguery was at a minimum; and the thinking and the expressions of her sons are characterized by the simplicity and the sincerity of naiveté. They were unconscious of sociology as an objective science, and of the theories of social evolution and progress —it never occurred to them that continued scientific development may affect social relations. They were at the peak of mental health: theirs was an atmosphere exuberant with the consciousness of expansion; they were going forward—a continent of land stretched before them; and the future was identified with freedom, growth, power, wealth. Their way of life was qualitatively the highest attainable, and they lived in "the best of all possible worlds"; there was a relative absence of property consciousness, as each had a subjective attitude concerning his own individual estate; and they implicitly took for granted their place in the "beautiful monotony" of the feudal framework. They believed in biological superiority: they were sensitive, virtuous, cultured— while the lower classes were ignorant, rough and often brutal; this was traced to qualities of blood, which they associated much more with social class than with nationality; and they considered themselves congenitally superior to commoners. Thus rule was to be by a blooded aristocracy, and they opposed leveling. They thought in terms of class liberty, and they identified citizenship and freedom with station, and ability and virtue with external connections such as ancestry and property—not with the inner man. They did not live by "the book"—scripture or ledger: culture never came from the mart—and economic independence or disdain of "the budget" was their due, since they associated cultural pursuits with material comfort and leisure; insouciance was a mark of station, for to do things for money was "mean"; and condescension was an acknowledged virtue. Aristocracy was above labor: labor was a "curse"; the "field of honor" was identified with the sword —never with the plough, and labor was servile and was viewed as degrading. A straight line could be drawn between proprietor and slave: the proprietor was European, civilized, patrician—while the slave was African, primitive, proletarian; and never the twain did meet, as each remained —strictly, and forever—in his own world; the proprietor was a Cavalier, which the slave could never be. Aristocracy represented everything that was noble and good, and it was the duty of men of honor to espouse liberty and fight tyranny. They believed in human uplift, but never in terms of social revolution or on the "meaner sort's" own initiative; rather did they identify it with endeavor from above or social philanthropy. They wanted a world where time stood still: the absence of social dynamism was the sum of all good—nothing was to disturb the quiet of the land; they were suspicious of any kind of change, which they felt would be to their detriment, and they preferred to continue—to rely on the wisdom and the safeties of—the past. They dreaded to hear the ways they lived by brought into question: the federal political relation was embedded in sacred tradition—it was part of their subjective life; and they were horrified by the events that rendered federalism objective, and forced them to take cognizance of it as a question in issue. They were men of the country, not of the city: their economic theory was purely agrarian; they were interested in moral and political problems, but they dreaded sociology; artifice—with its vast conglomeration of cities, buildings, machines, people—was a hopeless complexity, from which the simple feudal mind recoiled; and they were traditionally opposed to social upheaval, and were horrified by mobs and tumult. They had great respect for the Anglo-Saxon civil law, and the petty grievances and the excitement incident to litigation relieved somewhat the insipidity of plantation existence. The absence of towns, of diversity of pursuits and of the important learned professions practically precluded opportunities for social contrast and friction with their broadening effects on the mind, and with the absence of specialization the Virginian combined the functions of statesman, judge, teacher, soldier and healer.

They were guided by esthetic, not by use, values: they took pure delight in loveliness and harmony for their own sake; there was a "beautiful equilibrium between man and nature"; they drank in the beauty of the world around them to the point of intoxication; and they delighted in admiring the natural scenery and the landscape, and they appreciated the mountains and the countryside and, to a lesser extent, the seashore. They exalted quality—they could afford it and were unstinting in its acquisition, and they were careful that man's work added more than it took away from the beauty of nature. Their love of beauty found expression also in architecture: foreigners were imported to design the home magnificent on the lines of classical construction; they built primarily for appearance, rather than for utility; some designated their mansion houses after alleged ancestral homes in England, while a few adopted Latin and other exotic names; and in the building of a church,

"The purest style of Grecian architecture would be displayed in a cornice, an arch over a doorway, or especially in the 'alter-piece' behind the chancel."

The area of the patrician mansion house was meticulously kept as they cultivated hedgerows, lawns, orchards, flower gardens; and a few also built small parks for the keeping of deer and other harmless animals. Life and art were entirely human, never mechanical; the aristocratic atmosphere was most favorable to sensitivity, and the mansion houses were radiant with imported beauty and quality. Their portraits, done by England's best, decorated the walls; their libraries, furniture, wearing apparel, musical instruments, engravings, also came from the home country; and they had statuary from Italy, paintings from France, rich intricately woven carpets from Persia, porcelain from China. They were concerned about fashions in dress, which were set by the royal family—with those of the Stuarts continuing in Virginia almost to Independence. They were self-conscious about, and took great pride in, their personal appearance—

and they took very good care of their persons: they seemed convinced that art need not be separated from the individual—a thing apart, on canvas—but that he may himself be a work of art; and the patrician was resplendent in expensive dress, in jewels, and in equipage. Everything of beauty and quality in the arts—which made up the best part of their lives—was imported, and this broadened their mental outlook as they realized that value is universal. The mansion house—at times an atmosphere of splendor and gayety, at other times of tragedy and gloom—was the essence of the Virginian's being; it was the *raison d'etre* of the estate—its removal may have brought about the disintegration of the plantation; it supplanted the church as the center of sacredness, and of the values of peace, beauty, love; it became the symbol of the liberal mind and the open heart—nobody was ever turned away, although there was a sharp consciousness of the distinction between the front and the rear entrance; it was the place of the patrician birth, upbringing, education, marriage, entertainment and interment; it was the center and symbol of his prestige, power and prosperity and was, in fact, more than a home—it was a seat of government. The perpetuation of the family name was a sacred duty: the soil of the family seat was consecrated by the dust of his fathers, and was therefore revered; and the idea of its alienation was tantamount to treason.

The cultivated gentleman was a tradition in colonial Virginia: they respected culture as a value, and considered it the prerogative of the select few. Their ideal of the complete gentleman was: to have many accomplishments rather than to be expert in one, to be equally versed in the arts of war and of peace, to enjoy sports, to be skilled in music, to know literature, to speak several languages, to be dignified yet civil to all men, to have been to college, and to have traveled. Education was regarded as a formality—and they ordinarily acquired it for polish and ostentation, rather than for under-

standing or use. The gentleman was not to be associated
professionally with the useful avocation: to become a physician, lawyer, minister, teacher, engineer, scientist—to be
employed and paid for his services, was generally beneath
the dignity of quality. Their occasional engagement—especially in their younger days—in surveying, map-making,
law practice, was noblesse oblige. They yearned for, but
never achieved, a court of their own: they emulated Versailles—more than the Court of St. James, and they had
great respect for the French aristocracy as the source of
refinement and elegance; George Washington at fourteen
years of age,

"had written out carefully the old French 'Rules of
Civility and Decent Behaviour', and steadily practised them."

It was the mode for gentlemen to be patrons of the arts,
of letters, and of the sciences: the masters of brush and pen,
past and contemporary, had worked in order to submit their
creations to the pleasure of aristocracy; and the praise that
some of them sometimes undertook to bestow on writers,
painters, composers, sculptors, was supercilious and condescending.

This—the Virginian view of life—was sacred tradition,
not intellectual conviction: it was immanent—a matter of
emotional content not easily lending itself to rational expression; yet it was eventually brought to consciousness
and objective understanding by the contrast elicited from
the contact with forces external and alien.

Towards the outsider the Virginian aristocrat affected
the air of condescending aloofness characteristic of the
gentleman of leisure: things in general were expanding and
his own affairs improving; he employed a steward under
whom were several overseers, and with his interests well
managed he could free his mind from the vulgar concerns

of life. He was usually attired in a broadcloth dress coat with gold and silver buttons, knee-breeches, shirt ruffles, a white cravat flowing through a golden ring, a wig over which was a gold and silver laced hat, silken hose, and shoes graced by huge buckles. An historian speaks of,

> "The old Virginia gentleman's ... sword, which used to be left in a sword-rack at the church door when he went in to kneel before the Prince of Peace".[20]

To have an "affluent style of life, great landed estates, troops of dependents, lordly deportment, far reaching authority", was the ambition of every aristocrat. It was a mark of station to be of a good, ancient family; keep one's genealogy, have a coat-of-arms, military title and college diploma; own many slaves, be surrounded with flunkeys and squander money; and, at the end, be buried with pomp and vainglory and vaunt one's virtues on an elaborate tombstone. To serve as a Burgess or county official was an aristocrat's inheritance, and was not always desired; the presidency of the Council was the highest post a colonial could attain, and some of them were not above the use of bribery to achieve membership in that body.

In earlier days—when the Cavaliers experienced the status of refugees and had to fight for their conquest of Virginia; when title to land was insecure, slaves to exploit were few and the foundations had first to be laid for what later developed into George Washington's social milieu—the state of mind was different. There was a condition of penury, and fortunes had to be built from meagre stakes. This meant struggle, and the grandfather of the strutting, sporting aristrocrat of pre-Revolutionary days was a shrewd business man, penny minded, hard working, absorbed in the personal supervision of his estate and not above shady dealing. The Assembly had to legislate against false weights and measures; and against the perpetration of fraud in the packing for export of tobacco, pork, beef, pitch and tar, as this allegedly caused a drop in prices, was "to the great prejudice of the trade of this . . . dominion", and "may destroy the credit of the country". They became extravagant in their individual living since that was the way of aristocracy but their governmental fiscal measures, especially as in relation to outsiders, show throughout a high sense of economy.

The contemporary Beverly—no doubt influenced by the London atmosphere—in discussing Virginia's plant life seems much more concerned with commercial possibilities than with natural history: his mind is on turning plants into various commodities and, says he of an abundantly growing acorn, "I believe the making Oil of them, would turn to a good Account". He also speaks of iron works and water power. He laments the indifference of his countrymen to towns and trade, and points to many such neglected opportunities:

"I should be ashamed to publish this slothful Indolence of my Countrymen".

Yet he dreads industry and husbandry:

"the natural Production of that Country, which the Native Indians enjoy'd, without the Curse of Industry, their Diversion alone, and not their Labour, supplying their Necessities. . . . none of the Toils of Husbandry were exercised by this happy People".

"the Indians; happy . . . in their simple State of Nature, and in their enjoyment of Plenty, without the Curse of Labour."

The modern trend from agriculture to commerce was reversed in colonial Virginia—the commercial activities relatively increase as one goes backwards in time. Wertenbaker says that William Byrd the Second "is more the Cavalier than his father, less the merchant", while William Byrd the Third "was . . . an excellent example of the Cavalier of the period preceding the Revolution". The Virginians of the time of Robert "King" Carter, who died in the year of George Washington's birth, are described as, "an aristocracy founded on landed wealth, but an aristocracy that also engaged in trade, and profited by commerce without letting business become an end in itself." [49]

Their attitude towards woman was ungentle, while militarism and duelling were repugnant to them.

The rise from the condition of distressed Cavaliers to that of lordly aristocrats changed all this, and affluence brought self-confidence and consciousness of station. They "stood on their rank": they developed the traditional contempt of the feudal landowner for the merchant, and they were full of wise reflections on the "base nature" of common folk. They sneered at the few traders in the colony, who were chiefly Scotchmen, and at the slave dealers; considered them a distinct class with whom they wanted no social intercourse, and they resented the term "Scotchman" as an epithet; while citizens of other colonies were identified as "foreigners". They took for granted implicit obedience and loyalty from inferiors: to the average commoner the patricians were a legend, whose names were mentioned with bated breath; men competed for the honor to be near them, and to live and to die for them; and those who sometimes had their contact, such as stewards and clerks, were very careful of their manners towards their betters—and addressed them as "Honour'd Sir" and "Your Honour". They understood the psychology of the mean whites—and of the frontiersmen (called Buckskins), held them in contempt, and knew how to control them. The relations of the classes are portrayed by romance in terms of the condescending good nature of the "gentle" towards the ignorance and roughness of the "simple". Colonial Virginia never having been invaded they were removed from whatever fighting took place, were indifferent to militarism and did not exalt the way of life of the soldier, and they hated to leave the comforts of home for the trials and privations of the frontiers, forests or military campaign. Their feudal economy was based on a home grown staple, they did not have to venture into the unknown in search of goods or customers, and they had no interest in exploration and discovery. George Washington was sixteen years old before he saw a natural Indian. They were convinced that "time and the great wait for no man": never called on to obey orders or exercise self-repression they were often self-indulgent, without a sense of duty and irresponsible. They were pompous: they loved to pose, and the most renowned masters of the art of silhouette had them for subjects. They had no reason to resist feminine pulchritude, and they were philanderers. They knew no athletics, fought few duels, gambled at cards and dice, drank excessively, and some were not above delight as onlookers in the brutal sports of bear-baiting, the cock-fight and the prize fight.

> "In his (George Washington's) early life profanity
> was regarded as a symptom of familiarity with poor
> whites and negroes; it was ungentlemanly among
> Virginians, though the habit was sometimes caught
> from English officers." [50]

Duelling, and gambling—which "was carried to a frightful extent by all classes" [51]—were prohibited by law. The ban on gambling was largely ignored, and they indulged more for thrill and pastime than for gain; gamblers could sue to recover their losses, but it was the code of honor among gentlemen never to have recourse to the courts.

The ministers of the Establishment fell under the existing influences, and they accepted slavery and followed in the ways and practices of their masters. Says the Reverend Edward D. Neill:

> "With a vestry elected by a community of godless
> planters, the most orthodox minister was liable to be
> complained of, suspended or removed, by the secular
> power, while a wine bibbing or horse racing parson
> could be retained for years by a vestry of jolly and
> loose living parishioners." [52]

259

The Puritan influence in Virginia was not easily shaken off
—and a year after Bacon's Rebellion the Assembly enacted
various penalties for,
> "such ministers as shall become notoriously scan-
> dalous by drunkingnesse, swearing, fornication or
> other haynous and crying sins".

What aggravated this condition was that the ministers
came from England and the best did not leave, the absence
of a Bishop's control, and lack of companionship apart from
the upper class. The instructors at the college were little
better.

Under civilization as a way of life the individual man
developed the ability to produce more wealth than is necessary for his own preservation. A few men were enabled to
appropriate the surplus for themselves, and the civilized
society throughout pre-technology had a conical form of
organization. This created an aristocracy—a leisure class
of men who were freed from the economic burden, and who
had the opportunity to devote their time, mind and effort
to an understanding of the world around them. Thus it was
under civilization that man rose to his noblest achievement
—the awareness, the appreciation, and the attempt at an
understanding, of the good, the beautiful, and the true:
and it was this endeavor that developed man's rational
faculties, brought out his ability to think in abstract terms,
and enabled him to become mentally creative—to achieve
culture. The European was convinced that the civil slave
society with its opportunities for cultural achievement was
qualitatively superior to the primitive tribal society with its
freedom for all of jungle ranging. Civilized people were
never subjected to slavery under Christianity. The primitive
did not show creative aptitudes, and the European sincerely
believed that in "civilizing the savage" he was uplifting him.
Thus aristocracy finds historical justification in the fact
that without leisure the sensitive and the profound couldn't

have been cultivated, and that throughout civilization, in all times and climes, it has been the creator, the patron and the custodian of culture.

Colonial Virginia had her being during the economy of scarcity in pre-technology, and when "wage" or free labor was only in its beginnings—and she was not unique in the fact that she had an aristocracy, which rested on the back of repressed labor. During the War of Independence many Virginians were beginning to become conscious of their institution of slavery. Virginia was then slave surfeited, and the price of Negroes had sharply declined. The slaves' cheapness, plus the anxiety of secessionist libertarians to counteract British incitation of slave revolt,[53] to emulate the States that were moving towards abolition, and to avoid the charge of hypocrisy, gave rise to a wave of humanitarianism: they began to show an aversion to use of the word "slave", as they preferred "servant" instead; and some proprietors manumitted a few of their slaves, while a number even expressed abolitionist ideas. Arrangements were also made enabling philanthropists to help slaves purchase their freedom.

Before 1776, however, abolitionism had not reached the stage of a political force, the institution had not yet become "peculiar", and there was little self-consciousness concerning it among the Virginians. Their understanding of man as a natural—rather than as a social—being, brought the conclusion that men are divided into their respective classes by qualities of blood, and it was therefore in the nature of the African to be a slave. They were, however, anxious to be regarded as "kind" to their Negroes. Their attitude on slavery is expressed by William Byrd, who died in 1744:

"Our negroes are not so numerous or so enterprising as to give us any... uneasiness, nor indeed is their labour any other than gardening, and less by far than what the poor people of other countrys undergo. Nor are any crueltys exercised upon them unless by great accident they happen to fall into the hands of a brute, who always passes here for a monster." [54] The deplorable condition of labor throughout the world at the time was inherent in the social organization of pre-technology. The patrician shunned, and considered himself above, the brutality and ignorance that existed among the lower elements of the population—gentleness distinguished him from the common herd. Although excessive indulgence did sometimes bring undesirable incidents, life as within the upper class was on the whole gentle; to the limited extent that the patrician had personal contact with slaves, especially household help, there is no doubt of his kindliness towards them; and the aristocracy was an important influence for moderation in the Virginia social milieu.

The atmosphere of primitivism that was created by the African mind hung like a pall over the colony—and rendered inevitable its influence, at least to some extent, on the masters. This is discernible in some of their manners, speech expressions, forms of dancing, and in their superstitions on the curing of various bodily ailments. It is said of the upper class:

"Iron rings were worn for fits ... an iron ring was used at Mount Vernon on Patsy Custis".
Several varieties of the wooden musical instrument, which is said to have originated in Africa, were to be found in most of the mansion houses.

The Cavaliers faithfully followed Governor Berkeley's ban on popular education, and there were no free schools in Virginia. The schools of the time were in the hands of the Church; and the colony's disability to ordain, and her inhabitants' indifference to religion and dispersed way of living discouraged the rise of public institutions of learning. Moreover, the absence of social consciousness rendered incomprehensible the idea of universal education as a state responsibility. Sir William Berkeley regarded culture and popular education as antithetical: he was conscious and proud of aristocracy as the traditional creator, patron and custodian of culture, and he feared popular power or democracy as productive of demagoguery and destructive of the sensitive and the profound. He refused to exchange culture for democracy—hence his denunciation of free schools and printing was actuated by a concern for the preservation of culture.

There was plenty of learning in the colony: appreciation of things sensitive—especially of the humanities—as a mark of aristocracy, had always been shown primary consideration by the Cavaliers; and Virginia's second century is the most cultured period in her history. In adopting measures for the maintenance of William and Mary College, a state institution, the Assembly said:

"the supporting and encouraging so hopeful a work, is of the greatest importance to the people of this colony, for the advancement of learning, and the good education of their youth".[55]

Virginia's most important institution of learning was the mansion house, in which an atmosphere of respect for culture always prevailed; and the young patrician was brought up in this atmosphere. The mansion house was the citadel of Virginian tradition and values, which were the aristocrats' most coveted possession. Their fear to entrust the education of their youth to an atmosphere apart from that prevailing in the mansion house was among the main reasons for the absence of public schools. Each mansion house had a study, in which there was usually a large library; and the tutor was an invariable member of every aristocratic household. William Byrd the Second had the largest library in America. Councillor Carter owned nearly fifteen hundred books. Jefferson estimated the value of his books burned at his home "Shadwell" at £200 sterling. The College of William and Mary accumulated a library of about three thousand volumes. John "Locke's 'Works' were to be found on the shelves of every Virginia library of any pretensions", and the works of the French philosophers "figured prominently among the French publications" in the Virginians' studies. An inscription on a tombstone dated 1766 says:

"He was distinguished by his love of letters, which he improved at Cambridge and the Temple".

It was in the days before world communications, mass literacy and the popular publication: events were of hardly more than local importance; and there was only incidental interest anywhere in "what's new", and in sensationalism and current facts—the stuff that newspapers are made of. Eighteenth-century publications catered to the upper classes, and they were intellectual. There is abundant evidence that many Virginians subscribed to and read some of the best of England's literary periodicals—and their weekly publication, the Virginia Gazette, was not without some literary content. The patricians who participated as actors in the staging of amateur plays had to study and memorize their parts. Many of their wills are neatly drawn up.

"Until the reign of Queen Anne, the English language was extremely variable and unsettled. The best informed men, writing at the same period, would spell the same words very differently."

The influence of the Renaissance raised English to the status of a classical language. But it took some time before developments in England became prevalent in the colony.

They had always been ambitious to make their capital a cultural center. As early as 1666 a play, "Ye Beare And Ye Cubbe", was staged in Jamestown. But the times were fraught with popular disaffection, and the authorities were uneasy about public gatherings. The actors, who were evidently colonists with a bent for the theatre, were arrested; but when the political innocence of their "speeches" was established, they were released. During the eighteenth century Williamsburg became the capital of the colony. The observer Jones wrote of the town in 1724:

"Here dwell several very good Families ... They live in the same neat Manner, dress after the same

264

Modes, and behave themselves exactly as the Gentry
in London".

The Virginians were proud of their capital: it was an
index to the best in the colony, and they lavished luxuries
on it as their wealth increased. They regarded their capital
as a miniature London—as "the seat of learning and the
abode of wealth" it became Virginia's political, social and
cultural center, and there were scenes of brilliant entertainment when, during sessions of the Assembly, members
came in bringing relatives and friends. In 1752 William
Shakespeare's "The Merchant Of Venice" and "Othello",
as well as several farces, were staged in the capital by a
traveling company of professional actors, and the music
was furnished by "Mr. Pelham, who taught the harpsichord
in the town". Williamsburg became one of the prominent
places of theatrical performance in colonial America, and
the plays and players were criticized in the Gazette. An
organ was imported for the church in 1752. Some of the
royal officials and members of the College faculty and of
the aristocracy were intellectuals, and they sometimes held
gatherings for discussion; their Governor Fauquier, 1758-
68, is referred to as,

"The genial, dissolute, free-thinking Fauquier, who
gathered about his table the rising genius of Virginia—Jefferson, Wythe, Mason and the like".[51]

The governor's discussion sessions seem an emulation of
the ancient Hellenic study groups. Bacon's Rebellion stim-
ulated a good deal of literary activity. The following passages from T.M.'s account of the Rebellion, published in
1705, have been described as "worthy of Clarendon":

"the drum beat for the house to meet, and in less
than an hour Mr. Bacon came with a file of fusileers
on either hand near the corner of the state house
where the govern'r and councill went forth to him;
we saw from the window the govern'r open his
breast, and Bacon strutting betwixt his two files of
men ... flinging his right arm every way ...; if in

265

this moment of fury, that enraged multitude had faln upon the govern'r and council we of the assembly expected the same imediate fate".

"in this hubub a servant of mine got so nigh as to hear the governor's words, and also followed Mr. Bacon, and heard what he said, who came and told me, that when the Govern'r opened his breast he said 'here! shoot me, foregod fair mark shoot'. often rehearsing the same, without any other words".[56]

No doubt Governor Berkeley had a flair for the theatrical: his act brings to mind the scene in William Shakespeare's "Julius Caeser", where Caeser;

"plucked me ope his doublet and offered them (the common herd) his throat to cut."

No contemporary writer on the upheaval of 1676 "approaches, in literary power, that unknown 'Bacon's Man' who wrote upon his master a really noble epitaph." [57]

Bacons Epitaph, made by his Man.

Death why soe crewill! what no other way
To manifest thy splleene, but thus to slay
Our hopes of safety; liberty, our all
Which, through thy tyrany, with him must fall
To its late caoss? Had thy rigid force
Bin delt by retale, and not thus in gross
Grief had bin silent: Now wee must complaine
Since thou, in him, hast more then thousand slane
Whose lives and safetys did so much depend
On him there lif, with him their lives must end.
  If't be a sin to think Death brib'd can be
Wee must be guilty; say twas bribery
Guided the fatall shaft. Virginias foes
To whom for secret crimes, just vengeance owes
Disarved plagues, dreding their just disart
Corrupted Death by Parasscellcian art
Him to destroy; whose well tride curage such,
There heartless harts, nor arms, nor strength
        could touch.

Who now must heale those wounds, or stop
    that blood
The Heathen made, and drew into a flood?
Who is't must pleade our Cause? nor Trump
    nor Drum
Nor Deputations; these alas are dumb,
And Cannot speake. Our Arms (though near so
    strong)
Will want the aide of his Commanding tongue,
Which conquer'd more then Caeser: He orethrew
Onely the outward frame; this could subdue
The ruged workes of nature. Soules repleate
With dull Child could, he'd annemate with heate
Drawne forth of reasons Lymbick. In a word
Marss and Minerva, both in him Concurd
For arts, for arms, whose pen and sword alike
As Catos did, may admireation strike
Into his foes; while they confess with all
It was their guilt still'd him a criminall,
Onely this difference does from truth proceed
They in the guilt, he in the name must bleed.
While none shall dare his obsequies to sing
In desarv'd measures; untill time shall bring
Truth Crown'd with freedom, and from danger free
To sound his praises to posterity.
    Here let him rest; while we this truth report
Hee's gon from hence unto a higher court
To pleade his Cause where he by this doth know
Whether to Caeser he was friend, or foe.[58]
But feelings ran high, and Bacon's Man was answered by
another anonymous poet.

Upon the Death of G.B.*

Whether to Caeser he was Friend or Foe?
Pox take such Ignorance, do you not know?
Can he be Friend to Caeser, that shall bring
The Arms of Hell, to fight against the King?

* During the upheaval Bacon was referred to as "General Bacon".

(Treason, Rebellion) then what reason have
Wee for to waite upon him to his Grave,
There to express our passions? Wilt not bee
Worse then his crimes, to sing his Ellegie
In well tun'd numbers; where each Ella beares
(To his Flagitious name) a flood of teares?
A name that hath more soules with sorrow fed,
Then reched Niobe, single teares are shed:
A name that fil'd all hearts, all ears, with paine,
Until blest fate proclam'd, Death had him slane.
Then how can it be counted for a sin
Though Death (nay though myselfe) had bribed bin,
To guide the fatall shaft? we honour all
That lends a hand unto a Trators fall.
What though the well paide Rochit soundly ply
And box the Pulpitt, into flattery;
Urging his Rhetorick, and strained elloquence,
T'adorne incoffined filth, and excrements;
Though the Defunct (like ours) nere tride
A well intended deed until he dide?
'Twill be nor sin, nor shame, for us, to say
A two fould Passion checker workes this day
Of Joy and Sorrow; yet the last doth move
On feete impotent, wanting strength to prove
(Nor can the art of Logick yield releife)
How joy should be surmounted by our greafe.
Yet that wee Greave it cannot be denide,
But 'tis because he was, not cause he dide.
So wep the poore distressed, Ilium Dames
Hereing those nam'd, their City put in flames,
And country ruin'd; If we thus lament
It is against our present Joyes consent.
For if the rule in Phisick, trew doth prove,
Remove the cause, th' effects well after move,
We have outliv'd our sorrows; since we see
The causes shifting of our miserey.
    Nor is't a single cause, that's slipt away

That made us warble out, a well-a-day.
The Branes to plot, the hands to execute
Projected ills, Death Jointly did nonsute
At his black Bar. And what no Baile could save
He hath committed Prissoner to the Grave;
From whence there's no repreive. Death keep
    him close
We have too many Divells still goe loose.[58]

The influence of Shakespeare, especially of his "Julius Caeser," is here evident.

The period was one of social upheaval; men were jarred from their accustomed ways into untrod paths, and their writing is full of bewilderment over the instability of the times. A contemporary philosophized:

"Thus doth fortune sport her self with poore mortells, som times mount them up in to the aire (as Byes do Tennis balls) that they may com with the greater violence downe, and then a gaine strike them against the earth that they may with ye grater speed mount up in to the Aire".[59]

The natural beauties of Virginia, and the development of a profound patriotism, induced a number of native attempts at poetry of which some have literary merit. The anonymous writer of the following poem, which was inspired by the Potomac River, shows a thorough familiarity with that part of the country:

Potomack, in thy silver stream
At silent night I love to lave,
Unseen, save by the lunar beam,
As light I wanton o'er thy wave.

Here, in thy waters fair reclin'd
I court illusion's changeful sway,
To sweet delirium all resign'd,
Reality fades fast away.

But what soft voice steals on my ear

As wrapt I lie in languid dream?
And see! a graceful form draws near—
It is the Genius of the stream.

'Mortal!' he cries (his liquid voice
Sweet as the blue wave's softest sigh),
'Still are my humid haunts thy choice,
Still wilt thou to my green banks hie!

'When Nature spoke, and this fair flood
Rush'd from its dark and secret source,
The frowning rock, impervious wood,
Alternate bending o'er its course,—

'Then rov'd my new-born shores along,
The tawny sons of savage life,—
Here raised the war-whoop loud and strong,
Here desp'rate met in deadly strife.

'And here full many a warrior rude
In tortures drew his parting breath,
But still with spirit unsubdued
Pour'd fearless forth the song of death.

'Near yon wild willow is the spot
Where oft they formed the mazy ring;
And yonder stood the warrior's cot,
Who styled himself Potomack's King.

'There from the sun's meridian ray
An oak's broad shadow gave relief,
Where oft thy ancestor would stray
And woo the daughter of the Chief.

'And often that same Indian maid
(The white man's bride, as records tell)
In childhood's lovely season play'd
O'er these soft scenes thou lov'st so well.

'At night when summer's ardent heat
O'er all a listless languor leaves,
Like thee she sought some cool retreat,
And slyly stole amid my waves.

'And often with her rustic bow,
When Autumn's varied beauties smil'd,
Then to my greenwood sides would go,
And wander there a huntress wild.

'I've seen full many a fleeting race
Since then arise to bloom and fade,
Through time's illimitable space,
And sink in dark oblivion's shade.

'But none like thee in all that time
So oft have sought my lonely shore,
So loved my verdant banks to climb,
Their mossy beauties to explore.

'To none than thee more dear the sight,
The music of my noble flood,
And none have with more warm delight
So oft upon my margin stood.

'For this I bade yon sycamores
In clusters o'er my beach to rise,
And when thou sought'st thy native shores,
To guard thee from intrusive eyes.

'For this I bid my waters bright
To soothe thy ears with murmurs low,
Whene'er by day or silent night
Thou com'st to mark their graceful flow.' [60]

The poem seems to have a feminine touch: it reveals the
values of the Virginians—the worship of nature, the ap-

preciation of beauty, the profound love of life, the yearning for languor and solitude. The Indian is already the stuff of the historian, and the romance and legend of the poet.

The following poem, whose author is unknown, was found among George Washington's early copy-books and, in the opinion of the historian Conway, may have been written by Captain Washington:

TRUE HAPPINESS

"These are the things which once possessed
Will make a life that's truly blessed:
A good estate on healthy soil,
Not got by vice, nor yet by toil;
Round a warm fire a pleasant joke,
With chimney ever free from smoke;
A strength entire, a sparkling bowl,
A quiet wife, a quiet soul,
A mind as well as body whole;
Prudent simplicity, constant friends,
A diet which no art commends;
A merry night without much drinking,
A happy thought without much thinking;
Each night by quiet sleep made short;
A will to be but what thou art:
Possessed of these all else defy,
And neither wish nor fear to die." [61]

When Governor Fauquier died in 1768 the Gazette published the following rhyme:

"If ever virtue lost a friend sincere,
If ever sorrow claim'd Virginia's tear,
If ever death a noble conquest made,
'Twas when Fauquier the debt of nature paid."

During the eighteenth century Robert Beverly wrote his "History Of Virginia"; the Reverend William Stith, president of the College, later contributed a more elaborate "History Of Virginia"; William Byrd the Second, conciliar aristocrat, well educated, wrote historical discourse enlight-

272

ening to posterity; and a few kept diaries and wrote correspondence which, in an age of rudimentary printing, were important forms of literary expression.

The plantation was a tiny world in itself—the social microcosm—in which there occurred the multiplicity of problems arising from the complexities of human relationship. Problems of class, race and sex relations; law enforcement, religion and morality; ethical standards or concepts of good and bad, right and wrong, success and failure, reward and punishment—were all there. The thinking aristocrat was in a position to contemplate, and to try to deal with, the problems arising in his tiny social world.

The General Assembly, whose membership turnover was quite large, showed remarkable efficiency and foresight in organizing, controlling and expanding the colony. The legislation was often indicative of a familiarity with, and an attempt to profit from, the experiences of the ancient slave societies, and the laws are generally written in language that is clear and precise. Their Code of 1705—which is among the most important, and draconic, documents in American history—reveals them as well informed on the theory and workings of the feudal society; it laid the foundations for what was later identified as "The Sociology Of The South". Their statutes abound in Latin phraseology. The rules of court procedure were carefully thought out and explained. The Assembly was a medium for the development and expression of the qualities of political leadership, and some of its members' polemics anent secession evince a thorough knowledge of the problems of government. The War of American Secession is the most important single event of colonial history. America was emerging from the anonymity of remoteness and subservience to the identity and dignity of sovereignty—she was reaching for equality with the other countries of the world. The leading figures of Virginia and of the other colonies had the feeling that they were making history: they were taking their first step on the world stage; and they were animated by an excitement and self-consciousness that caused them to put their best foot forward.

But social and political thinking is not as profound as religious thinking: Virginia produced no theologians—and her prevailing atmosphere was not such as to develop a Jonathan Edwards.

Some of the Virginians approached the accepted standards of the complete gentleman. A few attained them: they were as much concerned about values, as they were about valuables; they were fired and illuminated by the masterpieces of the past; and they regarded culture as life—it was never a thing apart. They preferred the aristocracy of mind—virtue, culture, talent—to that of power—blood, wealth, privilege. They therefore attempted to cultivate music and the fine arts—and they devoted their time to reading, philology, philosophical speculation, contacting distinguished contemporaries, matters of state, and experimentation. They were not internationalists, and they disdained popularity; they preferred to appreciate universality—

"The philosopher is the man who is in love with the spectacle of all time and all existence, and that is what delivers him from petty ambitions and low desires".

They had a sense for the intrinsic, and they appreciated it regardless of origin—everything in their lives symbolized the universality of value. They knew that,

"We children of a day imagine our contests are the sole things that move the world. Alack! our fathers thought the same; and they and their turmoils sleep forgotten":

they were fully aware of the underlying universal principles of government and statesmanship; they felt that their political localism emanated from ideals that are profound and eternal; they had no inner doubts about their ability to make a case in reason and justice for their position; and they sensed that their words and acts were of far-reaching significance. Their nature environment encouraged the contemplative life: they loved to go on long solitary walks, and lose themselves in communion with the silent vastness about them; quiet contact with nature has its effects upon human achievement and quality, for "great things are done when men and mountains meet". They were introspective: there was plenty of opportunity for the mind to revert to cherished incidents, which brought forth smiles of satisfaction—and to unpleasant experiences, which caused the ego to well up in bitterness. They were articulate: they are an index to the mind of their time and place, as they reduced the Virginian world view to rational expression; and they were dedicated above all else to the preservation of their way of life. They indulged moderately or not at all, and occasionally played at cards or chess but seldom gambled; were dignified in bearing, refined of speech and polished in society; and they were always responsible in their relations with others. They eschewed the cold haughtiness that is often characteristic of aristocracy: they preferred to be tender to women and children, condescending towards underlings, philanthropic towards the unfortunate, and liberal in politics; but they were not democratic, which is equalitarian. Unused to contradiction and sensitive to the most trivial slight they never participated in combat, physical or oratorical. They walked in the way of the Hellenes: they believed in the rational principle or self-restraint, and they regarded wrath and sensuality as irrational; and it was a matter of honor with them not to lose their temper, although they could be stern when necessary. Everything in their tradition tended towards the abhorrence of violence—and Virginia of the First Secession produced first-rate statesmen, and indifferent generals. They loved the solitude of their plantations and the wilderness about them, and as free-thinkers they preferred to worship God in the open. Their way of life developed leadership qualities, and it was easy for such a person to fall into a position of command as statesman or military officer.

The Virginians were the beneficiaries of—but not contributors to, the body of knowledge that they had inherited from the revival of learning in Europe: colonial Virginia did not produce a culture of her own—quality was exotic. This was due to her historical recency, the struggle to establish herself, absence of cities, and her colonial status. There was insufficient time for the development of a distinct Virginian identity. As a colony she was culturally as well as politically subservient; she constituted the preservation of England's pre-Elizabethan sociology up to Independence. For a long time "home" was Virginia's sole contact with civilization, which enabled her to escape the deteriorating influences of the frontiers.

The Virginians were neither original nor creative in their thinking, and their culture was basically English. Ancient Greece and Rome were an important influence in their life for they followed their English "cousins'" ruling on the superiority of the classics of antiquity, and they stocked their libraries with them; Latin and Greek distinguished the gentleman, and those who attended college at home and abroad studied these languages as required subjects; and the ancient, especially the Roman, influence is apparent in the virtues they emulated, in the busts they had made of themselves, in the pseudonyms of their polemics, in their laws on slavery, and in the authorities they cited in arguing law cases. That they were familiar with the classics is evident from their style of writing, which is often copied from the classicists, especially from Shakespeare. Thus a young lady writes to her girl friend:

"Oh my Marcia how hard is our fate! that we should be deprived of your dear company, when it would compleat our Felecity—but such is the fate of Mortals! We are never permitted to be perfectly happy. I suppose it is all right, else the Supreme Disposer of all things would have not permitted it".

They emphasized form of expression and reveled in the

use of superlatives: "charm of beauty", "brilliancy of wit"; and they loved to affect the air of suffering nobility, which is Shakespearian. This attitude, however, is stilted; they had the language expressive of deep feeling, although there was usually little to apply it to. They felt with sincerity their individual longings and tragedies but, before the troubles that led to Independence, there were no social problems expressive of the sufferings of "the people".

During the eighteenth century the sense of spacial remoteness was strongly embedded in men's minds, and distant places and peoples were regarded with fear and disdain. Europeans thought of America as remote, mysterious and uncivilized. The English aristocrats always had an air of arrogance towards their colonials in America, and they constantly harped on the Virginians' alleged descent from convicts and commoners. Daniel Defoe, in his "Moll Flanders", thus describes the convicts in Virginia:

" 'tis that cursed place (Newgate prison in England) ...that half peoples this colony."

"many a Newgate-bird becomes a great man, and we have... several justices of the peace, officers of the trained bands, and magistrates of the towns they live in, that have been burnt in the hand."

The colonials were disdained as uncultured, and as mentally insufficiently trained to appreciate things sensitive and profound. The Virginians admired and envied the old world for its culture; their intellectual conversation was entirely European, and most of them had a feeling of inferiority towards Europe's upper classes. Thus Robert Beverly, in the preface to his book, is extremely humble and apologetic:

"I am an Indian, and don't pretend to be exact in my language... Truth desires only to be understood, and never affects the Reputation of being finely equipp'd."

But many Virginians resented their "cousins' " disdain, and in the bosoms of the more sensitive ones there rankled the bitterness of the mortally wounded.

The Virginians' Cavalier traditions, together with the mastery, isolation, leisure and indolence of plantation life, resulted in a *weltanschauung* wholly unlike that prevailing in the industrial and farming world; they can be understood only if their values are appreciated. Virginia was dedicated to the perpetuation of feudalism when the world around her was rapidly departing from it; the foreigners who visited her were struck by the contrast, and they wrote much more about her than her native sons.

Colonization is war with nature, and Virginia as a transplanted way of life was a triumph over space, water, wilderness, mountains. As the oldest of the Anglo-American colonies she was the pioneer in empire building, in representative government, in the establishment of total feudalism, in the labor system, in the conquest of the Indians, in the westward movement, and in the liquidation of piracy. She had turned a state of nature into a civilization, and she had survived social rebellion. Her feudal sociology with its world outlook was stabilized and gave her a feeling of uniqueness and self-consciousness. She was always the leading colony in territory, population, wealth and power. Virginia was at one time understood to comprehend almost half the present United States, for her land claims included what are now West Virginia and Kentucky and the area above the Ohio River—now the states of Ohio, Indiana, Illinois, Michigan and Wisconsin— as well as western lands clean through to the Pacific Ocean. In every respect she was far ahead of the other southern colonies: had originally claimed Maryland and North Carolina, been the model and inspiration in their efforts to establish themselves, helped to populate some with her own inhabitants, assisted a few against external foes and internal insurrection, benefited economically from their early dependence, and was traditionally identified as in a paternalistic role towards them. Strong as was the colonies' particularism it was strongest in Virginia. She was none too proud of the fact that England was the progenitor of social dynamism in the modern world, although London was no threat to the colonial status quo. Yet the outer world was taking a different form of social organization, and it was suspected as invasive—she was beginning to develop the feeling that her sociology was on the defensive: she was already under English merchant domination, and her chief rival in western ambitions was industrial Pennsylvania; and she was always in fear that her way of life might be threatened by forces from without. Her relative remoteness from rival imperialist and from aboriginal foes dispensed with the need for assistance from England or cooperation with other colonies; as the leading colony she was characterized by the aloofness that accompanies superiority; and the plantation economy emphasized her isolationist ideology. She regarded political association with other jurisdictions as "foreign entanglements": she was very chary about obligating herself in the slightest to any intercolonial organization; she rejected the proposal for a resident Bishop of the Anglican Church in America because her clergy would come under his jurisdiction, which she considered an invasion of her sovereignty; at first refused to acquiesce in the continental post-office; declined to send a delegate to the Albany Convention in 1754 of the Anglo-American colonies; and was averse to military cooperation to the extent that a law forbade her militia to leave her territory. She was always in closer touch with England than with any of the other colonies. Prior to the ferment that led to secession from the Empire no proposal for continental federation ever came from a Virginian. London was partial to her because she was economically the most valuable of the colonies; her lack of manufactures obviated an important sore spot; her political and church organization most closely resembled that of the mother country; Virginians had more personal ties in the old home than any of the others; and she was a royal colony with relations direct. Of the colonial ruling classes Virginia's was held genuinely aristocratic as it was land based, and she was homogeneously English and Anglican. The Virginians in every way identified themselves with traditionally ascendant groups (Cromwell's interregnum was considered an aberration); and theirs was an attitude of haughtiness and disdain, or—if some inclined to philanthropy and liberalism—of condescension, towards most everyone else in America. The ruling classes of other colonies were not nearly as prosperous, and they largely stemmed from inferior and persecuted groups.

With the development of Anglo-America, however, Virginia was forced into a measure of continental cooperation. As population increased settlements pushed out, distance was gradually reduced and communications improved, which threw people into greater proximity. Itinerant missionaries of various sects crossed boundaries in their attempts to convert the natives and one another, and intercolonial migration arose. Soon provincial newspapers appeared, and the colonies began to show some interest in one another as information on various subjects was exchanged. George Washington and Benjamin Franklin began to acquire a continental reputation.* The northern colonies had to fight French and Indians, and their sacrifices safeguarded those southwards who sometimes helped with money, men or supplies. New England's victory over the French at Louisbourg in 1745 was celebrated throughout Anglo-America. Virginia eventually joined the continental post-office, and a colonial was appointed postmaster-general whom she also recognized. During the wars on the French Virginia had to obey London's orders to cooperate: she participated in the Carthagena expedition, contributed men towards raising the "Royal American Regiment", and was quite active in the attempts on Fort Duquesne. During the wars provincial militia entered one another's territory and

* By 1758 these men were also fairly well known in Europe.

280

mingled. With the organization of land companies the economic interests of colonials began to transcend boundaries. Treaties with Indians were made by Virginia together with the other colonies concerned in the locale, and there were sectional extradition agreements for the return of fugitives. Virginia entered into several agreements with Maryland to regulate the size of the tobacco crop, and she materially assisted South Carolina in her Indian wars.

The colony under the federal political concept meant simply the establishment of another autonomous jurisdiction, while under the national principle in government the colony is subordinated or associated with repression. Anglo-America was originally founded, and it achieved organic integration, in terms of the federal principle. England was the pioneer in economic capitalism and in political nationalism. From the Revolution of 1689 Parliament definitively supplanted the Crown as the governing body of the British Empire: the principles of the Revolution were extended to include Anglo-America; London began to treat the colonies in terms of the national political system, under which they became overseas "possessions"; and this introduced a radical change in the British-colonial connective principle. The responsibilities of imperial power required the introduction of centripetal organization or control from above, and Britons began to think definitely from the political whole to the part. Thus London's unilaterally-imposed change in the connective principle constituted the violation of the colonies' local autonomy—in fact, of most everything fundamental in colonial tradition and life.

With the fall of the French power in America the colonies' western boundary became a vast open domain; London could no longer recognize their local autonomy on frontier problems as this would be handing them imperial power; and Parliament issued the Declaration of 1763, which completely deprived the colonials of freedom in relation to trans-Allegheny lands. But London's attempts to stabilize the colonies in this and other respects could be consummated only through the full application of centripetal organization, which violated local autonomy. Moreover, the practical application of the new way was basically dependent for elucidation upon experience, and the British were themselves not yet quite clear on the exact workings of their altered relations with Anglo-America.

From the Revolution of 1689, certainly from the Hanoverian accession to the British throne in 1715, the colonies began to writhe under London's new dispensation—they were adamant in their interpretation of the Empire as a federal organization or union of autonomous States. The Virginians—who had been removed from England's political changes—had no way of understanding the meaning of nationalism: they suddenly found themselves confronted with a renunciation of the mutual political respect inherent under federalism, and an asserted London supremacy, which they had never hitherto experienced; they were convinced that the abolition of local autonomy would concentrate power in the hands of the central government to the extent of rendering it despotic; and London's new attitude appeared to them as "tyranny". The evolution of British nationalism created the contrast which eventually made the Virginians conscious of their federalism: they maintained that the ancient liberties guaranteed to them in their charters—which were granted by the feudal-minded Stuart kings—were being violated, and they resisted London's nationalism with their traditional, now attenuated, federalism.

The American Revolution of 1776 was a protest against the English Revolution of 1689. The colonials repudiated the authority of Parliament within their jurisdictions: according to the British prime minister, Lord North;

"The language of America is, we are the subjects of the King; with parliament we have nothing to do."

They maintained that Parliament ruled England—it did not rule the Empire. They understood the British Empire as an association of several autonomous jurisdictions under a common Crown, but not under a common legislature: Virginia was a member of this association and its legislature had power exclusively within its own jurisdiction; England was another member, as were Pennsylvania, Canada, Ireland, Barbados, Massachusetts and others, and the power of the legislature of each was purely local and in no way extended within another's jurisdiction. According to James Madison:

"The fundamental principle of the Revolution was, that the Colonies were co-ordinate members with each other and with Great Britain, of an empire united by a common executive sovereign, but not united by any common legislative sovereign. The legislative power was maintained to be as complete in each American Parliament, as in the British Parliament." [62]

The Virginians maintained that their General Assembly's power was a matter of its own dictation and that without its consent no external power had the right to impose mandates concerning western lands, navigation, taxation, manufactures, paper money; to involve them in wars, and to raise and maintain troops or requisition property within their jurisdiction. Their courts affirmed the supremacy of Virginia law, and denied to the statutory and common law of England any force except such as was given it by the explicit act of their legislature. They claimed they had received their grants and charters from the Crown, not from England's legislature or Parliament, and they owed allegiance to the Crown, not to Parliament, because, how could subjects owe allegiance to subjects? Since the colonials regarded the London Parliament as a foreign agency and repudiated its authority they held the reigning king responsible for the invasion of their local autonomy, and they argued that the traditional commitments of the British Crown could not be contravened by succeeding kings. The Virginia Assembly felt it had the same rights against the king as the Parliament in London.

Under her new order Britain could either have recognized the colonials as equals with proportionate representation in Parliament and admission into her aristocracy, or forced them into a subordinate position. If the colonials had to have nationalism they demanded it on the former status, claiming that as British subjects they were entitled to the rights of Englishmen. They alleged no objection to paying money, but denied that a legislature in which they were not represented could tax them. Thus while the principle of an overall legislature was non-existent in their tradition the colonials were willing, although not without misgivings, to accept it. But the British were disinclined to grant equality for traditional reasons, while communications made colonial representation in Parliament impractical. It was held in some powerful places at home that Anglo-America was conquered territory whose inhabitants were on an inferior status:[63] but England's attitude on the whole was not without some consideration; she demanded colonial subordination, yet she expected it to be filial—not servile. The Virginians' very lives symbolized everything Anglo-Saxon: they were intensely traditional, they were pacifistic, and they abhorred rebellion, militarism and war. Yet they couldn't understand that Englishmen had forfeited their traditional rights when they left home to turn a wilderness into a civilization in order to create and to expand the British Empire. They held Anglo-America an extension of England, and declared that Englishmen in either place should regard those in the other as equals and not as objects of exploitation.

The colonial government of the eighteenth century was marked by the bickering resulting from opposing basic approaches to the same problems, which gave each the impression that the other was deliberately obstructive. The royal officials' approach was national and centripetal, or in terms of the Empire as a whole; while the colonials' approach was federal and centrifugal, or in terms of each colony as an end in itself. The colonies regarded the infringement of their local autonomy by the national principle as subjugation. England's political vicissitudes had undermined her prestige as she set the colonies examples in social revolution and disrespect for traditional ways and authority. In the eighteenth century the home country was ruled by people who were ideologically alien to those who before had been in power, and the colonies were required several times to change their allegiance. All this tended to weaken the bonds of attachment to the old country; and the preparations of New England to resist the Stuarts by force and of Virginia and Barbados to do the same against the Commonwealth, had set precedents for colonial revolt.

By 1776 there had already developed a Virginian tradition: time had always been friendly, and hers was a story of consistent quantitative growth; and she had built up a sense of achievement and pride of strength that gave her a feeling of self-confidence. Problems concerning London jurisdiction arose mainly in relation to frontier lands, and to the intricacies of fiscal obligation—about which the resident royal officials could know little, and were helpless, without local cooperation. Her inter-colonial rivalry—especially as in relation to transmontane lands—was sharp, but it was respected as a family affair. The London foreign office was pretty well in the dark on hinterland doings especially as they tapered to detail, and Royal Indian Commissioners had to be sent to the frontiers to take charge.

Virginia's political tradition was particular as in relation to Anglo-America, and federal as in relation to the Empire—she repudiated the London Parliament's authority within her jurisdiction. She regarded the right of jurisdictional withdrawal—of secession, as inherent in the federal type of political association: it seemed the only defense—there was no thought of submission—against the catalytic implications of the imperial principle—revolutionary nationalism's inexorable encroachment on traditional local autonomy; moreover, it was the de jure recognition of a virtual de facto condition—the Virginians had had things pretty well their own way all along. Virginia officially announced her secession from the Empire fully seven weeks before July 4, 1776: this meant revolt against the Crown, as well as repudiation of the Crown's pre-emptive right to land in America; Virginia had set a precedent— she established the tradition of secession in American life.* She was in no position to take it for granted that the rest of the colonies would follow suit. She knew that she would have to stand up militarily to the most powerful imperial entity of the time: yet she felt that it was in the stars for her to go forward—her freedom and expansion were not at bottom matters of military decision; and she took her courage chiefly from her tradition of consistent growth and her practical independence. The War of American Secession involved the three political principles—nationalism, federalism and particularism. The British were for union— on the national principle, or colonial subordination. The colonials were divided—federalists and particularists. The united empire loyalists represented the union cause: they were consistently traditional; they wanted to continue the past, to save the union—on the federal principle. The rebels, as in relation to London, repudiated the principle of union—they wanted particularism, or state sovereignty. Virginia's severance of her Empire links constituted the enunciation of her status as a sovereign political entity, but this was short lived—she accepted the Articles of Confederation and sent delegates to the Continental Congress. This meant the re-acceptance of the federal principle: she could not escape association with the other political jurisdictions in North America, which was bound to bring the hated external complications necessitating compromise; but this time she would be in a leading role.

* This tradition was renounced by President Andrew Jackson a little over a half century later when he said—"Our federal union; it must be preserved."

References
CHAPTER THREE
THE MIND OF COLONIAL VIRGINIA'S ARISTOCRACY

1 Bruce, Social Life, 79, 80.
2 Norwood Young, George Washington: Soul Of The Revolution, 33.
3 Wertenbaker, Pat & Pleb, 58.
4 *Ibid.*, 99.
5 VCSP 1; ix, x.
6 Journal Council Col. Va., 1; 13.
7 Bruce, Social Life, 252.
8 Wertenbaker, Pat & Pleb, 120.
9 J. B. Van Urk, Story Of American Fox Hunting, 1; 32.
10 J. F. D. Smyth, Tour In USA, 1; 66.
11 Fithian, 286.
12 Conway, 27.
13 Stanard, 120.
14 Francis P. Gaines, The Southern Plantation, 181.
15 Conway, 123.
16 Stanard, 185.
17 Lodge, 74.
18 J. C. Spruill—Women's Life & Work In Southern Colonies, p177.
19 Smyth, 1; 41, 2.
20 Conway, 118.
21 Claude Bowers, Jefferson & Hamilton, 93.
22 Kimball, 69.
23 S. H. Gay, James Madison, 12.
24 Spruill, 74.
25 Waddell, 275: Conway, 185.
26 Fithian, 248.
27 Lodge, 83.
28 Fithian, 121.
29 Neill, VC 283, 4.
30 *Ibid.*, 264.
31 Beverly, Bk, 3; 44, 5.
32 Conway, 142, 3.
33 *Ibid.*, 194.
34 *Ibid.*, 75.
35 Trent & Wells, Colonial Prose & Poetry, 3; xiii.
36 Bruce, Social Life, 219, 20.
37 *Ibid.*, 218.
38 Meade, 1; 297.
39 Hugh Jones, 73.
40 Kimball, 149.
41 Hartwell, 14.
42 VCSP 1; 173.
43 Lodge, 72, 3.
44 *Ibid.*, 90.

[45] FT v3, Clayton's Va., 35.
[46] VCSP 1; 260.
[47] Ripley, 122.
[48] I. S. Harrell, Loyalism In Va., 26, 7.
[49] Robert Carter, Letters Of xiii.
[50] Conway, 189, 90.
[51] Lodge, 86.
[52] Neill, VC 169.
[53] George W. Williams, History Negro Race In America, 1; 336.
[54] Glenn-1;41.
[55] HS4;429.
[56] FT v1.
[57] Trent & Wells 2;148.
[58] FT v1.
[59] *Ibid.*, An. Cotton, 11.
[60] Conway, 21-4.
[61] *Ibid.*, 88.
[62] James Madison, Writings, 4; 533, 4.
[63] George Chalmers, History Revolt Of The American Colonies, 1; 413.

CHAPTER FOUR
COLONIAL VIRGINIA'S LABOR BASE
Part One:
GENERAL BACKGROUND

Man is universally and eternally a social animal. During pre-technology the problem of production of wealth—the relation of man to nature—had not yet been solved, and the economy of scarcity was universal: there was a dearth of the goods of life; their acquisition—the need to "make a living"—was the primary pre-occupation of man; and things of economic value constituted the main object of reward. The individual man under civilization had developed the ability to produce more wealth than is necessary for his own preservation: a few men were enabled to appropriate the surplus for themselves; this resulted in the conical or class system of society—men were divided economically into the owning or "rich" class, which was based on the principle of "private property"; and the "poor" or laboring class, which was rendered propertyless by the dearth of wealth. During this era civilized man's social organization, while always vertical, took different forms. Labor was living—human and animal; it was not mechanical. Human labor constituted society's permanent mass base, and it took a different form in each type of social organization. The labor terms "slave", "serf", "peasant", "farmer", are synonymous in an occupational sense, each denoting a laborer in the ground: but each of these terms, to the extent that it describes a peculiar relation—legal, political, economic, social —of the laborer in the ground to the ground, is distinct, in that it points to a given sociology. Thus the labor system was not an isolated phenomenon: it was the foundation of a social superstructure—the heart of the social organism, and it is an index to the particular sociology of the time and place; a change in the form of labor was basic, as it implied a social revolution. No particular labor system was good or evil in itself, or in terms of absolute values—conclusions concerning its quality must be the result of comparative study. The world of pre-technology was ruled by social forces other than labor—the warrior, priest, landowner, trader, each having a social pattern of his own. Man has a natural aversion to labor: labor in all its forms—including "wage", which is dissociated from land—was throughout pre-technology fundamentally forced; it had no human rights; it was universally regarded as economic resources, and it was included as within the meaning of "capital". Labor had no positive practical program, or social pattern, of its own: the concept of the "proletarian" sociology, with its own institutions and values, had to wait on the development of technology; labor never ruled, and the form it took was determined by the particular social force in power. A change in the system of society was introduced with the succession of a given ruling class by a rival class—such as land by capital: this brought with it a change in the labor form as a matter of course; labor as such was passive—it did not lie within the power, or the responsibility, of labor to change the labor system. Thus the absence of proletarian social thought precluded labor from challenging the rule of its masters, and it could not be a social revolutionary force. Labor self-assertiveness, which sometimes did take place and was often explosive, was a protest against the severities of its immediate living and working conditions: labor had the power to bring about a quantitative improvement in its condition—as within the limits of its particular form; but the qualitative change from one form of labor to another— or the overthrow of the entire social super-structure—was not within the power of labor.

Anglo-America was founded during pre-technology: the private-property class-system was the most advanced form of social organization, and it was this form that the founders introduced in the colonies.

America was won for civilization by the laborer with the axe. It was officially held in Virginia that land is valueless without laborers to work it:

"should their intailed slaves be taken in execution and sold . . . their lands would be rendered useless, and they wholly unable to support their families".[1]

The sociology of Cavalier Virginia, which revolved around the plantation economy, was predicated upon a blend of land and labor; their legal status seems to have been reciprocally determined, and the alteration of the legal status of the one carried with it that of the other. Yet the conversion of the abundant forests into arable land, and its fructification, presupposed labor—and it seems that labor maintained a primacy throughout the colonial period. A writing on Virginia of 1697 says:

"their Servants and Slaves (are) the most considerable Part of their Estates";

and three decades later the General Assembly declared,

"the greatest part of the visible estates of the inhabitants of this colony, does generally consist of slaves".

It happened sometimes that entailed lands were docked to enable their alienation for the purpose of buying laborers, but never the other way—and it was upon the sons of the soil and of toil that the existence and expansion of the colony rested.

The labor system in America, like everything else, had to be planned—and it had to be forced. The aboriginal population of the new world was too sparse to furnish a labor base, and this had to be laid through the abduction of natives from other continents—namely, Europe and Africa. Those who came from the British Isles were from the distressed elements of the lower classes, most of whom had never been gainfully employed; the Africans in their native habitat had never been exactly "workingmen"; these people had to be broken from a condition of relative idle freedom to one of constant labor routine; and labor in colonial Virginia was throughout a statutory class—men had to be condemned to labor by law. The colonial labor system consisted fundamentally either of Europeans indentured into temporary slavery, or of non-Caucasians subjected to permanent slavery. Thus colonial labor was always regarded as inherently disaffected, and was suspected of tendencies to disturb social serenity. Wage labor was never sufficient to constitute a social force.

Pre- and post-Restoration Virginia were different worlds: the Puritan sociology was institutionally and ideologically adapted to indentured servitude as a labor system; while the Cavalier sociology—once it had taken root—was thus adjusted to chattel slavery.

The Puritans were the time's social revolutionary force— capital control was rebel victory. When they founded Virginia they intended to organize it according to their way of life, and they tried to establish towns and manufactures. Under the use economy of Puritanism efficiency is a value: wage labor takes the place of forced labor because manufacture requires skill necessitating forethought and care, which cannot be exercised without a promise of reward and presupposes worker education; the worker must concentrate mentally in making an article, and he is handling high-priced and dangerous tools; and there is an introduction of speed-up, which tends to feverishness. Work and play are strictly separated, and the daily hours of work must be limited because the absence of relaxation induces fatigue. In addition, wage labor opposes bondage alleging that it lowers wages. The development of the Puritan economy would have resulted in a society with bourgeois characteristics such as graduated income and wealth; the rise of new classes with conflicting economic interests; and the need for workers possessing skill, whose difficulty to replace gives them value and empowers them to wrest concessions to social rights. The "working class" is a phenomenon of the civilized society: the European was traditionally a working-man, and he continued as such—although under different conditions—when he came to the colony; the free hired status, working for wages—was the height of labor achievement; with the acquisition of skills labor began to win respect as human; all of which was enabled by the rule of capital which European labor preferred. The Puritans intended to introduce England's apprentice system in America: under this system the workers in Virginia were used as field laborers, but they were promised an opportunity to learn a trade—in the days of the Company skilled workers in various trades were sent to the colony under contract to instruct the settlers. The inescapable recessiveness of a colony, however, frustrated immediate plans, and apprenticeship sank to "indentured servitude"—a form of bondage, which was established by statute and created a "master-servant" relationship. Thus the Puritans introduced the system of white bondage, which formed Virginia's labor base up to nearly the end of her first century—during which time her laborers were referred to as "servants". Indentured servitude was a temporary condition: the servant of pre-Restoration Virginia felt himself needed, and he developed a sense of belonging in the Puritan world; and there was a legitimate place for him within the social framework, as he was eventually absorbed into the commonalty freeman class.

The Puritans never thought of chattel slavery in relation to their labor system. There is no chattel slavery in the English common law. The Anglo-Saxon people had no tradition in chattel slavery—both as labor system and as traffic; the colony founders had had their origin in an atmosphere of class, but not of race, consciousness; their mind was a *tabula rasa* concerning slavery in general, and Negro slavery —with its social complications—in particular. The few Africans and Indians who were brought into the colony before 1660 were thought of as labor, not as race; they were not considered as in a special category, and they were bought on the same basis as European labor. Yet the imported non-Caucasian failed as a temporary bondsman, because his primitive values rendered him unfit for a place as freeman within the civilized society. The Puritans did not make chattel slavery their labor system fundamentally because it was out of place in their social order. There was always a moral revulsion under Christianity to the enslavement of fellow Christians: this found its most extreme expression in the Puritans, who had great reverence for the Mosaic law—under which coerced labor for those of one's own nativity is limited to seven years. Moreover, the founders were in great fear for the preservation of their civilized values, and they had to confine themselves to European labor as they couldn't risk the introduction of a primitive force in their midst. Thus non-civilized labor was insufficient to constitute a distinct social force, and pre-Restoration Virginia was ideologically monolithic—it had no group of people that could be regarded as outside the framework of civilization.

When the Cavaliers came to power in 1660 they found Virginia's social organization—and its labor system, alien to their way of life. Their sociology was total feudalism, which is inherently static—everything is rooted: there is no place within it for the free landless individual; and the status in relation to the land, of labor especially, must be stratified. The existence of a class of people whose status is temporary and changing was feared for its socially disturbing implications. Under the feudal agricultural economy the skilled worker is a small minority, and efficiency is not a primary value: there is a relative absence of a sense of time, and therefore no rationalization of labor; the worker usually goes about his tasks with a certain amount of leisure, there is no strict separation between work and play, and no limit is necessary on the daily hours of work. The Cavalier sociology was institutionally and ideologically adapted to chattel slavery, which is static, as a labor system: and the new masters therefore immediately and systematically proceeded to transform the status quo ante, and to lay the labor base necessary for their erection as a feudal proprietary class. The laboring masses throughout the world were held to their condition by tradition, but there was no tradition in America. Legislation therefore had to be relied upon: the Fourth Revision of the Virginia Code in 1662 made chattel slavery a statutory law, and drew up a slave code; the Cavaliers were the first to introduce human slavery as a basic social institution under Christianity. Yet they too were averse to the imposition of slavery on their own race and religion: the European lower classes were regarded as largely rebellious towards the rule of land, and it was feared that they would be the same way in America especially if they were subjected to the hopelessness of chattel slavery; while by the seventeenth century the civilized world had had over a century of experience in ocean navigation, which put other continents within practical reach. It was therefore thought that the stratification of the labor class in Virginia could best be achieved by imposing the legal category of slavery on persons who are differentiated from the masters by an obvious, ineradicable mark—such as the biological mark of color. This introduced a new principle in the life of Virginia, and a new mental attitude on the part of the European towards the African: it created a race problem—labor was to be rooted in its place by both the law of nations and the law of nature. But the change had to be gradual: the Cavaliers' substitution of primitive for European labor presupposed a sense of permanence and stability concerning the cause of civilization in America, as well as of their control of the colony—which they at first did not have; the freshly imported African was barbaric and balky, and the docility of labor could be expected only with the preponderance of slave-born generations; the slaves were evidently a small minority during Bacon's Rebellion as there is no mention of labor trouble despite the derangement of authority; and the importation of Africans did not begin in earnest until the Cavaliers were sure of their control. Thus there had to be a transition period, during which the new masters had to rely on civilized labor: they took over and continued the prevailing labor system—indentured servitude, which they found well organized and established; and from the Cavaliers labor in Virginia took on a dual form. But white servitude was always out of place under feudalism; with time it began relatively giving way to chattel slavery, and by the eighteenth century use of the word "slave" had become general.

Chattel slavery came to be based on the principle of the racially unassimilable individual such as the African, with the fundamental objection to it being the permanent threat to the civilized way of life. Indentured servitude comprised the assimilable and therefore freeable individual with the fundamental objection here, however, being that discharge meant the rise of a class of freemen which could ultimately become a menace to the feudal way of life. Land feared capital, above all else—as social revolutionary: the man of civilized values, whether native or acquired, was really the menace to the Cavalier way of life; civilized labor was identified with capital—during the Rebellion the servants almost all supported the rebel cause. The Cavaliers evidently had more confidence in their ability to overcome the enemies of civilization than those of feudalism: of the two types of labor they needed and preferred the first, and their descendants consistently held to it.

European servitude had to precede primitive slavery as a labor base. The civilized way of life had first to become rooted in America: home labor was easier to procure; it was a local problem, while African labor—especially in view of imperial rivalries—was an international problem presupposing complex organization and huge investments. Thus up to 1660 Virginia's labor traffic was based entirely on Europe, after which it began to be based primarily on Africa. In Europe abduction was considered illegal and immoral: her economic stability would have been disrupted by a constant drain on her reserves of common labor; and although the man hunters could to quite an extent operate clandestinely, the servant traffic could never achieve the sufficiency and reliability that the labor-hungry colonials had to have. In Africa, however, there was no native force that could stand in the way of abduction, while the European governments sanctioned the traffic in Negroes. The slave traffic to America started by supplying Spain's colonies, but because of her subjugation of the American natives the commerce was relatively small. But when the Cavaliers made chattel slavery their labor system they laid the foundations for the transformation of the slave traffic into an organized business which built up international ramifications, and lasted two centuries. There was also a domestic labor source which consisted chiefly of the natural increase of the slaves, to some extent the Indians, emigrants from other colonies, and the children of the indigent class within the jurisdiction. Batches of women had been shipped to the colony in the early days to be "bought"[2] by the colonists, in order to lay the base for the creation of a domestic labor supply.[3] Thus the three world ethnic groups—Caucasian, Mongolian and Ethiopian—were all represented among the slaves in Virginia.

Part Two:
INDENTURED SERVITUDE

Virginia's white laboring people came and were brought over under two categories: voluntary servants under contract; and coerced or "spirited" involuntary servants indentured by the "custom of the country". There was a qualitative difference in the status of these two categories. The voluntary servants consisted of skilled workers who bound themselves out to a master, usually for from three to five years: some were fairly literate, and the papers of agreement—which seem like a contract, rather than strictly indenture—were drawn up at the place of origin; they entered the country as prospective freemen, and they enjoyed a privileged labor status throughout the history of the colony. But Virginia's agricultural economy—especially from 1660 —required overwhelmingly the brute laborer or "those that worke in the ground", and they were brought over as coerced or involuntary servants indentured by the "custom".

The British Isles during the seventeenth century were an almost inexhaustible source for indentured servants. England was in the throes of social change, a condition of instability prevailed, the nether elements of the population got the worst effects of the transition, and there were many more unemployed than jobs. Said the Reverend Patrick Copland in a sermon delivered in London in 1622:

"For I have heard many of the painfullest labourers of your Cittie, euen with teares, bemoane the desolate estate of their poore wiues and children, who, though they rise early, taw and teare their flesh all day long with hard labour, and goe late to bed, and feed almost all the week long vpon browne bread and cheese, yet are scarce able to put bread in their mouthes at the week's end, and cloathes on their backes at the yeare's end; and all because worke is so hard to come by".[1]

It is declared that in England alone in 1688,

"over one million persons, nearly a fifth of the whole nation, were in occasional receipt of alms, mostly in the form of public relief paid by the parish." [2]

People were in a constant state of protest, as they had to resort to anti-social acts—crime, vice, beggary—in order to live; and, since about three hundred offenses were capital, it seems that a policy of physical extermination of the labor surplus was deliberately being followed.

Transportation to the colonies—sometimes described as "assisted emigration"—introduced the principle of mass emigration, which alleviated England's unemployment problem and contributed importantly towards solving her chronic social-revolutionary condition. With time the word "transportation" acquired a secondary meaning, and colonial bondsmen were sometimes referred to as "transports". These people were at first enticed with lies; they were required to pay the regular apprenticeship fee on the promise to be taught a trade in Virginia, which was declared to be only a few hours sail from England. But that this was fraudulent soon became common knowledge. All the colonies had to be supplied, and with volunteers too few coercion was resorted to. Paupers on the parish charity rolls; vagabonds, beggars and waifs in the streets and alleys of England's cities; men and women criminals of whom many would have hung; all were herded together, sold to the slave traders and packed away to the colonies. Ballagh declares that:

"In 1661 . . . power was given to Justices of the Peace to transport felons, beggars and disorderly persons." [3]

As the opposing forces in the social commotions and civil wars which agitated the British Isles alternated in possession of power they sold many of their political, religious and war prisoners to the colonies as servants. Says Ballagh:

"Of the Scotch prisoners taken at the battle of Worcester sixteen hundred and ten were sent to Virginia in 1651. Two years later a hundred Irish Tories were sent, and in 1685 a number of the followers of Monmouth that had escaped the cruelties of Jeffries. Many of the Scotch prisoners of Dunbar and the rebels of 1666 were sent to New England and the other plantations." [4]

Roundheads after the Restoration and prisoners taken in foreign wars suffered a like fate. But the method that yielded best results was kidnaping. Bands of body-snatchers roamed the English cities, London and Bristol especially, and "spirited" away whomever they could lay their hands on. They used violence on many, while others were victimized with lies and liquor. Boys and girls in their teens, who were commonly referred to as "kids", were especially desirable because they fetched higher prices. In 1680 the Virginia Council declared:

"all English children imported be tithable at fourteen years of age and no sooner."

It is said that minors who were heirs to property were thus disposed of by interested parties.[5] Of the "considerably more than 100,000 persons (who) migrated to" Virginia during the seventeenth century, from one thousand to sixteen hundred came annually as servants. The Secretary of the colony wrote, in 1635:

"of hundreds of people who arrived in the colony, scarce any but are brought in as merchandise, to make sale." [6]

The traffic was sufficiently notorious to influence the literature of the period. The lower classes were in constant panic of the "spirits". John Hammond in his "Leah And Rachel", published around 1655, describes an incident in England:

"The other day, I saw a man heavily loaden with a

burden of Faggots on his back, crying, Dry Faggots, dry Faggots; he travailed much ground, bawled frequently, and sweat with his burthen: but I saw none buy any, neer three houres I followed him, in which time he rested, I entered into discourse with him, offered him drink, which he thankfully accepted of (as desirous to learn the mistery of his trade) I enquired what he got by each burden when sold? he answered me three pence: I further asked him what he usually got a day? he replied, some dayes nothing some dayes six pence; some time more, but seldom; me thought it was a pittiful life, and I admired how he could live on it; and yet it were dangerous to advise these wretches to better their conditions by travaile, for fear of the cry of, a spirit, a spirit." [7]

There were mass riots in London against the authorities' alleged collusion with the man hunters.

"The ladies of the court, and even the mayor of Bristol, were not beneath the suspicion of profiting by this lucrative business." [8]

This fear persisted into the next century. Wrote Hugh Jones in 1724:

"the common People here (England) have . . . such despicable Notions of Virginia, &c. and are under such dreadful Apprehensions of the imaginery Slavery of the Plantations".[9]

The overwhelming bulk of Virginia's white laborers were of the coerced and "spirited" class who, on arrival, were placed on auction blocks and sold to the highest bidder. They were without contracts previously drawn up, and the Virginia government cooperated with the man hunters by officially regulating the status of people so imported as "the custom of the country". Had a "spirited" servant escaped to England there was no law under which he could have been held, and he would have had a case in law against his abductors.

During the eighteenth century the servant traffic was

better organized. Civil disorders in England had subsided, and there were fewer prisoners of war to sell; the British ruling classes began to object to the draining of their labor markets of surplus laborers; and kidnaping was declining. But the traffic in felons increased. Says Ballagh:

> "in... 1717 Parliament passed a statute over the most vigorous protests from the Virginia merchants in London, making the American colonies practically a reformatory and a dumping-ground for the felons of England. In 1766 the benefits of this act were extended to include Scotland ... and in 1768 the more speedy transportation of felons was ordered." [10]

The purchase of convicts in Virginia was tax free so as to encourage their sale.

British agents negotiated with the petty princelings of the war-torn Palatinate and Switzerland for the transportation of their convicts and surplus serfs. Companies were organized, fake advertising was resorted to, and shiploads of these people—who were generally called "boors"—and of Huguenots, were sent to the colonies. Says Ballagh:

> "dealing in servants had become a very profitable business. The London merchants were not slow to see the advantages of such a trade; a servant might be transported at a cost of from £6 to £8 and sold at from £40 to £60, and a systematic speculation in servants was begun both in England and in Virginia. Regular agencies were established, and servants might be had by any one who wished to import them." [11]

Their passage across the ocean was regarded as the shipment of goods, and there was no privacy. Knittle writes about a trip of Palatines to America in 1710 which lasted six months, and says:

> "Probably because of the low transportation rate, the people were closely packed in the ships. Many of them suffered from the foul odor and vermin; some below deck could neither get fresh air nor see

the light of day."

"Crowded in these foul holds with little or no provision for the most elementary sanitation, the immigrants were decimated by this dread disease
(typhus)." [12]

Servants shipped on consignment, who were generally
skilled workers—and those sent to stock the frontier lands
granted to European nobles, fared best of all when they
reached their destination. But ordinary laborers had no
choice of master and occupation: the usual method was for
a ship captain to buy a load of servants, transport them to
America and vend them along the coast for whatever they
brought, which broke up families. In the bargaining and
on the auction block the servants were weighed, felt, tested,
and they were happy to be bought as this meant delivery
from the ship. One of the voluntary servants wrote in
1773 about the,

"Soul drivers. they are men who make it their business to go on board all ships who have in either
Servants or Convicts and buy sometimes the whole
and sometimes a parcell of them as they can agree,
and then they drive them through the Country like
a parcell of Sheep untill they can sell them to
advantage".[13]

Servants were also obtained from within Virginia. For
a while debtors were condemned to servitude, and army
deserters were reduced to the same status for a period of
five years. But the chief source of native servants was
the legal category of "bastardy". The white or mulatto
child of parents not married in the Established Church was
held a bastard. These, together with indigent orphans, were
indentured to the parish up to their thirtieth year. It was
a practice to kidnap the mulattoes at the end of their terms
and sell them into slavery.

The area in the Shenandoah valley which was settled by
Scotch-Irish and German frontiersmen during the early
eighteenth century was granted by the Virginia General

Assembly in 1736 as a proprietary estate to the aristocrat Robert Beverly. This reduced most of the settlers to the legal status of "tenants," under which they were in a relation of serfdom to the proprietor.

Up to the introduction of private property in 1619 the Virginia Company alone owned servants. With the establishment of the government, and the dissolution of the Company in 1624, the great majority of the servants became the property of private owners, and a few were owned by the parishes. While differences in the time of servitude of the "spirited" were based on their age its duration was generally the Mosaic seven years: convicts were indentured for from seven to fourteen years, and were the cheapest labor obtainable; there was no legal indenture for life in Virginia at any time.

The freemen could always be held liable in their relations with servants either to the government or to the master and, eventually, to the servant himself. The master's right to service was based upon his payment of the servant's transportation to the colony, as well as providing him with the essentials of life. The master was to use his servant humanely, place no undue burdens upon him, and provide for him properly. The servant's duties to his master were to obey his orders, work faithfully for him, protect his property, and refrain from incontinence and absconding. On the servant's discharge the master was required by law to provide him "freedom dues," which generally consisted of two bushels of Indian corn, thirty shillings (in 1748 increased to £3.10s) in money or goods, and a musket worth at least twenty shillings. The freedom dues were forfeited if the servant misbehaved.

In law the servant was a legal being in contractual relationship with a master to whom he had bound out his service—not his person, and thus was not property; his term of servitude was limited and he could be manumitted;

while he could not hold public office or vote he had civil rights, could make a contract, own personal property, bring suit, act as a witness and serve in the militia; the master could punish him only within limits; and he had the right to protest against improper board and treatment. De facto, however, the servants were slaves, and while the individuals changed the class remained. Their status de jure was ignored; they had no legal being in the community, and they deteriorated to the condition of personal property. They lost their civil rights under the English common law, and were not permitted to correspond with anyone outside the colony; and they were treated as things, not persons. As personalty they were bought, sold, exchanged, auctioned, loaned, hired out, stolen, given away as gifts, used as security on loans, paid or seized for debts, considered assets in the bankruptcy and liquidation of estates, bequeathed in wills. During the seventeenth century they constituted the most valuable item of taxation. Their right to make a contract was ignored and they couldn't own property, trade or marry, and they were not trusted with arms and didn't serve in the militia. In religion they were chiefly Nonconformist; under the Puritans readers were required to "catechise children and servants," but when the Cavaliers rendered Separatism illegal in Virginia the servants were deprived of religious rights and of the opportunity to worship. The laws for their protection were hardly better than those for horses, and under the fugitive servant act it was not murder to kill them. Says Bruce:

> "the labor of slaves ... was cheaper than the labor
> of indented white servants, although the latter class
> of persons stood upon the same footing as the former
> as long as their terms continued." [14]

Law and fact, however, coincided in penalizing sex relations between servants, although this hardship was gradually mitigated for the men with the increase of black females.

England's colonies always had enough capital with which to acquire and employ the best agricultural equipment of the age: animals—horses, oxen—not men, pulled the plow; and horses were never hitched to the plow by the tail (which was the case in some parts of the world at the time). Most of the people that were sent to the colonies for indenture had never been strictly wage earners. Their life potential at home was very low, and they were in a debilitated condition at the time of their impressment—this was aggravated during transportation, and in 1636 it was said in the colony that diseased immigrants brought and spread epidemics. They were not used to laboring—and the strenuous labor they were put to, together with the change of climate, caused great mortality among them. Virginia's first century, whose energies were concentrated chiefly on the attempt to take root, is the period of feverish labor—of which indentured servitude had to bear the brunt. The foundation of colonization is reclamation: in pre-technology this was based on the axe; it was the most back-breaking and dangerous task of all, for in removing the trees and brush a dust was scattered through the atmosphere that was fatal to vast proportions of the workers as well as to some of the masters. There is a difference in reclamation between the initial area for settlement, and subsequent additions for expansion: feverishness in the clearing of forests for arable had its peak in the founding days, when the Company had full charge and allowed little other activity until 1619; and at the time of the Restoration—which seems like a second founding—when the Cavaliers immediately pushed westwards and converted the best part of tidewater into vast proprietary estates. This renders understandable the awful mortality of the early days, as well as Governor Berkeley's statement in 1671 that more than eighty percent of Virginia's white laborers died within a year of their arrival. Pioneering has its implications: the Puritan could be unconscionably exacting, and the Cavalier could be disdainfully indifferent—but the basic trouble was inherent; America had to be won for civilization; reclamation was excruciating, labor discipline had to be severe, and the bondsmen were in a physically inferior condition—the colony sank its roots in the flesh, and the blood, and the bone, of labor.

Although indentured labor was on the whole very profitable, it had many drawbacks. The importation of labor was based on the master's investment: the organization and transportation of a shipload of laborers took about six months, during which time they had to be quartered and fed without producing; on arrival in the colony many of them crumbled up within a year, and the master got months rather than years of service from most of his laborers. This made indentured servitude expensive: the servant traffic was none too reliable, the moral and legal opposition to impressment could be a practical obstacle, and there was no certainty and fixity of labor supply; while the breaking-in process—the abrupt change from a condition of idle freedom to one of forced arduous labor, and acclimation—had constantly to be repeated. They were not as well adapted to labor under the hot sun as the Negroes, and the discharge of surviving servants meant the rise of a new class that did not clearly fit into the feudal framework.

In addition to this, the servants gave plenty of trouble. The ordinary tendencies to anti-social behavior, especially in view of their background at home, no doubt did exist among them—and their instances of aberration in the colony cannot entirely be traced to disaffection with their status. Running away was a serious problem:

> "servants ... would run away in 'troops,' enticing the negro slaves to go with them ... under the liberty given them on the plantations, and with an accessible back country, it was not a difficult matter to accomplish."

This was especially serious at harvest time, since laborers were so scarce that their flight often consigned large quan-

307

THE SOCIOLOGY OF COLONIAL VIRGINIA

tities of unharvested crops to ruin. Moreover, the runaways usually took with them a good deal of the master's goods. Punishment for absconding was doubling the time of servitude plus restitution in labor time of the expense incurred in their capture, and lashes on the bare back. From 1660 the act of a white servant inciting slaves to abscond became a grave offense; in addition to extending his indentures the servant had to make good, with an extra two years of labor time, the slaveowner's loss of the absconded Negroes' services since the slave, as a property for life, could not be punished by extension of labor time. For the second offense the servant had the letter "R" branded in his cheek and was shackled on one leg, and if he turned out to be a hopeless case he could be executed. The servant who laid violent hands on his master or overseer had two years added to his term. Various other infractions were also punished by extending the period of servitude. The servants were so situated that they always had easy access to their master's goods, and they were often guilty of stealing. Thus freemen were penalized for buying merchandise from, or selling—especially liquor—to, servants, without their master's consent, as this encouraged them to steal.

Another serious trouble from servants was sexual incontinence. Sex contact between them was made unlawful because it was much cheaper to buy them, and since their marriage would hamper free disposal of them as property it was predicated upon their owners' consent. If a free person married a servant without the master's consent he had to pay a fine or make good in labor time. No court in Virginia had the power to grant a divorce; and when servants married clandestinely the woman's term was doubled, the man's had one year added and the minister who performed the ceremony was punished. But the chief source of trouble was from promiscuous sex contact. To quote Bruce: "many of this class of women were exposed to improper advances on their masters' part as they were, by their situation, very much in the power of these masters, who, if inclined to licentiousness, would not be slow to use it. In the corn and tobacco fields, and in the barns, the female agricultural servants of English birth were also thrown into a very close and promiscuous association with the lowest class of men to be found in the Colony, and the opportunities thus constantly arising, no doubt, led to frequent immoralities; and the same was true of the social intercourse after hours of labor for the day were over; and also during the various holidays, including Sundays, which the servants and slaves enjoyed."[15]

When a servant became pregnant she was for some time disabled from laboring; not owning her own time and labor there was no way for her to bring up the child; and she might be chronically weakened or die in childbirth — all of which was to the master's debit. The child had to be taken from its mother, but since Christianity does not permit exposure (which was the case in ancient Greece) the parish took responsibility for its care. With time the problem became increasingly burdensome, and stringent measures were adopted to keep servants from sex contact. Says Bruce:

"If a woman gave birth to a bastard, the sheriff . . . was required to arrest her, and whip her on the bare back until the blood came. Being turned over to her master, she was compelled to pay two thousand pounds of tobacco, or remain in his employment two years after the termination of her indentures." [16]

The mother could avoid the whipping if she was willing to serve another six months. In 1662, however, the Assembly found it necessary to enact the following legislation:

"Whereas by act of Assembly every woman servant haveing a bastard is to serve two yeares, and late experiente shew that some dissolute masters

have gotten their maides with child, and yet claime
the benefitt of their service, and on the contrary
if a woman gott with child by her master should
be freed from that service it might probably induce
such loose persons to lay all their bastards to their
masters; it is . . . enacted . . . that each woman
servant gott with child by her master shall after
her time by indenture or custome is expired be by
the churchwardens of the parish where she lived
when she was brought to bed of such bastard, sold
for two years, and the tobacco to be imployed by
the vestry for the use of the parish." [17]

If the master wanted the extra two and a half years of
the woman's service he had to turn over 2500 pounds
of tobacco to the parish for the child's care. If the father
of the bastard was an unrelated freeman he had to
reimburse the parish in money, kind or labor; and if
he was a servant he had to indemnify the parish after
his discharge in labor time. All bastards were indentured
to the parish until their thirtieth year; and the offspring
of such bastards, if non-Caucasian, also had to serve the
same period. Punishment for the mother was much more
certain and severe if her infant was a mulatto. An act
of 1691 declared:

"if any English woman being free shall have a
bastard child by any negro or mulatto, she pay the
sume of fifteen pounds sterling . . . and in default
of such payment she shall be taken into the possession of the Church wardens and disposed of
for five years . . . and that such bastard child be
bound out as a servant . . . untill . . . the age of
thirty yeares, and in case such English woman
that shall have such bastard child be a servant, she
shall be sold by the said church wardens, (after
her time is expired . . .) for five yeares". [18]

In order to escape punishment many pregnant women committed abortions on themselves with improvised field instruments, some gave birth in secret and abandoned or killed their infants, and a number of women were tried for infanticide of whom some were hanged.[19] The law was much more severe on women than on men servants for sexual incontinence. Medical doctors were scarce and their fees generally exceeded the value of a servant.[20] A crime against the master was considered a crime against the community, and since the state was controlled by the masters the servants could be punished by both. Minor servant offenses were to be corrected by the masters, while the more serious ones were tried in the county courts. Their crime and punishment show resentment against subjection to the condition of forced labor. Thus their punishment was always with a view to humiliation, or the breaking of the ego; and it included lashes, which varied in number with the offense; shackling, standing in the stocks or pillory, lying in bolts and tying neck and heels, and "breaking them on the wheel";[21] mutilation—such as branding, and cutting off the ears; and whipping while being led to the gallows. In 1630 a servant was sentenced to be "drawn and hanged".[22]

The indentured servants in Virginia were held in contempt: by the Puritans, allegedly because they didn't want to work; and by the Cavaliers, who regarded labor as congenitally ignorant, vulgar, brutal. They lived under the rule of the lash—"well laid on". They couldn't pay fines, and they had to expiate their ordinary infractions of the many restrictions imposed upon them with "blood, sweat and tears" at "the publick whipping-post". The sheriff's fee for whipping a servant was twenty pounds of tobacco, which had to be made good by the victim in labor time. Their abusive treatment became widespread, and caused a contemporary to write:

"Negroes being a property for life, the death of slaves, in the prime of youth or strength, is a material loss to the proprietor; they are therefore, almost in every instance, under more comfortable circumstances than the miserable European." [23]

When the Cavaliers came to power they showed some uneasiness concerning the coercion into labor of Europeans many of whom had a tradition as rebels—they were especially in fear of Oliverian servants because of the conspiracy of 1663. With the introduction and growth of African slavery the Europeans began to develop a consciousness of values and race—the behavior patterns of Virginia's white labor were civilized, while those of black labor were primitive. The European servant and the African slave were on about the same footing in terms of class—but ideologically and racially, which were much stronger motivations, the servant had an affinity with the master: this became the foundation for divisive tendencies among the laborers which, being deliberately encouraged from above, precluded them from achieving unity of purpose; and European labor began to feel itself on a preferred status. In the Fourth Revision the Assembly declared:

"the barbarous usuage of some servants by cruell masters bring so much scandall and infamy to the country in generall that people who would willingly adventure themselves hither are through feare thereof diverted, and by that meanes the supplies of particuler men and the well seating of his majesties country (are) very much obstructed".[24]

Ship captains were required to improve the conditions for servants in passage: those brought in for "the custom" were given a chance to prove that their indentures had been previously drawn up; and masters were forbidden to appropriate goods brought by or sent to their servants, which was recognition of the latter's right to own personal property. As the colony moved towards a solid foundation and began to flourish the lot of the servants showed consistent improvement: laboring became more normal, as feverishness and driving subsided; more labor—both human and animal—and more implements, were used to clear smaller tracts over longer time periods; they were required to work from sunrise to sunset, but they were allowed several hours intermission in the summer to escape the midday heat. Permission from the court was required to whip them on the bare back, which punishment could be averted if the master was willing to pay a fine and take it out of the servant's time; the county courts, which were empowered to draw up and impose indentures, prevented masters from taking advantage of their servants in the renewal of indentures as this required judicial validation; sick and disabled servants could be provided for by the parish until recovery, when they had to make good in labor time; and the whispering attending the surreptitious burial of deceased servants became notorious enough to elicit a law commanding their public interment.[25] Laws had to be passed against the manumission of disabled servants by masters who sought to evade responsibility for their care, and, conversely, the bent of some masters towards leniency is evidenced by a law fining them for remissness in correcting their servants. As early as 1660 a discharged servant brought suit to recover his freedom dues. The Code of 1705 gave servants the right to complain to the county court against their masters' abuse "without the formal process of an action"; if the abuse continued the servant could be sold for his remaining period by the sheriff to another master; but if the court held with the master then the expense of court proceedings was added to the servant's labor time so as to discourage unjust servant complaints. All servants, except "popish recusant convicts",[26] were permitted to testify in court. In 1748 the punishment for unmarried mothers of two years additional labor time was reduced to one year; it was enacted that indigent orphans and the bastards of all non-slave women be indentured to twenty-one years

of age if male, and to eighteen years of age if female—
after which they were to be free; and "no servant shall
receive more than forty lashes at one time", which was
subsequently changed to one lash on the bare back for
each five shillings fine. Penalties were provided for the
selling of white Christians into slavery, and it became
illegal for non-Christian whites to own European servants.
The freedom dues for the voluntary servants were enumerated in the articles of agreement or contract, while
the involuntary servants were presumably provided for
under "the custom" until the Code made their freedom
dues legally incumbent. In 1713 the Assembly permitted
each servant to own one horse, if the master gave written
consent.

The indentured servants were generally dissatisfied with
their condition: in the old country their adjustment to
and protest against adversity had taken the form of mass
crime, vice, beggary; but this did not happen in the colony,
and the protest of disaffection had to find other outlets.
The labor protest was without a positive practical program
as within the civilized community: labor as a class could
not escape its indentured status as it could not be a social
revolutionary force—it had what to move from, but not
what to move towards. The servants had the choice of
remaining and trying to improve their lot within the
jurisdiction, both as a class and as individuals—or of
flight: they could hope to recross the ocean back to their
condition in England; or go westwards where they could
settle on the frontiers under conditions intermediary between the civilization of Virginia and the primitivism
of the Indian tribe; or they could settle to and become
absorbed in aboriginal life.
    Some condemned felons slated for servitude are said
to have preferred execution.[27] A servant in Virginia wrote
about his fellows in 1623, saying:

"Oh that they were in England, without their limbs,
. . . though they begged from door to door".[28]
But the intention to go back "home" could never be more
than a dream—the settlement was tightly sealed against
escape. Virginia has many rivers, and all incoming and
outgoing vessels were carefully watched. The person anxious to get away might be a servant, or a debtor, or a
political malcontent seeking outside help. Shipmasters were
forbidden to take anyone out of the jurisdiction without
a Secretarial pass, on the penalty of assuming the runaway's obligations. There was also great fear, especially
during the colony's first century, that disaffected elements
would be armed and comforted by confederates on incoming ships. Lawful departure required the posting of a
bond of £2000 sterling with the Secretary of the colony,
and giving sufficient advance notice so that the person's
intended leaving could be published in the parish church.

But Virginia's ever-present frontiers were wide open,
and they couldn't effectively be sealed against escape. The
servants' chief protest against their condition took the
form of absconding: large numbers of them fled towards
the wilderness; and their apprehension, punishment and
return was the state's responsibility. County inhabitants
and ordinary keepers were required to report all strangers,
and they were rewarded for helping in the arrest of runaways. Servants off their master's plantation had to have
permits, travelers in the colony had to carry papers of
identification not to be taken for fugitives, and arrangements were made with neighboring Indians and colonies
for the apprehension and return of escaped servants.
Many of them, however, made good their flight especially
towards the frontiers of North Carolina. A few whites
were seen by fur traders living among the Indians—but
the vast majority of the escaped servants settled on the
frontiers, and they became "frontiersmen". The frontiersman brought with him a state of mind—the values of

civilization: the African, like the Indian, preferred to adjust himself to nature—but the European intended to adjust nature to himself; the dead weight of the primordial atmosphere could have made it the path of least resistance for him to go native — but he did not change his mind, and he never severed his ideological ties with the European settlements; although he was severely tried he tenaciously held to his civilized values, and he eventually had his way.

There was never a general servant uprising in the colony —there are no indications of labor trouble during the derangement brought on by the Indian massacres and Bacon's Rebellion. The servants' lack of a positive practical program; their hope that they could improve their lot as a class and as individuals as within the social status quo; as well as the opportunity for flight—constituted the safety valves that averted a general explosion. Flight to the frontiers meant the permanent substitution of freedom in the wilderness for bondage under the civilized way of life, and the great majority of the servants preferred to make the best of their status under civilization. Some servants managed to hide their identity by removing to another county, and there were attempts to counterfeit "freedom papers". There were also numerous individual acts by servants of sabotage and arson against the master's property, and of assault and murder on their overseers and masters. It is declared that:

"A dangerous conspiracy among servants (was) discovered Oct. 13, 1640." [29]

"There seems to have been a seditious feeling in York (county) in 1661".[29]

"The indentured white servants, the refuse of the camps of the late civil war, and the alleys of London . . . were now so numerous as to be a constant source of anxiety to the planters. In Gloucester County there appears (1663) to have been a combination for a general uprising, which failed by one

Birkenhead, a servant . . . becoming an informer." [30]
"many evill disposed servants in these late tymes
of horrid rebellion taking advantage of the loosness
and liberty of the tymes, did depart from their
service, and followed the rebbels in rebellion".[31]
"following . . . the Rebellion of 1676, there was im-
minent danger of an open insurrection on the part
of the servants." [32]

During Bacon's Rebellion both sides were anxious for man
power, and they made a bid for servant support. But the
arming of an enslaved class is tantamount to its emancipation, and the servants who became soldiers had to be
promised their freedom. The overwhelming number of
the servant soldiers, however, were on the losing side,
and the victors punished them as runaways; they had to
make restitution in labor time to their masters for services
lost and goods plundered. In 1729 an allowance of £300
sterling was granted by the Assembly to Thomas Lee,

" 'towards lessening the loss of his dwelling house,
outhouses and goods' which had been burned by
transported felons".[33]

The following year the Assembly declared:

"divers wicked . . . persons, intending the ruin and
impoverishing of his majesty's good subjects, have
. . . secretly, in the night time, and at other
times, frequently practised . . . unlawful and wicked
courses, in burning tobacco-houses, warehouses,
storehouses, and houses and places where . . . grain
is kept".[34]

In order to guard against revolt servants were prohibited
to gather in groups, and to carry weapons.

The great majority of the servants died in bondage,
while those who survived the first term were usually
intimidated, tricked or penalized to their status indefinitely.
As to the convicts, wrote a contemporary, "they frequently
there (Virginia) meet with the End they deserved at

317

Home". There were a number of disputes over servants'
claims to expiration of indentures, and since the masters
were the makers, interpreters and enforcers of the law
"the custom of the country" never worked to their detriment. Discharge from servitude was an involved process
requiring a certificate of freedom from the court, and
those discharged were generally skilled workers and clerks
under voluntary indentures who were sufficiently intelligent
to know their rights. They had, however, given the best
years of their lives to the masters, and freedom found
most of them physically emasculated with egos snuffed
out. The freed servant was protected: there was a serious
penalty for reselling him into servitude; but if it appeared
that he would become a public charge through inability
to support himself then resale could officially take place.
Discharge under the Cavaliers was held to a minimum
because labor was at a premium to the extent that legislation was enacted punishing masters for seducing one
another's servants, but by about 1720 a condition of labor
sufficiency had been attained and with the spread of black
slavery white freemen began to increase.

Indentured servitude was the labor system of the Puritan
sociology. Labor was a universal duty—there was no class
of people in the trader world that was per se above work.
The Puritan could be an exacting taskmaster: the values
were material; labor—like everything else—was rational-
ized, and it was usually a case of all work and no play;
but the master did not spare himself—the awful mortality
of the founding days respected no classes. Servitude was
at the bottom of the social scale and was looked down on,
but for reasons other than the fact that it was labor: it
was never a pariah class per se, and the likely servant
had a good chance of getting some consideration; but the
Puritan was unrelenting towards those whom he regarded
as shirkers—the transported anti-social character could

not abruptly adjust himself from a life of idleness at home to one of honest toil in the colony. The Puritan mind was saturated in, and life flowed from, religion: this was inherent in the master-servant relation, and gave it paternal-filial characteristics—the labor status was not confined to servility. Life in the Puritan world revolved around the principle of the "master's household", which was the unit of social organization: "household" had a broad meaning; it included the master's family—as well as domestics, foremen, clerks and tutors, who were in a "personal trust" relationship with the master. The principle of paternalism prevailed— there was a sense of responsibility towards labor which reached out, to some extent, even to the field hands. This gave the servant a sense of belonging—he had a community of interest with the master. Labor was expected to reciprocate with a filial attitude, and the ethics of the period condemned a man as an ingrate if he betrayed his master. The indentured servant was outside the social milieu, but he was not forever condemned: on delivery from the status, for which there was plenty of opportunity, he was admitted into the social order as one of "the People"; and he became a freeman and citizen, and he acquired property rights and the ownership potential, as well as the right to marry—which absorbed many women of the class. Thus the servant did not have to associate freedom with flight from the jurisdiction, and absconding was at a minimum. There were more freemen in pre-Restoration Virginia in proportion to population than at any subsequent time—and there were no mean whites, and no frontiersmen, on a social scale.

When an indentured servant was discharged he was legally entitled to freedom dues, which are enumerated in the Statutes. Nothing is said about a plot of land. The government had jurisdiction over public domain, which was wilderness. Wilderness is natural resources that has to be transformed into arable land through reclamation—

which presupposes capital investment: the conveyance of a forest tract to anyone without capital would have been meaningless, as it is a physical impossibility for an individual to create arable by himself with an axe; while the cost of creating and stocking a farm unit rendered its giving away as part of the freedom dues an economic impossibility, especially as there were many discharged servants. With the establishment of Virginia as a civil community in 1619 the principle of monolithic authority disappeared: the creation, stocking and conveyance of a farm unit became solely the responsibility of private capital; the government did not engage in the creation of farm units, it had no say as within a private estate, and the legislated freedom dues for discharged servants couldn't include a land grant. The indentured laborer had small value as compared with skills, yet the social conditions of the time did give him some hope of eventually achieving unencumbered ownership of a farm. The domain owner had many prepared farm tracts for which he was anxious to get occupants: he could do so chiefly by entering into an arrangement with the discharged servant known as the "leasehold"—which was in principle a mortgage, under which the leaseholder could in time pay off the mortgage and achieve full ownership of the property. The owner could make much more money from a man as leaseholder than he could by working him as a servant: he therefore singled out the servants that appeared to be normally intelligent and responsible, and he manumitted them so as to make them leaseholders; and manumission went on as a normal business practice. The leasehold couldn't be legislatively mandatory: it resulted in a complex master-occupant relation of long duration; the master had to use some judgment in selecting a leaseholder, and he could do this only for a few.

The craftsman, being "under papers", was on a privileged labor status: he had to be voluntary—the type of man who is willing to work—as skill cannot be coerced, and he was never "bought"; he was respected, and had to be offered inducements to emigrate as he was none too numerous and not easy to get; and he had to be content if he was to give the best in him. The skilled workers rendered the domain owner indispensable services; gave him an income from their work for the independent farmers; and trained apprentices for him, towards whom they were in a relation of "master". The legislated freedom dues did not apply to them, as the benefits for skill were contained in the contract previously drawn up. The colony had comparatively few craftsmen: their services to the domain owner were sufficiently valuable to warrant the conveyance to each of them, at the termination of the contract, of a family farm unit in fee simple independent title unencumbered— which made the craftsman a property owner; and skill was a form of capital, as it was a way to the acquisition of property.

In all these instances of land conveyance, whether encumbered or not, the grantee became a fee simple independent farmer. The rise from the condition of bound labor to the status of freeman property-owner was a remarkable, and a complex, achievement: it was an achievement in sociology, not in legislation; the impoverished person did come by a plot of "land" in the only way he could have done so—in terms of the economic arrangement of that day. The advancement of the servant to the status of leaseholder as within the corporate farm estate is of primary importance in the economic evolution of America—it is the seed from which eventually developed the fee simple independent farming system.

With the rise of the Cavaliers—and the social revolution they brought about in Virginia—new principles were introduced in master-servant relations: the Puritan attitudes on land and labor were erased; the head right, the leasehold, the farmer, and manumission—disappeared.

Indentured servitude was retained: but labor ceased to be a value, and became a pariah class per se; and the attitude of paternalism, the inner sense of responsibility towards labor, the relationship of trust between master and servant —all this was succeeded by the condescension of aristocracy. Servitude was a dynamic labor system, and it was bound up with the Puritan way: it was alien to feudalism, which is static; and the slave labor system was introduced, to which servitude began to give way. Primitive slave labor was socially below civilized indentured labor, and the burden gradually began to shift from white to black shoulders: there was a consistent increase in the colony's wealth, and insouciance displaced rationalization; all of which eventually brought an improvement in the servants' treatment in passage, as well as in their living and laboring conditions in the colony. The Cavaliers showed some consideration for white women servants: the severity of their punishment was very much reduced; and laws were passed exempting them from taxation if they were used for household work—and very few such women were worked in the fields. The craftsman had a degree of independence whatever the social system, and his appreciation continued under tradition: but the change in the land laws applied also to him; he lost his status as fee simple independent farmer; he was conveyed an agricultural unit as a commonalty freehold on a sub-infeudated entailed status, for which he had to pay rent in perpetuity.

The servants seem to have preferred the Puritan way: when Bacon's Rebellion broke out they had been under the Cavaliers for some time—they were almost all on the rebel side. They felt themselves out of place under feudalism: labor as such was a thing apart—a condemned status, and was held in contempt; and they lost their sense of belonging, and their community of interest with the master. Freedom from servitude was confined to termination of indentures, but this still left them outside the social milieu—the openings for admittance into "the People" were tightly sealed. The few who survived their terms and received freedom papers were put on a "tenant" status, under which they had no civil rights and no economic opportunities; and they were without influence on the social order. Says the contemporary Jones of the servants in Cavalier Virginia:

"when they are free, they may work Day-Labour,
or else rent a small plantation for a trifle almost; or
else turn overseers . . . or follow their Trade".

Most of the discharged servants, however, became mean whites and frontiersmen—and it was feudalism that produced these groups on a social scale. Wage labor in colonial Virginia was never large enough to become a factor.

From about a decade before secession from the Empire Virginia became surfeited with black labor, and her legislation and judicial decisions became increasingly liberal towards white labor. Indentured servitude began to lose its characteristics as slavery: it was withering away, rather than changing to another labor form; and by the winning of Independence it had practically disappeared as a social force.

"the white servant . . . was the main pillar of the
industrial fabric of the Colony, and performed the
most honorable work in establishing and sustaining the earliest . . . of the English settlements in
America."

Part Three:
CHATTEL SLAVERY

Colonial Virginia was peopled by aboriginals from two continents—Europe and Africa. The Europeans and the Africans were characterized respectively by the civilized and the primitive way of life. According to Charles Darwin:

> "The difference between savage and civilized man is greater than between a wild and domesticated animal."

The initial contact of the continentals made each conscious of the other's appearance: Europeans, Africans and Indians are not known to have had color sentiments while each was confined to its own habitat; and the color consciousness that was created by their early contacts aroused curiosity, rather than feelings of attraction or revulsion. But the first thing that each became conscious of as a *barrier* was values: the ways of doing things, behavior patterns, ambitions, hopes, fears, aptitudes—of each, were different and mutually incomprehensible; and none of them had the intention to relinquish his way. Civilization and primitivism are natural enemies: the behavior of each in terms of his own way appears aberrative to the other; on contact one must in time give way to the other, as there is no rational foundation for a composition of differences; the relation of European and African in colonial Virginia involved the survival of each as an ideological entity; and coercion was the only alternative of both—one had to impose his way on the other.

The patent purpose of European colonization was to project its heritage—civilization, into America: the success of the venture could not be taken for granted—the settlers were caught up within a primordial macrocosm, against which there had to be a constant struggle; the coming of the African en masse meant the introduction of a physical and ideological force for primitivism into the heart of the colony. With the rise of feudalism the importation of Africans became a policy of state: from the latter part of Virginia's first century the Europeans began to develop a confidence concerning the basic safety of their heritage; and Africans were beginning to be brought in en masse. The Africans brought their mind with them into the colony—Virginia became the scene of a basic duality in ideological atmosphere, as the values of primitivism and of civilization both prevailed. The absence of a common denominator between the ideologies precluded mutual understanding, and there could be no mingling: mind dictated segregation—each was a world in itself; and the Virginia-born generations of Negroes were brought up fundamentally within their own atmosphere. This difference in mind eventually became identified with physical characteristics, or race—and ideological segregation preceded and induced race consciousness.

Segregation was vertical: the heritage of Europe dominated that of Africa; the sociology of colonial Virginia was contained within the civilized atmosphere; primitivism was a nether world—it was outside the social milieu; and the attempt of the European to adjust the Africans to his ways could be made only through coercion, which took the form of chattel slavery. The man of Europe had developed the ability to produce more of the goods of life than was necessary for his own individual preservation: this surplus wealth was crystallized into capital; and he brought capital with him to America, as well as the knowledge how to produce it. The transportation of the primitive—who had never been a "workingman" in his native habitat—to the colony, brought an abrupt change in his way of life—from the freedom of jungle ranging to the restraints of civilization:

> "the Negro arrived in Virginia, not only as a
> wretched slave ... but also an indescribably raw and
> bestial savage, as hideous in aspect as he was brutish
> in instinct and mean in intelligence.";[1]

he did not show the competence and the initiative to produce
beyond his own immediate physical needs; and he clung
tenaciously to his primitive ways. The colonial mind tended
to explain everything in natural, rather than in artificial—
or social, terms. The transplanted European had intimate
contact and experience with "naturals" from other continents: he was convinced that his development of civilization and Christianity, and his ability to subdue and bend
the primitives to his way, were marks of superiority—
which he traced to natural causes. The African came to be
regarded as a biped animal, not as a human being: the
"slave" was a phenomenon in nature—in physiology, not
in sociology; the master did not have the feeling that he
was beating a fellow human being into slavery—rather
was he acquiring a being who was born a slave; and he
regarded his relation to the slave as that to an animal.
The slave statutes were simply the de jure recognition of
a de facto condition. With the passing of time and the
obliteration of origins the Negro in Virginia became a slave
per se, both to himself and to the European.

The rise of chattel slavery, and its predominance over and
eventual substitution for indentured servitude in Virginia's
labor system, followed historically and logically the Puritans' displacement by the Cavaliers. The historian Wertenbaker declares that this change caused a social revolution in the colony:

> "from 1700 to 1720 . . . (Negro slavery) actually
> accomplished the overthrow of the old system of
> (indentured) labor and laid the foundations for a
> new social structure." [2]

Thus from apprenticeship developed indentured servitude, from which in turn came chattel slavery.

Slaves were reduced to their status by custom, statutory law and judicial decision. They were obtained by purchase, as in the case of Negroes and Indians brought in by traders; natural increase, where the mother was on a slave status; capture, or enslavement of prisoners of war; and condemnation, where law violators were punished with enslavement. The Code of 1705 finally provided that,

"all servants imported . . . into this country, by sea or land, who were not christians in their native country . . . shall be accounted and be slaves, and as such be here bought and sold".[3]

This law, which was re-enacted in 1748, automatically condemned the aboriginals of the world outside of Europe to slavery within Virginia's jurisdiction.

Chattel slavery as a labor base is characteristic of feudalism, but the slave traffic is commerce and was participated in by commercial states. Thus colonial Virginia used chattel slaves but did not engage in the slave traffic, while with Great Britain and New England it was the other way. The British were late in entering the business, they achieved leadership in it, and were among the last to abandon it. With the establishment of the American colonies and improvement in oceanic transportation Charles Second, one year after the legalization of chattel slavery in Virginia, chartered the "Company of Royal Adventurers trading to Africa", and this was reorganized ten years later as the "Royal African Company"; these were Crown monopolies. The expulsion of the Stuarts was followed by the abolition of Crown monopolies, and all British subjects were permitted to engage in the trade. An historian declares:

"At the opening of the eighteenth century the African slave trade was the foundation on which colonial industry and the colonial commerce of European

THE SOCIOLOGY OF COLONIAL VIRGINIA

countries rested. It dominated the relations between the countries of Western Europe and their colonies; it was one of the most important factors in the wars of the century; it played a considerable role in the domestic affairs of the nations involved in it. The century saw . . . the growth of industries dependent upon African markets".[4]

Africa's chief contacts were for the first time transferred from East to West.

The international slave traffic drained entire sections of Africa of their population. The tribal societies, some of which were themselves based on slavery and commonly engaged in the slave trade, were fairly well advanced: they were for centuries subject to raids by man-hunters from the west; some of them were destroyed, others were emasculated and the cultural development of the dark continent was aborted. The Negro writer Du Bois says that in the fifteenth century, before the slave traffic began—

"there was no great disparity between the civilization of Negroland (Africa) and that of Europe".[5]

The slave companies employed many agents and kept a corps of personnel regularly stationed on the African coast; forts were built for protection against traffickers of rival nationalities; and coast natives were employed to raid the interior and bring the prisoners to the slave dealers. The native raiders were paid in tobacco, whose use they had been taught and for which they developed a craving.

The captured Africans were driven aboard ships, and while in transport the horrors of the "middle passage" occurred. Wrote an observer in 1702:

"I was overnight on a ship, which several days before had come from Guiné with 230 slaves. . . . a hundred of them died on the journey to Virginia."[6]

The arrival of Negro cargo was advertised, and the following notice appeared in the Virginia Gazette in 1772:

"Just arrived from Africa, the Snow Nancy, James

E. Colly Commander, with about two Hundred and
fifty fine healthy Windward and Gold Coast Slaves,
the Sale of which will begin at Osborne's, on James
River, on Wednesday the 29th Instant (July) and
continue until all are sold. Merchants Notes, payable
at the General Courts in Williamsburg, will be
received in Payment. John Lawrence, William Call
and Co." [7]

In 1769 it was enacted that all ships bringing laborers,
many of whom suffered from diseases which were "frequently propagated among the inhabitants of this colony",
were to be quarantined before unloading. While the ships
were in Virginia the unsalable sick and crippled Negroes
died, and their bodies were thrown into the rivers. This
happened often enough to cause the Assembly several times
to legislate against it,[8] and to require that the corpses be
buried on land.

Indians also were enslaved in Virginia. The natives'
chief complaint against the whites was the appropriation
of their land and sharp practices in trading, as well as
coercion into slavery and sexual abuse of their women.[9]
After the Indian massacres of 1622 and 1644 the Virginians
realized that it was cheaper to recognize them as human
beings and dicker with them. In earlier days captured
aborigines were used as indentured servants on the allegation of saving their souls. The Fourth Revision legalized
and regulated an Indian slave traffic. The rebel Bacon
advocated their enslavement, and this was put into practice
after the Cavaliers established themselves. On the suspicion
that neighboring Indians had murdered several white people Governor Berkeley is declared to have decided that,

"it was necessary to exterminate every member of
these tribes except the women and children, who
might be spared in order, by their sale as slaves,
to defray the expenses of the campaign." [10]

In 1711 press gangs (called "rangers") were organized by

329

the Assembly and sent to the frontiers to capture Indians
for sale into slavery, and it became legal to buy any offered
for sale by white traders and by natives who had taken
their fellows captive. The captured Indians were sometimes transported to the West Indies and other colonies
for sale into slavery. But the Indians didn't want to be
enslaved, and they failed as a labor supply. The Europeans'
rivalries kept the natives always well supplied with firearms, which they used when necessary in their own defense
—and it was this that saved them from slavery. They
could be used more profitably as fighters, hunters and
trappers, and as guides in exploration. The colonials'
weakness made Indian wars serious affairs, and restraint
was often exercised for fear of retaliation; and by cultivat-
ing their good-will the fur trade would be promoted, and
they could be used as allies against rival interests. Moreover, the Indians' local nativity facilitated their escape,
and precluded their apprehension. White and African labor
was a disorganized mass kidnaped with little trouble, but
the Indians had sufficient organization to enable them to
fight and to inflict casualties and sometimes defeat; and
the recognition implied and concessions made in drawing
up trade and peace agreements with them, created a feeling
of respect that the masters could not entertain for imported
labor.

With the Cavalier seizure of power the importation of
labor, especially of Africans, began to assume immense
proportions. The price of slaves rose from about £18 per
head in 1676 to as high as £35 per head in 1700, yet the
supply hardly kept up with the demand. Virginia exploited
slave labor much more profitably than the colonies north
of her:

"he (Negro slave) was useless in the system of in-
    tensive agriculture in vogue north of Maryland." [11]
Bassett points to,

"the extreme profitableness of tobacco planting in
connection with slave labor. How great this was
we have seldom realized." [12]

The slave was most profitable when he was always doing
the same kind of work, which encouraged the mono-crop
agricultural economy. Slavery was tobacco:

"the tobacco trade . . . rested almost entirely upon
the labor of the savage black man".[13]

By about 1750 Virginia had around a quarter of a million
slaves, which was probably more than half the number
of Negroes in the continental Anglo-American colonies.

During the seventeenth century the relatively few Negro
slaves were, like the white servants, regarded as personalty
and could be alienated and encumbered. This implied a
domestic slave traffic, the auction block and separation
of families, but it also meant good usage for salability and
the right to manumission. By the end of the century, how-
over, African slavery was beginning to assume institutional
proportions and the Code of 1705 changed the legal status
of the chattel slaves. Land and slaves were now economically inseparable, the laws of primogeniture and entail
were made rigid, and slaves were declared "real-estate-
entailed" [14] who were alienable only by government permission. Said the Virginia General Assembly:

"the true design of (this) act . . . is, to preserve
slaves for the use and benefit of such persons to
whom lands and tenements shall descend . . . for
the better improvement of the same: which cannot
be done, according to the custom and method of
improving estates in this colony, without slaves".[15]

"the said slaves unsold, together with all their future
increase, shall continue annexed to, and go and
descend with the residue of the said tract of land,
in fee tail".[16]

Entail secured slave property against distraint, and thus
protected estates from liquidation. The tithe on slaves was

a realty tax as land and labor were legally indistinguishable; and together they were held in "fee taille" or, as developed after Independence, in fee simple.

Under certain conditions, however, the slaves were excepted from their status as realty-entailed: they could be seized in satisfaction of judgment if no personalty were left; their alienation did not require a deed; they did not escheat—on failure of lineal heirs the slaves did not revert to the state but were inherited by the collateral descendants; and their ownership in numbers sufficient to equal the value of a freehold did not qualify one for citizenship. Negroes brought in and held for sale were classed as personalty. As the docking of entails on the commoner freeholds increased a category of fee simple slaves was introduced. All property transfers in slaves—through sale, exchange, gift, will—had to be in writing and recorded in the county court, for the protection of creditors.

With the slaves annexed to the land the domestic slave traffic was virtually abolished, but they were subjected to harder usage and their right to manumission was nullified. Says Fiske:

> "No master was allowed to emancipate one of his slaves, except for meritorious services, in which case he must obtain a license from the governor and council . . . by an act of 1699 the freedman was required to quit the colony within six months; for obviously the presence of a large number of free blacks in the same community with their enslaved brethren was a source of danger." [17]

Manumission—which had now become entirely an act of philanthropy—was considered both a private and public concern; the government subjected the slave to his condition, and it always reserved the final say on his freeing. "Meritorious services" usually meant the betrayal of conspiracies; this was sometimes further rewarded with permission to remain in the colony, and the master was reimbursed by the state for the slave's value. Slaves freed without official consent were resold into slavery for the benefit of the parish. All non-Caucasians—those with any degree of African or Indian blood—were regarded as unassimilable, and they were either enslaved, expelled or exterminated.

Although Englishmen engaged in the slave traffic, all inhabitants of the homeland were free; human slavery was regarded as a traditionally un-English institution; and English justice declared that when a slave set foot on the British Isles he was automatically free, for there was nothing in Lex Britannica which could hold him to his status. Virginia therefore legislated in the Code of 1705 that slaves leaving her jurisdiction do not thereby become free.

The everyday life of the Negro slaves is described by eye-witnesses. One of these was Thomas Anburey, a lieutenant in the British army of General Burgoyne during the Revolutionary War. On Burgoyne's surrender at Saratoga in 1777 the prisoners of war, of whom our commentator was one, were marched down to Virginia where they were quartered until released. Being an officer privileges of freedom, on parole, were extended to him. Anburey wrote letters home on his observations in Virginia during 1778-9, excerpts from which are here presented.

"Thus the whole management of the plantation is left to the overseer, who as an encouragement to make the most of the crops, has a certain portion as his wages, but not having any interest in the negroes, any further than their labour, he drives and whips them about, and works them beyond their strength, and sometimes till they expire; he feels no loss in their death, he knows the plantation must be supplied, and his humanity is estimated by his interest, which rises always above freezing point."

"It is the poor negroes who alone work hard, and I am sorry to say, fare hard. Incredible is the fatigue which the poor wretches undergo, and that nature should be able to support it; there certainly must be something in their constitutions, as well as their color, different from us, that enables them to endure it."

"They are called up at day break, and seldom allowed to swallow a mouthful of hominy, or hoe cake, but are drawn out into the field immediately, where they continue at hard labour, without intermission, till noon, when they go to their dinners, and are seldom allowed an hour for that purpose; their meals consist of hominy and salt, and if their master is a man of humanity, touched by the finer feelings of love and sensibility, he allows them twice a week a little fat skimmed milk, rusty bacon, or salt herring, to relish this miserable and scanty fare. The man at this plantation, in lieu of these, grants his negroes an acre of ground, and all Saturday afternoon to raise grain and poultry for themselves. After they have dined, they return to labor in the field, until dusk in the evening; here one naturally imagines the daily labor of these poor creatures was over, not so, they repair to the tobacco houses, where each has a task of stripping allotted which takes them up some hours, or else they have such a quantity of Indian corn to husk, and if they neglect it, are tied up in the morning, and receive a number of lashes from those unfeeling monsters, the overseers, whose masters suffer them to exercise their brutal authority without constraint. Thus by their night task, it is late in the evening before these poor creatures return to their second scanty meal, and the time taken up at it encroaches upon their hours of sleep, which for refreshment of food and sleep together can never be reckoned to exceed eight."

"When they lay themselves down to rest, their comforts are equally miserable and limited, for they sleep on a bench, or on the ground, with an old scanty blanket, which serves them at once for bed and covering, their clothing is not less wretched, consisting of shirt and trowsers of coarse, thin, hard, hempen stuff, in the Summer, with an addition of a very coarse, woollen jacket, breeches and shoes in Winter. But since the war, their masters, for they cannot get the clothing as usual, suffer them to go in rags, and many in a state of nudity."

"The female slaves share labor and repose just in the same manner, except a few who are term'd house negroes, and are employed in household drudgery."

"These poor creatures are all submission to injuries and insults, and are obliged to be passive, nor dare they resist or defend themselves if attacked, without the smallest provocation, by a white person, as the law directs the negroe's arm to be cut off who raises it against a white person, should it be only in defence against wanton barbarity and outrage."

"Notwithstanding this humiliating state and rigid treatment to which this wretched race are subject, they are devoid of care, and appear jovial, contented and happy. It is a fortunate circumstance that they possess, and are blessed with such an easy satisfied disposition, otherwise they must inevitably sink under such a complication of misery and wretchedness." [18]

"Having mentioned that there are mulattoes of various tinges, it may not be amiss to inform you from whence it arises, and no doubt, but you will be surprized, when I tell you it is by the planters having intercourse with their negroes, the issue of which

being a mulatto, and having a connection with that
shade becomes lighter; as an instance, I remarked
at Colonel Cole's, of whom I have made mention;
there were mulattoes of all tinges, from the first
remove, to one almost white; there were some of
them young women, who were really beautiful, being
extremely well made, and with pretty delicate features; all of which I was informed, were the Colonel's
own. I could not help reflecting, that if a man had
an intercourse with his slaves, it was shameful in the
extreme, to make his own offspring so; for these
mulattoes work equally the same as those who come
from Africa: To be sure, you may say, it is a
pleasant method to procure slaves at a cheap rate.
I imagine there could not be less than twenty or
thirty mulattoes of this description, at Colonel Cole's,
notwithstanding he has a very agreeable and beautiful wife, by whom he has had eight children." [19]
Another observer was Philip Vickers Fithian. He was
a native of New Jersey who went to Nomini Hall in Virginia where he acted as a tutor to Councillor Carter's children. He stayed there during 1773-4, keeping a diary and
writing letters home. When the Revolutionary War broke
out he joined the Continental forces and was in Washington's army when he died in December 1776. The following are excerpts from Fithian's writings.

"And Mr. Carter is allowed by all, & from what I
have already seen of others, I make no doubt at all
but he is, by far the most humane to his Slaves of
any in these parts! Good God! Are these Christians?—When I am on the Subject I will relate
further, what I heard Mr. George Lees Overseer,
one Morgan, say the other day what he himself had
often done to Negroes, and found it useful; He said
that whipping of any kind does them no good, for
they will laugh at your greatest Severity; But he
told us he had invented two things, and by several

experiments had proved their success.—For Sullenness, Obstinacy, or Idleness, says he Take a Negro, strip him, tie him fast to a post; take then a sharp Curry-Comb, & curry him severely til he is well scraped; & call a Boy with some dry Hay, and make the Boy rub him down for several Minutes, then salt him, & unlose him. He will attend to his Business, (said the inhuman Infidel) afterwards! But savage Cruelty does not exceed His next diabolical invention—To get a Secret from a Negro, says he, take the following method—Lay upon your Floor a large thick plank, having a peg about eighteen Inches long, of hard wood, & very Sharp, on the upper end, fixed fast in the plank—then strip the Negro, tie the Cord to a staple in the Ceiling, so as that his foot may just rest on the sharpened Peg, then turn him briskly round, and you would laugh (said our informer) at the Dexterity of the Negro, while he was relieving his Feet on the sharpened Peg!—I need say nothing of these seeing there is a righteous God, who will take vengeance on such Inventions!" [20]

"I find it is common here for people of Fortune to have their young Children suckled by the Negroes!... Mrs. Carter said that Wenches have suckled several of hers—Mrs. Carter has had thirteen Children." [21]

"At Supper from the conversation I learned that the slaves in this Colony never are married, their Lords thinking them improper Subjects for so valuable an Institution." [22]

"Mr. Carter entertained us with an account of what he himself saw the other Day, which is a strong Representation of the cruelty & distress which many among the Negroes suffer in Virginia!... As Mr. Carter rode up he observed Mr. Turburville's Coach-Man sitting on the Chariot-Box, the Horses off—... he had occasion soon after to go to the Door when he saw the Coachman still sitting, & on examination found that he was there fast chained! The Fellow is inclined to run away & this is the method which This Tyrant makes use of to keep him when abroad; & So Soon as he goes home he is delivered into the pityless Hands of a bloody Overseer!" [23]

"Before Breakfast I saw a Ring of Negroes at the Stable, fighting Cocks, and in several parts of the plantation they are digging up their small Lots of ground allow'd by their Master for Potatoes, peas, &c; All such work for themselves they constantly do on Sundays, as they are otherwise employed on every other Day." [24]

"About ten an old Negro Man came with a complaint to Mr. Carter of the Overseer that he does not allow him his Peck of corn a Week—The humble posture in which the old Fellow placed himself before he began moved me. We were sitting in the passage, he sat himself down on the Floor clasp'd his hands together, with his face directly to Mr. Carter, & then began his Narration—He seem'd healthy, but very old, he was well dress'd but complained bitterly—I cannot like this thing of allowing them no meat, & only a Peck of Corn & a Pint of Salt a Week & yet requiring of them hard & constant Service." [25]

"A Sunday in Virginia ... by five o-Clock on Saturday every Face (especially the Negroes) looks festive and cheerful—All the lower class of People, & the Servants & the Slaves, consider it a Day of Pleasure & Amusement, & spend it in such Diversion, as they severally choose—" [26]

"Yesterday a Negro Child about six years old sickened ... in the morning it expired! It is remarkable that the Mother has now lost seven successively, none of which have arrived to be ten years old!—The Negroes ... seem all to be free from any terror at the Presence of Death..." [27]

The masters had no regard for sex in their slaves. An

historian says:
  "Female slaves being exempted (from taxation), the
  custom of employing them as field hands instead of
  men became so general that an act was passed to
  cover the case." [28]
Towards the end of the colonial period the patricians
began to expand their estates by acquiring interior holdings, and the overseer became a factor. There was a rapid
increase in the number of plantations which were regarded
purely as investments and expected to yield dividends; and
since the overseer was held responsible for this and for
the prevention of servile insurrection, he was himself hardly better than a slave. Usually a Nonconformist stemming
from the low whites he was often illiterate and rough; he
was paid on a percentage basis; and the responsibility of
driving unwilling workers and attending to many other
duties caused him to degenerate into drunkenness and brutality. He was held in contempt by the upper class, his socially intermediary position isolated him, and he largely replaced the master in absorbing the slaves' resentment when
they saw in him the direct cause of their condition. Jefferson speaks of,
  "a seculum of human beings called overseers, the
  most abject, degraded, and unprincipled race, always
  cap in hand to the Dons who employed them".[29]
Some of the large plantations, such as George Washington's Mount Vernon, employed a medical doctor to look
after the slaves. Most of the black and white laborers,
however, had to shift for themselves when ill or injured.
The few medicines at the master's household and the few
individuals who used grandmother remedies rendered some
assistance. Although a few slaves reached old age their
sub-human level of existence shortened their average life
span. Slave life was thought of fundamentally as natural,
not social. Their births and deaths had simply a property
signification. The sanitary conditions in their quarters were
deplorable. They were regarded as cattle who were in-

capable of acquiring moral responsibility—and they had no sense of sex morality, and they mated promiscuously. An act of 1662, re-enacted in 1748, declared that a child took the legal status of its mother. This made slave descent matrilineal—"a woman named Sarah and her five children". There was a kind of "family" as in relation to slaves: the father was unknown; they had no contraceptives, and births were separated by the natural period of gestation; "pickaninnies" toddled about the congested quarters, wandered and mingled; and the Negro "mammy" was none too alert, and she was none too concerned about which was her own. Thus the slave family was a loose biological entity, and afterwards—with the adoption of Christianity some slaves staged Christian marriages—it acquired also the characteristics of a religious entity. But the slave family never got legal recognition as such, since this would have interfered with its members' distribution as property.

The observer Smyth says that the slave's hours away from labor,

"never exceed eight in number, for eating and repose. But instead of retiring to rest . . . he generally sets out from home, and walks six or seven miles in the night . . . to a negroe dance, in which he performs with astonishing agility, and the most vigorous exertions, keeping time and cadence, most exactly, with the music of a banjor . . . and a quaqua . . . until he exhausts himself, and scarcely has time, or strength, to return home before the hour he is called forth to toil next morning." [30]

The slaves who were located on the aristocrat's seat or were owned by smaller planters generally found the plantations more like homesteads than factories. Most of Virginia's Negroes during the seventeenth century were freshly transplanted, and being of primitive manners and unintelligible speech they were fit only for brute labor. But during the next century most of the Negroes were slave-born; they were usually docile, which caused them to bring a higher price than the imported ones; and they eventually supplanted the white servants as workers around the mansion house. These were picked for meekness and loyalty, and they fared best of all and often acted as informers. Some of them attended the master on trips away from home, but for the majority of the slaves the world was rimmed by the plantation.

The religion of the slaves is described by Du Bois:

"The Negro priest early became an important figure on the plantation and found his function as the interpreter of the supernatural, the comforter of the sorrowing, and as the one who expressed, rudely but picturesquely, the longing and disappointment and resentment of a stolen people. From such beginnings arose and spread with marvelous rapidity the Negro church . . . It was not at first by any means a Christian church, but a mere adaptation of those rites of fetish which in America is termed obe worship, or 'voodooism'. Association and missionary effort soon gave these rites a veneer of Christianity".[31]

The Negroes dissociated religion from ethics, and they saw no connection between their prayers and moral conduct in experience. They preferred to get together by themselves, led by one of their own, and they engaged in prayers which consisted of rhapsodical moanings. They were credulous, and full of crude superstitions: they believed in luck charms and were in fear of ghosts, "hants" and the devil; and they were convinced that a snake hung up would bring rain, that deceased mothers came out of their graves at night to admonish their sons against sin, that the haunted house was the scene of nocturnal orgies, and that the wearing of iron rings would ward off and cure fits. The masters were at first opposed to the Africans' baptism in the Christian religion alleging that, although they partook of human characteristics, they were too little removed from the beast to acquire moral and spiritual responsibility. It was feared that the baptism of slaves would be tantamount to their emancipation because, how could one Christian enslave another? This was settled when the legislative bodies of England and Virginia passed resolutions declaring that the baptism of slaves will not alter their status of bondage. From about the beginning of the eighteenth century the slaves in Virginia adopted Christianity en masse, and slavery proved to be the most powerful proselyting agency known. The Negro church, unlike the Church in Europe, had no dogma, theological seminaries and ordained clergy, and owning no property it was without political and economic power. The interceding influences of priests of religion as between master and slave were therefore non-existent in Virginia.

There was no difference in the slave's status de jure and de facto, and he had no legal being in the community. He was a thing—not a person: could act only as his master's agent, or as a "detachable limb"; was owned body and service; and no contractual relationship existed between them. His disability to contract incapacitated him from owning property, trading and marrying. The slave was legally completely defenseless in his own right; he could under no condition testify in court against any white person; the master had absolute power over him, and the man who killed his slave—which sometimes happened especially under correction—was not liable in the law on the theory that no one will deliberately destroy his own property. No white person was liable if his killing of a slave was held manslaughter. The slave's only legal defense was the right of a white person to testify on his behalf, and the owner or other free white who killed any slave was liable in the law if a white witness proved the act to have been malicious. The owner could testify for and defend his slave, and for certain servile crimes the owner was permitted by the court to pay a fine—in place of the sheriff's fee of twenty pounds of tobacco for whipping a culprit—which freed the slave from corporal punishment. Yet the slave's basic protection lay in his value as property—in law he was always a chattel, never a human being. The white man who killed another's slave—which sometimes happened in connection with dismemberment, especially castration—was liable in property damages to the owner. And the practice of stealing slaves for sale in remote parts was punished by death without benefit of clergy.

The slave (serf) labor system was inherent under feudalism—the rule of land. The Negroes in Virginia were fundamentally unhappy—they were per se disaffected: remotely, because they didn't want to be enslaved; immediately, because their living and laboring conditions were sometimes unbearable. The institution of human slavery was indefensible in idealism: but in realism—in actual experience, life—if respect and consideration are to be shown for everyone involved, it presented itself as an almost hopelessly complex problem. The emancipation of the slaves in Virginia, or the abolition of the slave labor system, could be achieved in one of three ways: through an act of the masters, through the power and the initiative of the slaves, or through the intervention of an external force. The proprietaries of land couldn't emancipate the slaves: the sociology of colonial Virginia rested on the slave labor system—they stood and fell together; the proprietaries were dedicated above all else to the perpetuation of their way of life. The slaves could attempt to bring about their own emancipation in one of two ways: through exodus—separation from the jurisdiction; or as within the jurisdiction.

The recently imported primitive African was raw material: the abrupt change in his way of life came as a shock, he longed to return to the freedom of his native jungles, he was spirited and balky, and he was the chief internal danger to the peace of the colony. With the succession of slave-born generations the Negroes showed an aptitude to adjust themselves to the ways of civilization, and they seem generally to have preferred their lot in America to jungle freedom. Primeval America was more friendly to human life than Africa. Slavery begets a feeling of dependence, and a fear of responsibility: the slaves were materially better off on the plantations in Virginia, where the necessaries of life—food and shelter, some access to healing medicaments, and immunity from dangerous beasts and insects—could be taken for granted; and their individual life span was probably longer. As the Negroes were beginning to come within and to appreciate the atmosphere of civilization they showed a preference for life in the white man's world: they had no desire to go to Africa; they did not associate freedom with flight, or separation from the civil community; they began to consider themselves an integral part of civilization, and as such they lamented their lot within it; only a comparative few ran away to the frontiers; and as the imported African in time began to become a small minority slave disturbances subsided.

Virginia was the scene of an ideological duality, as the heritage of Europe and of Africa both prevailed. Freedom for the Negroes as within the jurisdiction could express itself either in terms of the values, the restraints and the responsibilities, of civilization—or in terms of the values of primitivism. The adult non-Caucasian who was brought into the colony never acquired civilized values, and he remained forever unfit for the civil freeman status. Nor could a straight line be drawn as between the imported and the slave-born Africans: those who escaped to the frontiers were swallowed up by the wilderness—they "went native" as they had not yet thoroughly absorbed the civilized values with which to resist the world of nature about them, and the Negro was never identified as a frontiersman; left to himself he would have followed behavior patterns leading to primitivism. The great mass of the slaves were little removed from tribalism. The appreciation of the values of civilization—freedom within restraints, education, artifices, living standards—presupposes a profound developmental complex within the individual. The fundamental obstacle to the African's Europeanization was inherent in himself: there can be no abrupt break with the past; the attempt to "civilize the savage" on a mass scale is a very difficult undertaking which takes several generations to achieve. The masters did not have to make a positive effort to perpetuate the primitivism of the Negroes: rather did the effort lie in the purpose to bring about their ideological transformation. The colonial slave represented mind, primitive—race, African—and class, proletarian: he was feared most for his mind; the master regarded him as a force for primitivism, or inherently an enemy of civilization. Ideology is a more important drive in life than race or class: the slave revolt was primarily an ideological, secondarily a racial, and hardly at all a class, expression; it was not thought of foremost as black against white or labor against mastery—rather was it regarded as an alignment of the heritage of Europe and of Africa, or basically a struggle of values. The protest against an undesirable social condition cannot be confined to negativism—it must have a positive practical program which flows from the conviction that an improvement can be achieved. But slave group action had to take the primitive path—it had to be outside of the values of civilization: this to the European was aberration; there was no foundation for a rational composition of differences, and there was therefore no alternative to violence. Social revolution is a phenomenon of the civilized world: the Caucasian never saw the slave as a social revolutionist; rather did he see the slave uprising as an animal stampede—the running amuck of hordes of armed, deranged ape men over his country, his home, his women. The European's patent purpose in America was to preserve, protect and promote his values and culture: African self-assertiveness was regarded as catastrophe—the "wild" man had to be kept in his place; the forces of civilization in Virginia could stop at nothing to keep from being inundated by the black flood of primitivism; and masters and slaves lived in constant terror of each other.

Thus, given the preservation of civilization in Virginia, and of her feudal society—the slaves couldn't have achieved emancipation as within the jurisdiction: the abolition of the slave labor system through the power and the initiative of the slaves meant the erasure of the heritage of Europe, of which they had never been the custodians; this would have taken with it the masters' sociology—plantation system, property, patrician status. The slaves could achieve freedom as within the limits of the European way only through the efforts of a power outside of themselves—only if the rule of land was displaced by the rule of capital, whose labor system was wage or free. Capital had a positive practical program as within the civil society: it could free the slaves, and control them, and in time eradicate their primitivism. Thus the slave was a menace to civilization, while capital was a menace to feudalism—it meant the overthrow of the sociology of colonial Virginia. But the rule of capital presupposed external intervention: capital as a social force was alien to Virginia, and it was beyond the power and the initiative of the slaves.

The war in Virginia between European civilization and African primitivism was constant and unremitting: there was always an underlying dread of servile aberration; the African was feared as a savage, not as a slave; and the masters felt that their world was built on dynamite. White cooperation against black derangement was an implicit responsibility: it was spontaneous—it was swift and certain, and it was remorseless. During the French and Indian War Governor Dinwiddie said:

> "We dare not venture to part with our white men any distance, as we must have a watchful eye over our negro slaves." [32]

The slaves as a group were wholly inarticulate—they had

no right to peaceful protest, which confined their collective action to violence. The recently imported free-born Africans came to the plantations with comparatively live egos, they didn't want to give up their freedom of jungle ranging, and they were most susceptible to aberration: they were against slavery, and for primitivism; this the Europeans couldn't countenance—the irreconcilable enemy of civilization had to be exterminated. According to Henry Cabot Lodge:

> "a tone of dread is perceptible in the acts of the Assembly, to all of which the negro insurrection on the Northern Neck in 1687 gave terrible meaning. From that time forth the slave laws have but one quality, that of ferocity engendered by fear." [33]

The number of imported Africans in Virginia relatively steadily declined as time brought a vast increase in those who were local born—which eased somewhat the menace to civilization. The spirit of the slave-born Negroes was crushed: they seldom engaged in group aberration, and only as a last resort—yet as primitives they were regarded as fundamentally unpredictable, and they too had constantly to be watched; there were times when the severities of living and laboring conditions, and the excesses of overseers, were unbearable and drove them to derangement. The masters were in constant terror of "slaves . . . notoriously guilty of going abroad in the night", and of slave "secret plots, and dangerous combinations"; and the most careful preventive measures had to be taken against slave collective action for conspiracy and rebellion. In 1726 the Assembly declared:

> "great danger may happen to the inhabitants of this dominion, from the unlawful concourse of negros, during the Christmas, Easter, and Whitsuntide holidays, wherein they are usually exempted from labor."

A "concourse of negroes" at night was unlawful under any condition. Slave grouping in the daytime was permitted only for labor and tolerated for religious worship, while gatherings for funerals, feasts or any other purpose exceeding five individuals each were declared "unlawful meetings". The slave could not leave his master's plantation without a permit on pain of the lash; he could not visit another plantation without permission from both owners; a law of 1682 prohibited any Negro, bond or free, to remain on any visited plantation for more than four hours; and no more than five visiting Negroes were allowed on any one plantation at any one time. In 1738 each county commander was required to organize a squad of men who were henceforth,

> "to patrol, and visit all negro quarters, and other places suspected of entertaining unlawful assemblies of slaves, servants, or other disorderly persons. And such patrollers shall have full power to take up any such slaves, servants, or disorderly persons ... or any other, strolling about from one plantation to another, without a pass ... and to carry them before the next justice of the peace".

This ban, under which free colored persons were also included, was a measure against servant-slave cooperation. It was a duty of the patrollers periodically to search the slave quarters for weapons, and the slave caught with a weapon was disarmed and whipped. Slaveowners and county officials were liable for neglecting to take measures against "rallying slaves".

The mass protest of the Negroes—whether free or slave born—could be aimed only at the immediate, never at the basic, condition—and since their treatment varied with time and place their protest was spotty. In Virginia's decentralized economy each plantation forever confined most of its Negroes, they never knew the layout of the outside world, and this precluded contacts between them for coordinated action. A number of isolated uprisings occurred in the earlier days of mass slavery, when the freshly imported African was still dominant. In 1672 the Assembly declared:

"it hath been manifested to this grand assembly
that many negroes have lately beene, and now are
out in rebellion in sundry parts of this country".

Says Ballagh:

"An intended insurrection of negroes discovered in
the Northern Neck in 1687 particularly alarmed the
colonists . . . intended insurrections were discovered
in 1710, 1722, and in 1730." [34]

On the outbreak of a slave disturbance every possible precaution was taken to keep the news from spreading to the
other slaves, as this may have brought on what the
masters dreaded most of all—the general slave uprising. Discussions on the subject in the General
Assembly were held behind hermetically sealed doors,
every white person in the know dared not utter a word,
and few details on colonial Virginia's slave rebellions are
available. Everything possible, from promises of reward to
threats of the most excruciating torture, was done to induce slaves to betray their fellows' conspiracies. The
masters succeeded well in holding their labor's mass aberration to a minimum: the expression of the slaves' protest
was chiefly individual and isolated; and the servile insurrections that occurred were confined to single or contiguous counties—they were never general.

The tendency to crime—to anti-social behavior, among
the Negroes was about the same as it is among any other
people anywhere: their recent removal from jungle ranging, however, did aggravate the condition. Fear of punishment rather than hope of reward kept them at their work.
Although slaves were regarded as without independent will
or choice the facts of life dictated that they be held responsible for law violations, and colonial Virginia's punitive
laws are an index to their acts and to the state of mind
of the masters. Slave violence expressed itself usually in
terms of the individual act, which often took the form of
terrorism. In addition, their situation—and their thorough
familiarity with the inner layout of the plantation—gave

them easy access to the master's goods, and indications point to their perpetration of thievery and sabotage that caused serious losses to the estate. Running away was a common offense: runaway Negroes were outlawed and hunted like wild beasts, and they could be killed in their attempted apprehension. The following item appeared in the Virginia Gazette in 1767:

"Run Away from the subscriber in Norfolk . . . two young Negro fellows, viz. Will, about 5 feet 8 inches high, middling black, well made, is an outlandish fellow, and when he is surprised the white of his eyes turns red; . . . Peter, about 5 feet 9 inches high, a very black slim fellow . . . They are both outlawed; and Ten Pounds a piece offered to any person that will kill the said Negroes, and bring me their heads, or Thirty Shillings for each if brought home alive." [35]

While Virginia had agreements with other colonies and with the Indians for the return of absconding slaves it seems that quite a number of runaways escaped to the Indian tribes where some were adopted as members. Fur traders often reported seeing Negroes among the Indians. Runaway slaves constituted a property loss—and the problem evidently became serious for, says an historian:

"decided at this Treaty at Albany (1754) was that none of the runaway negro slaves should be harbored by any of the tribes; but should be returned to their masters, and the Indian so doing should receive 'one Good Gun and two Blankets for each Negro' ".[36]

Another problem was created by Negro fugitives who hid in neighboring woods and swamps and terrorized the plantations by committing depredations; a price was put on their heads and the owners were reimbursed by the state for those killed or executed. Fithian relates the following:

"Something alarming happened a few nights ago in the Neighborhood of Mr. Sorrels a House in Sight—It is supposed that his Negroes had appoint-

ed to murder him, several were found in his bed
chamber in the middle of the night—His wife
waked—She heard a whispering, one perswading the
other to go—On this She waked her Husband, who
ran to his Gun; but they escaped in the dark—Pre-
sumption is so strong together with a small confes-
sion of the fellows, that three are now in Prison—
The ill Treatment which this unhappy part of mankind receives here, would almost justify them in any
desperate attempt for gaining that Civility, & Plenty
which tho' denied them, is here, commonly bestowed
on Horses! . . . I sleep in fear too, though my
Door and Windows are all secured!" [37]

A law passed in 1748 declared:

"Whereas, under pretence of practising physic, Negroes have prepared medicine by which many persons
have been murdered or have languished, it is enacted that if any Negro, or any other slave, shall prepare, exhibit, or administer any medicine whatsoever, he shall be guilty of felony and suffer death".[38]

Fires were mysteriously numerous in Virginia. Says Waddell:

"Sampson Sawyer's negro woman, Violet, was sentenced to be hung . . . for burning her master's
dwelling house. . . . it was ordered also that after
the body was cut down, the head should be severed
and stuck upon a pole at the cross-road. . . . this custom seems to have been general in Virginia, at this
(1780), or an earlier period. The ghastly memorials
thus set up were doubtless to inspire a wholesome
dread in the minds of the negro slaves." [39]

In 1755 it was decided to build a brick wall around "the
public magazine (which) stands exposed to the designs of
evil minded persons".

Ordinary disciplinary measures were administered on the
plantation; but for serious crimes the slaves were tried—
"without the solemnity of a jury"—in the county or the

General Court. The slave could testify for or against another slave—which was necessary especially in relation to the betrayal of conspiracies—but to the extent that his testimony involved a white person it was invalid. Crimes that drew the death penalty without benefit of clergy were house-breaking at night, plotting insurrection or murder, manslaughter, burglary amounting to 20 shillings or more, and the third offense of hog stealing—evidently the slaves often had to poach to get enough to eat. The benefit of clergy was extended to slaves for certain crimes, but never to the same offender the second time. Execution, which was sometimes preceded by torture, usually was by hanging but sometimes they were burned at the stake [40] or drawn and quartered,[41] or "the criminal was hung and flayed, his skin being displayed".[42] A slave's crime against his fellows was never a capital offense. Other forms of judicial punishment depending on the offense were dismemberment, as in castrating the slave whose sexual self-control seemed dubious; mutilation, as in cutting off one or both ears and burning a hand; transportation, or sale to a slave colony such as the West Indies; chaining to place of labor and to quarters with an iron collar on the neck; stocks and pillory; transfer to less desirable type of work; and lashes on the bare back in varying number. In 1748 the Assembly declared:

"if any . . . (non-Caucasian) bond or free, shall at any time lift his . . . hand, in opposition to any christian, not being a (non-Caucasian) . . . he, or she so offending, shall for every such offence, proved by the oath of the party, before a justice of the peace . . . receive thirty lashes on his, or her bare back well laid on".[43]

The slave could not testify in his own behalf. Sometimes two or more punishments were inflicted on the offender. The scarcity and expensiveness of labor in the earlier days saved the lives of some slaves, but when Virginia achieved labor sufficiency and later became slave surfeited the condition of the Negroes in this respect tended to deteriorate.

This terrorism was effective, but the slaveowners' chief reliance was psychological. The principle of "divide and rule" was brought into play, and race consciousness began to become evident especially after 1660. The slaves also became divided as tendencies to group distinction arose among them, and the recently imported ones spoke different dialects. Religion, with its promise of an after life, was also found useful. Everything in their environment—from the crack of the whip under which they wilted to the denial of recognition as human beings—had for its purpose the extinction of the ego, and the master class did all it could to render their lives vegetative, to disable them from inquiring into the cause of their condition, and to degrade and brutalize them mentally and morally so that all self-respect, pride and courage were drained from them. Charles Darwin, while in a slaveholding country, describes his emotions when a slave thought that Darwin's gesticulation was intended as a blow:

"I shall never forget my feelings of surprise, disgust, and shame at seeing a great powerful man afraid even to ward off a blow directed, as he thought, at his face".

They were completely without a sense of time and place, and of events. The males were called "bucks" and the females "wenches": they had to be given individual names for their identification in property transfers and recordings, and for recovery in the event of their separation from the master; and among the names given them were Mingo, Cinchinello, Barebones, Basket, Jack, Tom, Moses, Rebecca, Pompey, Hannibal, Cromwell, Rosamund, Jupiter, Cupid, Minerva.

In the early days of continental contacts the institution of slavery proved to be the most effective medium for the mass transformation of primitives to civilization. The constant absolute domination by the European through slavery broke the Africans' will to revert to the ways of the jungle: their school for civilization was inherent in their experience as slaves; they had to be coerced into doing what and how the European wanted them to do; he had to bend them—to his way. Thus the black man failed to preserve his aboriginal way of life when he came to America: he acquired in time, through bondage, the civilized way of life— the white man's emphasis on mental development, and his religion, morality, language, artifices; slave labor was not unrequited. The *raison d'etre* of mastery was labor's ability to produce surplus wealth. African labor in Virginia was enabled to achieve this ability because it was provided by the European with an advanced system of agriculture; with sufficient domesticated labor animals; and with implements for laboring that were made of iron and steel, whose manufacture and repair presupposed craftsmanship. The masters also assigned slave boys to European craftsmen as apprentices: according to George Mason's son;

"my father had among his slaves, carpenters, coopers, sawyers, blacksmiths, tanners, curriers, shoemakers, spinners, weavers, and knitters, and even a distiller."

The slave's ability to produce surplus wealth was derived from the civilized social milieu of which he was a part—it was not inherent in himself. This surplus was taken away from him for the purpose of creating and maintaining a leisure class, but since his ability to create surplus was not inherent it cannot properly be said that he was robbed of the product of his labor.

The African as an animal could not have human intelligence—yet the facts of life forced the master, in his necessary dealings with slaves, to presuppose them as possessing basic human understanding. There was a slave code: the slave was presumed to know the difference between right and wrong, both in law and in morals; he could make himself intelligible through language, he showed normal aptitude in the crafts, his memory often had to be relied on, and it was realized that he could project his mind into the future—there were numerous efforts to influence his conduct with promises of reward and threats of punishment. The fact and the results of miscegenation proved the African to be biologically human. He showed an aptitude to adjust himself to a hostile environment. There were always some free and some literate Negroes in Virginia: these achievements were patent proof that they were civilized beings; and they constituted an index to the potentialities in their fellows. The conclusion that it was in the nature of the African to be a slave had to be discarded, as it was realized that there were always more free than enslaved Africans in the world. They were human beings in religion: their conversion to, and acceptance by, Christianity brought them recognition as "God's children"—human beings possessing redeemable souls. With the succession of slave-born generations the master sometimes expressed the feeling that the slaves' adjustment to his way of life benefited them: he evidently eventually came to believe that the Africans were basically human who had it in them, at least to some extent, to achieve civilization; and the European's mind concerning the African did undergo a progressive alteration—the Negro evolved from animal, to natural born slave, to human being. But the Negroes were regarded as childish minded: the sons of the soil and of toil were naive, in the sense of an absence of subtlety—as in relation both to connivance, and to the ability to think in abstract terms; and they were therefore put down as mentally inferior.

A slave code is in its nature harsh, and Virginia's was no exception. So long as a total ideological distinction existed as between European and African there could be no meeting of minds, and their relations had to be entirely physical: yet such a condition couldn't have lasted, as it is *contra naturam* for human relations to be confined always to physical brutality; and as the Negro began to absorb, to appreciate and to act in terms of the ways of civilization a foundation developed for an emotional, and to some extent even a rational, relation as between master and slave. There could have been no continuous driving of slaves everywhere as it is a law of biology that undue severity in the treatment of living beings discourages their procreation; slavery flourished in Virginia—her slaves were notoriously prolific; and her consistent growth in economic power attests to the basic loyalty of labor. The Negro never did Virginia any harm: he was very much desired, and the masters went to great expense in order to get him; he was pre-eminently the honest man—he never exploited anybody, and everything he ever had he earned through his own toil. He was kindly disposed towards the mansion house, and he regarded it as a source of the good and the just: when he felt himself in need—of medicaments, or of better treatment—his mind turned to the master in the big house; the slaves as individuals did have opportunities for peaceful protest; to repeat from Fithian—

"About ten an old Negro Man came with a complaint to Mr. Carter of the Overseer that he does not allow him his Peck of corn a Week";

it is worth noting that the slave had access to the person of the patrician. Pioneering has its implications, and the severity of laboring conditions was not always the master's fault. The "small Lots of ground allow'd by their Master"—which on the large plantation could have totaled up to about a hundred acres—had to be reclaimed, and implements for working them had to be furnished, by the master. The African laborers were spared the feverishness in reclamation of the founding days: the colonial economy always had an abundance of the best agricultural implements of the time, as well as sufficient labor animals—and slaves were never hitched to the plow; they had to be seasonally rushed as punctuality—meeting a deadline—was no value to them; and the somnolence of the Virginia atmosphere more or less affected all classes. Genocide was never perpetrated on the Africans in America: they always had enough at least of the basic necessaries of life; and contemporary records are clean of reports of mass mortality among them from starvation, exposure, epidemics—births always exceeded deaths. They were exempt from military duty—they had to labor, but not to fight. Virginia's labor troubles were not exceptional—her slaves' efforts at conspiracy and rebellion were comparatively few and minor. The African of primitive values was unconscious: awakening came with his acquisition of civilized values—but his self-consciousness was concentrated on race, rather than on his status as slave. The slave's state of mind was not that of a freeman suddenly enslaved, for most of them were born into that condition and knew nothing else: their tendencies to aberration cannot be traced fundamentally to a resentment over their basic condition, about which they could do nothing—they didn't have a positive practical program as within civilization, and they were never a social revolutionary force; moreover, the mean white was a living symbol to the slaves of what "freedom" would mean for them. Their group protest could never have been more than quantitative—as within the limits of their status they could hope to achieve some improvement. In view of the condition of eighteenth-century world labor the slave labor system does not appear as evil per se: the material condition and the state of mind of the slaves in colonial Virginia were about the same as those of the proletarian masses of the world at the time; like labor everywhere, and like the indentured servants and the mean whites all around them, the great mass of the slaves were normally quiescent; the wage labor system had not yet fully established itself as preferable, and there was no abolitionist activity to arouse them; and they had a subjective attitude towards, and were never self-conscious about, their condition in life. Their fundamental protection lay in their value as property: this was supplemented by religion as a reminder of the common destiny of man, by the humane and pacifistic aspects of Christianity, and by the tendency to a paternal and forgiving attitude towards those considered inferior. The master's power of life and death over his slaves was rarely exercised capriciously. Laws are enforced in spirit rather than in letter, and no doubt the law was much more often than not unenforced: in the everyday relations of master and slaves the law was remote, and the human element usually prevailed; time did bring a steady improvement in the masters' attitude towards, and in the conditions of, the slaves; and the indications are that the average slave lived his life through without being unduly oppressed. Says Hugh Jones:

"Negroes . . . do the hardest . . . Work; the most laborious of which is the felling of Trees . . . to which kind of Slavery our Wood-Cutters in England are exposed; only with this Difference, that the Negroes eat wholsomer Bread and better Pork with more Plenty and Ease, and when they are Sick their owners Interest and Purse are deeply engaged in their Recovery".[44]

The slave is mute: life under the lash is dulling; there is no recorded statement by a Negro slave in colonial Virginia concerning his own feelings about his condition. A slave people does not produce a culture, and the mind of the Negroes could at best be a reflection of the values and ethics of the masters. They could never rise out of their color: their complexion and economic status were marks of inferiority, most of them never knew of a world where they were otherwise regarded, and they were characterized by self-contempt. The feudal society's mania for the "quality" person penetrated to the slaves: a few of them had become sufficiently educated and refined to be regarded as fundamentally civilized; they acquired the attitude of class distinction, and there was a tendency to arrogance on the part of some slaves towards their fellows, the reasons for which were determined by the standards of the ruling class. To be in some favor with the master was to have a measure of protection. As time passed the masters began to associate the qualities of health, strength, appearance and intelligence in their slaves with the particular section of Africa that they came from: recordings of property transfers mention "choice slaves"; and the local nativity of freshly imported blacks advertised for sale was stressed and caused some difference in price. Thus Guinea Negroes were commonly regarded as the most intelligent. The Negroes who attended the person of the patrician constituted something like a slave aristocracy; and they accompanied him on trips off the plantation, which often took them to the capital at Williamsburg, sometimes on a journey to another colony and, more rarely, on a trip to England. These slave attendants had the master's confidence since they had to be entrusted with a measure of responsibility, and they were usually given some education. Some Negroes also acted as the guardians of young aristocrats during trips away from home. There were no slave teachers. The slave attendants of the members of the Assembly were safe from assault and arrest during its sessions. The Negroes who claimed aristocratic paternity, Quadroons and others with varying degrees of white blood, those of higher market value, the slave literates, the "little coloured pet", jockeys, grooms, musicians and foremen, and those who worked in the mansion house, also considered themselves in a favorable position.

As Independence was approaching and libertarian declamations were filling the air, the General Assembly arrived at the conclusion that the slaves' "punishment is often disproportioned to the offence, and contrary to the principles of humanity".[45] The African was progressing towards recognition as a human being: a slave was henceforth to be castrated only if he actually attempted rape on a white woman; the benefit of clergy was extended to slaves for housebreaking; and the death sentence could be passed on a slave only if at least four of his judges concurred. The apparent tendency to defraud the government by killing slaves allegedly as "outlaws" and then collecting for their value was discouraged by a law of 1772, which said that a slave would officially be recognized as an outlaw only if the county court had ruled him so prior to his killing. And it became legal for slaves on frontier plantations to carry arms if they had their master's consent and a county court license.

In pre-Restoration Virginia the population was almost homogeneously European: the basic ideology was mono-lithic, as the atmosphere in the settlement was one of total civilization; and the labor status was based on economic condition, rather than on race or blood. There were a few indentured non-Caucasians, of whom some had been born in the settlement: due to their fewness, and to the fact that there was no race consciousness, and no sentiment against miscegenation, the colored offspring were brought up among Englishmen—some, no doubt, in the master's dwelling; and they grew up as civilized persons. They partook of whatever opportunities there were for literacy —as well as for training in the catechism, which was of supreme importance in the Puritan household. This type of non-Caucasian was fit, and the capital economy rendered him eligible, for a legitimate place as within the social framework. Thus there was no race problem, and no force for primitivism or menace to the civilized way of life, within Puritan Virginia. This condition continued to some extent for a while after 1660: the Negroes as servants, and afterwards as slaves, were classified as personalty entitled to manumission, and some were freed into the commonalty with the right to settle in the colony and acquire property in land and labor; and the colored free-man was on the same status as the white one. It is recorded that a Negro was appointed executor of the will of a white testator. It is declared that:

"between 1635 and 1700, there were probably a number of persons of African blood in the Colony, who had raised themselves to a condition of moderate importance . . . There were certainly some who were able to write. It is known that patents to land were obtained by a few. . . . one hundred acres . . . were granted to Richard Johnson, a negro, upon the basis of head rights which were represented by two white men." [46]

"some negro . . . freemen owned indented negro servants." [47]

"a negro servant became the overseer of his master's servants." [48]

"The most remarkable property right possessed by free negroes was the right to acquire, own, and alienate slaves." [49]

It seems that during the better part of the seventeenth century there was greater consciousness of social distinction than of nationality and color, and the people who ruled the colony did so primarily because they were of gentle birth rather than because they were white men.

The rise of the Cavaliers and the establishment of feudalism in Virginia brought a radical change in the European's attitude towards, and in the status of, the non-Caucasians: slavery became the base of the social pyramid; the Africans as primitive, black and slave were outside the civil milieu—they were not people in a social sense; they became a nether caste subject to strict segregation, they were born and raised in their own atmosphere, and they lost whatever rights they previously had. The eye-witness Hugh Jones, whose writing on Virginia was published in 1724, says:

"The Children of Negroes and Indians . . . ought all to be baptized . . . tho' such (as the poorer Sort in England) be not taught to read and write; which has been found to be dangerous".[50]

When Jones was in Virginia the question of admitting Negroes to the Christian religion was troubling the masters:

they were in fear that conversion was tantamount to emancipation; and since the Church had control of education, admittance carried with it rights and opportunities for literacy. Yet there was no need for, and there never was, any law or custom in colonial Virginia which specifically denied literacy to slaves—Jones' "poorer Sort in England" were civilized beings, while Virginia's Negroes were primitive. Moreover, universal education as a mass right and state responsibility was then everywhere still in the womb of time, and the majority of the colony's white inhabitants, including many freemen, were illiterate.

Although the nurture of the slave-born generations within their own atmosphere effectively retarded their removal from primitivism, they did begin perforce to acquire the white man's ways: to the extent that they did so they became fit for freedom; and, although the mass of the slaves continued on the whole on a sub-civil level, there began eventually to emerge the "civilized slave"—whose numbers steadily increased with time. The emergence of the civilized slave introduced a new principle in Virginia, and gave rise to new problems. The Europeanized Negro was anxious above all else to preserve his new way of life—the most horrible calamity that could befall him was reversion to barbarism. Mind is stronger than blood: all civilized people, whatever their race and class, were equally in fear of the savage; and an unbridgable chasm yawned between the civilized Negro and the primitives; he saw his undeveloped fellows with the eyes of the European, and he knew full well what would happen if they got the upper hand—the motives of the "informer" were not confined to winning the commendation of the master. The civilized slave, who longed for freedom within the civil community, had his effects on the Europeans: they had a clear conscience in denying primitive freedom, which was out of place in their social milieu; but they felt morally constrained to take cognizance of the problem of civilized freedom. The manumission of individual slaves—with permission to settle in the colony—presupposed their thorough absorption of the white man's ways, and freedom for the slave in Virginia was introduced with the emergence of the civilized Negro. This began to bring into question the moral implications of slavery as a labor system, which was an important step towards the movement for mass emancipation.

In the course of time enough of Virginia's slaves were advancing towards the European way to create the kind of problems that required legislative regulation. In 1732 the General Assembly passed a law—which was re-enacted in 1748—introducing in Virginia the penal code that had prevailed in England up to 1606:

"where, by any act of the parliament of England, made before the fourth year of the reign of the late king James the first, the benefit of clergy is taken away from any offence, the same shall hereafter be adjudged to be taken away from the like offence, committed in this colony".[51]

The penal code of Virginia applied to her lower classes, especially to labor. Her passing of the above law seems to have marked an advance, since enough of her nether folk had evidently by then become sufficiently literate to render pertinent their eligibility to "benefit of clergy". The literate person is patently civilized: in 1740 the General Assembly took cognizance of, and made specific provisions for, the eligibility of offending slaves to this benefit.

The Cavaliers were extremely chary of freed bondsmen black or white, as there was little place for them within the feudal social framework. Free Negroes were not wanted: they were feared allegedly because they would be an undesirable example to the slaves—individual manumission could suggest the idea of mass emancipation—and interfere with their discipline and control; they could act as go-betweens in conspiracies for rebellion, be used as receivers of stolen goods, and through inability to support themselves become public charges. The doors to slave manumission were hermetically sealed—under the Code of 1705 the slaves became "real-estate-entailed", and their individual freeing was predicated upon an act of legislature. Thus with time there took place a steady increase in the number of civilized slaves who had no opportunity to achieve freedom.

Some non-Caucasians had become freemen before the Restoration: to be free was to be civilized—yet in 1668 the Assembly held that free Negroes,

> "ought not in all respects to be admitted to a full fruition of the exemptions and impunities of the English",[52]

which would seem to indicate that they previously had been so admitted; non-Caucasians were for the first time identified as in a special category; and laws were successively passed against Negroes owning indentured servants, holding any kind of office, and exercising the franchise. Thus the creation of a race problem—the introduction of the principle of race segregation and discrimination as a policy of state, coincides with the rise of the Cavaliers. While there were always some free Negroes in feudal Virginia, their number was severely limited—they totaled about two thousand in 1782. During most of the colony's second century the colored freemen's right to make a contract and own property was practically nil de facto; they were discriminated against in taxation; were regarded as pariahs, with whom white people could have no social relations; they had to serve in the militia as laborers since it was feared to teach them the use, and trust them with the possession, of arms; could not own any kind of weapon, and visit or meet with slaves; were liable to enslavement for varying terms for criminal acts and default in tax payments; and unless married within the Established Church their offspring were bastards indentured to the parish for thirty years—at the end of which term the offspring were usually kidnapped and sold into slavery. Although they avowed themselves Christian and showed some knowledge of the faith, they "are people of such base and corrupt natures" that none of them is "to be sworn as a witness, or give evidence in any cause whatsoever". From around 1765, however, the condition of the free Negroes began to improve: the Assembly exempted them from the status of "tithables", since such status is "derogatory of the rights of free-born subjects"; those classed as "housekeepers" were permitted to own arms; their kidnaping for sale into slavery was declared a crime; and they were permitted to testify in civil cases, as their disability to do so enabled them to evade payment of debt. They earned their living chiefly in the type of work where wage-labor was cheaper than slave-labor, and there were no Negro beggars. There was no caste distinction between the free and enslaved blacks.

A tendency towards the development of a form of social relation between masters and slaves seems to have resulted from their playing together as children; from use of the Negro wet nurse, and the feeling of tenderness for her on the part of the young aristocrat in the knowledge that she had nursed him; and from their sex relations. Whatever the social atmosphere, the emotion of fatherhood is natural: "The head of the house" also knew "that the handsome quadroon was really (his) daughter"; and there must have been numerous instances, hushed up—where the father obtained a passport for, and put money into the hands of, his shady offspring, and sent him to some European country to live. An eye-witness says, in describing the cock-fight:

> "Several houses formed a spacious square, in the center of which was arranged a large cock-pit; surrounded by many genteel people, promiscuously mingled with the vulgar and debased." [53]

Colonial Virginia seems to have been the first modern scene of race agglomeration on a large scale: Europeans,

Africans and Indians, and the variety of the progeny of their inter-breeding, introduced an unprecedented complication of complexions and appearances. Miscegenation was never either a sin or a crime: there is nothing in the Christian religion and in the English common law against it; and it was universally indulged in without a sense of guilt. In the Pocahontas incident an English freeman married an Indian girl. William Byrd advocated the inter-marriage of whites and Indians. William Thackeray in "The Virginians" has the Negro slave Gumbo, who accompanied his master on a trip to England around 1750, marry an Englishwoman. Fiske says:

"Usually mulattoes were the children of negresses by white fathers, but it was not always so. Some of the wretched women from English jails seem to have had fancies as unaccountable as those of the frail sultanas of the Arabian Nights." [54]

In 1640 a Virginia colonist had,

"to do penance in church . . . for getting a Negroe woman with child and the woman whipt."—

the fact that he had "to do penance in church" seems to indicate that he was punished for bastardy, rather than for inter-racial intimacy. With the rise of the Cavaliers miscegenation began to be regarded as against public policy: it became unlawful for whites of all classes to marry, or to have sex relations under any condition with, non-Caucasians; white servants became automatically free if their owner married a member of a race subject to slavery in Virginia; and a law of 1691 described mulattoes as "that abominable mixture and spurious issue". Such abstention by white females was rigidly enforced. The records mention the case of,

"Ann Wall, an English woman, who was arraigned (c.1690) . . . on the charge of 'keeping company with a negro on the pretence of marriage.' "

Thus miscegenation was a statutory offense—the laws punishing white mothers of mulattoes became very severe.

But Virginian justice was lenient the opposite way, and sex intimacy between white males and black females went on to the extent that the Assembly had to define the legal status of the complex variety of their progeny. The Code of 1705 therefore provided a great-grandmother clause:

"the child of an Indian and the child, grand child, or great grand child, of a negro shall be deemed . . . to be a mulatto." [55]

Thus the offspring of miscegenation which came to be known as "mulatto", "quadroon" and "octoroon" were held non-Caucasian, but beyond that it seems that the African strain was considered lost. Concerning the act of 1662, which declared that a child took the legal status of its mother, Ballagh says:

"Notwithstanding its effects it is clear that the purpose of the act . . . was designed to prevent race mixture rather than to create slaves."

Slaves were for most purposes realty-entailed and disabled from manumission and discharge, while indentured servants were personalty subject to both: and the child of the slave mother was automatically a slave, while the child of a servant was born into freedom; but the differences between them de jure were insufficient to create important differences de facto. Neither status implied civil rights or land tenure, while the hours and type of labor, and the lodging, food and clothing, were about the same. Yet the masters were bound to develop some differences in their attitude as between black and white labor, which in time tended to ease the latter's condition. The servants were civilized, while the slaves were primitive—the differences were basic, and precluded their cooperation as labor. African slavery created an ideological, a race, and a class, problem— and Negroes were oppressed both as primitive, as African, and as slave; while the servants suffered under the single disability of their economic status. Although purchased slaves usually cost about twice as much as servants they were economically far superior in Virginia's labor system. Slavery was a permanent and an inherited condition, which assured the master certainty and fixity of labor supply. Many of the imported Africans were used to the freedom of their native habitat—but the process of breaking them in was an initial task for afterwards they could be bred, raised and traded at home with future slave generations accepting their lot in life as "natural". They could not be freed, thus avoiding the danger in the rise of a class of freedmen. They acclimated with less mortality, were better adapted to work under a blazing sun, and their color was a badge of slavery precluding escape.

For about twenty years before the secession from the Empire conditions in Virginia were rapidly tending towards the abolition of the foreign slave traffic, and the establishment of a domestic slave traffic. The colony began to become slave surfeited: slaves were overstocking the plantations; they were being clandestinely moved from one county to another and confounded with fee simple slaves, since it was difficult effectively to enforce entail on "living things"; their price was declining; and their constant augmentation aggravated fear of insurrection. Virginia was rapidly approaching a condition where the breeding of Negroes for the slave market held forth promise of large profits, and William Byrd's prediction in 1736—"I fear this Colony will sometime or other be confirmed by the Name of New Guinea"—seemed to be coming true. During this period Virginia was in the process of acquiring vast areas of trans-Allegheny lands which were to be carved into plantations for the younger scions of her aristocracy, and this would necessitate the transfer of large masses of slaves. Moreover, the rapid territorial and economic expansion of the other southern colonies made them a potentially large market for slaves. The masters wanted freedom in the disposal of their property, and they called for the change of the slaves' status from real-estate-entailed to personalty so as to legalize their alienation. This would have also facilitated slave manumission. In 1748 the General Assembly passed legislation abolishing the slaves' status as realty-entailed and prohibiting their further importation, but the British interests in the African trade exerted successful pressure on the Board of Trade to veto these measures.

References
CHAPTER FOUR
COLONIAL VIRGINIA'S LABOR BASE

Part One
GENERAL BACKGROUND

[1] HS 8; 488.
[2] Trent & Wells, 2; 357.
[3] Craven, 95.

Part Two
INDENTURED SERVITUDE

[1] E. D. Neill, English Colonization Of America, 160.
[2] G. M. Trevelyan, Social History Of England, 278.
[3] JHUS, 1895: Ser., 13; 294.
[4] Ibid., 293.
[5] Lodge, 70.
[6] Neill, VC 107.
[7] FT 3: 18.
[8] JHUS, 296, 7.
[9] Hugh Jones, 116.
[10] JHUS, 295.
[11] Ibid., 299.
[12] W. A. Knittle, Early 18th Century Palatine Emigration, 146, 7.
[13] AHR, 6; 77.
[14] Bruce, EHV2; 60.
[15] Bruce, IHV 1; 45, 6.
[16] Bruce, EHV2; 35, 6.
[17] HS2; 167.
[18] HS3; 87.
[19] HS3; 516.
[20] HS1; 316 & 2; 109.
[21] J. E. Cooke, 89.
[22] HS1; 146.

[23] Documentary History Of American Industrial Society 1; 343.
[24] HS2; 117.
[25] HS2; 53.
[26] HS5; 480.
[27] Brown's Genesis, 740.
[28] Neill, VC58.
[29] Bruce, EHV2; 30.
[30] Neill, VC295.
[31] HS2; 395.
[32] Bruce, EHV2; 31.
[33] B. W. Bond, Quit Rent System, 250, 1.
[34] HS4; 271.

Part Three
CHATTEL SLAVERY

[1] Bruce, Social Life, 139.
[2] Wertenbaker, Pl. Col. Va., 126.
[3] HS3; 447, 8.
[4] E. Donnan, Slave Trade To America, 2; Intro.
[5] W. E. B. Du Bois, The Negro, 144.
[6] Va. Mag. Hist. & Biog., 24; 117.
[7] Donnan, 4; 160.
[8] HS3; 354-6.
[9] Wm. Byrd, Writings, 240.
[10] Bruce, IHV2; 86.
[11] Wertenbaker, 127, 8.
[12] American Histo. Ass'n 1901: 1; 561.
[13] Wertenbaker, 132.
[14] HS3; 333.
[15] HS4; 224.
[16] HS5; 394.
[17] Fiske, 2; 199.
[18] T. Anburey, Travels Through America, ed. 1923: 2; 191, 4.
[19] *Ibid.*, 2; 223.
[20] Fithian, 69.
[21] *Ibid.*, 70.
[22] *Ibid,,* 100.
[23] *Ibid.*, 135, 6.
[24] *Ibid.*, 151.
[25] *Ibid.*, 190.
[26] *Ibid.*, 202.
[27] *Ibid.*, 241.
[28] Ripley, 27.
[29] Kimball, 194.
[30] Smyth, 1; 46.
[31] Du Bois, 188, 9.
[32] G. W. Williams, Hist Negro Race In America, 1; 132.

[33] Lodge, 67.
[34] J. C. Ballagh, Hist Slavery In Va., 79.
[35] DHAIS 2; 86.
[36] Donehoo, G. P., Hist Pa., 1; 321.
[37] Fithian, 247, 8.
[38] HS6; 105.
[39] Waddell, 275.
[40] W. E. Woodward, New American Hist, 80.
[41] M. D. Goodwin, Colonial Cavalier, 260.
[42] Conway, 186.
[43] HS6; 110.
[44] Hugh Jones, 114.
[45] HS8; 358.
[46] Bruce, EHV2; 126.
[47] Russell, 33.
[48] *Ibid.*, 38.
[49] *Ibid.*, 90.
[50] Hugh Jones, 71.
[51] HS4; 325.
[52] HS2; 267.
[53] Dulles, 35.
[54] Fiske, 2; 202.
[55] HS3; 252.